The Campus History Series

GEORGETOWN COLLEGE

MEGAN LEMASTER

The Campus History Series

GEORGETOWN COLLEGE

MEGAN LEMASTER

ARCADIA PUBLISHING

ISBN 978-0-7385-1841-7

Published by Arcadia Publishing
Charleston, South Carolina

Printed in the United States of America

Library of Congress Catalog Card Number: 2005924082

For all general information contact Arcadia Publishing at:
Telephone 843-853-2070
Fax 843-853-0044
E-mail sales@arcadiapublishing.com
For customer service and orders:
Toll-Free 1-888-313-2665

Visit us on the Internet at http://www.arcadiapublishing.com

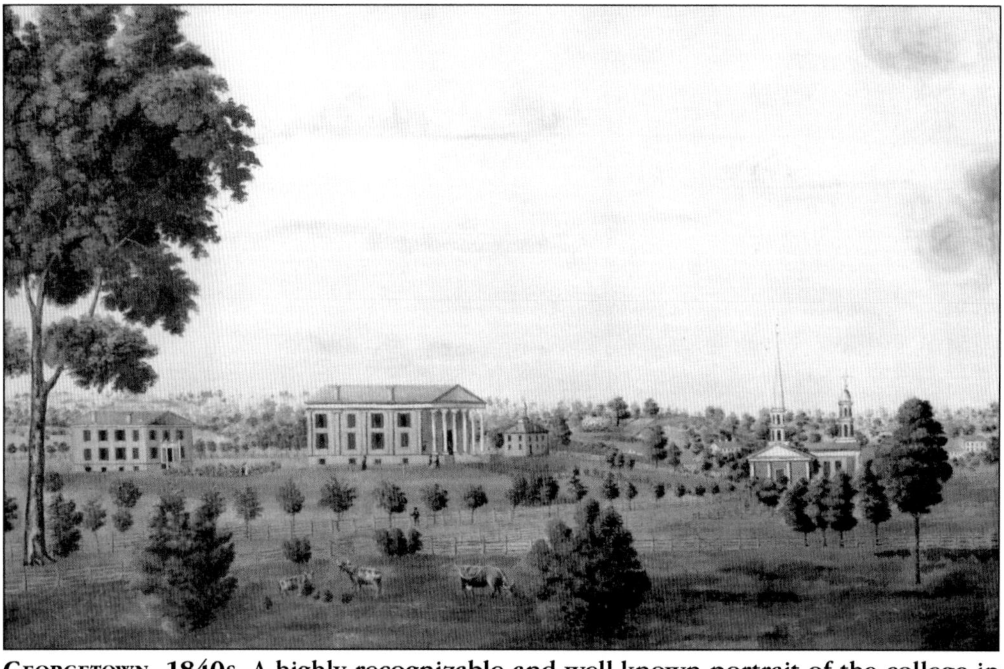

GEORGETOWN, 1840s. A highly recognizable and well-known portrait of the college in its infant stages, this 1840s painting of Georgetown lends a fairly accurate peek at the campus landscape of the time. The painting was completed by the talented Mrs. Esteria Butler Farnham, wife of Prof. Jonathan E. Farnham, who taught at the college. Mrs. Farnham taught art at the Female Seminary nearby and apparently possessed distaste for the brick columns of Giddings Hall, for in her painting they are white. Pawling Hall, newly constructed at this time, is shown at the left, and to the right of Giddings stands the old Rittenhouse Academy Building. To the far right in the painting is the original First Baptist Church of Georgetown, which has now been replaced with a structure more Romanesque in style.

Contents

ACKNOWLEDGMENTS

I would like to thank the following people for their assistance in the construction of this book: Ron Morgan, Doug and Becky Bishop, Jessica Ebehlen, Darren Neel, Alex Smiley, Anne Lee, Carla and Larry Cook, Dana and Clifford Dale, Zachary Wolfe, Travis Burton, and Roger Jasper.

This book would not have been completed if not for the grace of God and many other dedicated individuals. I thank Dr. Todd Coke for allotting study time for the project as well as his direction in writing; and special thanks to Dr. James Klotter and Ann Bolton Bevans for their expertise. I thank the Georgetown College administration for seeing me through on this project and especially Jim Durham, who has dedicated his time and efforts to the book's publication. I thank greatly John Toncray and Andrew Green with the Scott County Museum for the use of their photographs (especially the striking one featured on the cover), as well as Ed Boden and Steve Hockensmith for the use of their photography. I would like to thank Dr. and Mrs. Hambrick for the wealth of information volunteered and their willingness to share much of Georgetown's history. Many thanks to B. J. Privett for his countless hours of assistance. Finally, I would especially like to express my gratitude to Dr. Glen Taul, archivist and director of special collections at Georgetown College, who contributed much of his time and his knowledge of the college's history toward the production of this book.

WORKS CITED

Snyder, Robert. *A History of Georgetown College*. Georgetown, KY: Georgetown College, 1979.

Fields, Carl R., ed. Robin Oldham. *A Sesquicentennial History of Georgetown College*. Georgetown, KY: Georgetown College Press, 1979.

Meyer, Leland W. *Georgetown College: Its Background and a Chapter in its Early History*. Louisville, KY: Western Recorder, 1929.

Apple, Lindsey, Frederick A. Johnstone, and Ann Bolton Bevins. *Scott County, Kentucky: A History*. Georgetown, KY: Scott County Historical Society, 1993.

Georgetown News-Graphic. The Best of Scott County: The People and Events that Shaped Our History. Vancouver, WA: Pediment Publishing, 2000.

Scott County Genealogical Society. *Families and History: Scott County, Kentucky*. Paducah, KY: Turner Publishing Company, 1996.

INTRODUCTION

In 1787, a Baptist minister named Elijah Craig crossed the Appalachian Mountains from Virginia to Kentucky. He and his brothers had spent so much time on the road preaching they had become known as the "traveling church brothers." Craig settled in a place known as Big Spring, which he renamed Lebanon and then, later, George Town. In Georgetown, Craig established one of the state's earliest classical academies, as well as many of Kentucky's original mills and even the state's premier bourbon still. Known as the Rittenhouse Academy, the school was constructed *c.* 1816 but received its official charter, incorporating the trustees of the Kentucky Baptist Educational Society, in 1829, making it the first Baptist college west of the Alleghenies. This school quickly evolved into Georgetown College. The college was based on the model of Columbia College, founded by Luther Rice.

Georgetown's early years were not promising. The college's first president, William Straughton, died before he reached Georgetown. The next few presidents of the college, including Dr. Joel S. Bacon and Thornton Johnson, also faced barriers to building the success of the college and experienced denominational strife. In 1838, however, college president Rockwood Giddings finally provided the sound leadership the young college so desperately needed. A man of considerable financial skills, Giddings restored the financial foundation to firmer ground by increasing the college's endowment to about $70,000. The young but fragile president died only a year after he had taken office, and a recently built Greek Revival recitation hall was then renamed Giddings Hall in his honor.

The Civil War soon threatened Giddings's accomplishments. During the latter part of the conflict, the college was forced to close its doors and did not resume operations until the war ended. Fortunately, after the war, the college benefited from the leadership of Dr. Basil Manly, who led Georgetown through a difficult period of transition. Under his leadership, Georgetown rededicated itself firmly to the mission of Christian education. By 1875, the college had completely rebounded from the effects of war. Not only were one-third of its undergraduates studying for the ministry, they were paying $25 a year for the privilege. Under the leadership of Dr. Richard M. Dudley, who assumed the presidency in 1880, the period of good fortune continued. President Dudley tripled Georgetown's endowment and undertook an ambitious building campaign that transformed the façade of the campus. His efforts resulted in the construction of many new buildings, including a new president's home, chapel, library, gymnasium, and dormitory for women. With the assistance of J. J. Rucker, a pioneer of education for women, Dudley also initiated a coeducational program at Georgetown in 1891. Rucker went on to serve as the primary leader of the Georgetown College Female Seminary, which functioned as an alternative educational program before the college allowed admittance of women.

By 1925, Georgetown's enrollment had reached an impressive 400 students, all taught by 31 faculty members. Georgetown's progress came to a halt in 1930, however, when the campus was ravaged by a tragic fire. The school's gymnasium, constructed just six years before, was completely consumed by the blaze, which also destroyed the chapel, several offices and classrooms, and the college's 50,000-volume library. The Great Depression further deepened Georgetown's sorrows, driving the school, like so many other small academic institutions of its kind, to the brink of financial catastrophe. However, certain aspects of the college remained positive. Throughout the 1930s and 1940s, Georgetown's athletic teams marched from victory to victory and the Carnegie Corporation granted the school $5,000 for music scholarships. The music initiative facilitated the creation of Delta Omicron, a music society for women. Social organizations also blossomed during this time. Several fraternities and sororities were founded, including Lambda Mu and Sigma Kappa.

As a consequence to the infamous "Sherwood Affair," in which the legitimacy of college president Henry Sherwood's baptism was questioned, Dr. Sherwood resigned in 1941. The day after he did so, Pearl Harbor was attacked, signaling the beginning of World War II. As a result of the war, enrollment plummeted as young boys made the decision to serve their country. At home, Georgetown students battled through "indirectly fighting this war to end war." In the *Georgetonian*, students were quoted as saying, "Our weapons are textbooks." The end of World War II brought scores of veterans to the college due to the GI Bill. As a result, adequate housing became a giant dilemma.

Because of the immediate need for new structures on campus, an anticipated new chapel was finally built in 1948. It was named for John L. Hill, former dean of the college. The beautiful new chapel symbolized the purpose embedded within the framework of the college, "a call to worship and a call to excellence."

The baby boom in the 1950s propelled massive increases in the college's student body, which led to a recommendation at the Kentucky Baptist Convention to request a branch college of Georgetown in Louisville. This idea caused quite a stir, and the trustees terminated the sponsorship of the project. A building boom flourished with the erection of the Nunnelley Music Building, Cooke Memorial Library, Calhoun Hall, Lewis Auditorium, and two new matching dorms for both men and women, known now as Knight and Anderson Halls. These buildings proved to be essential because of the increased influx of students, numbering almost 1,000 in 1960. The construction of a student center in 1965 provided students with a new cafeteria, the Grille, mailroom, and bookstore, and a state-of-the-art science center was constructed in 1968, housing multiple floors of classrooms, labs, a small planetarium, and a greenhouse. A new "mall-like" plan for the building of dorms, initiated by Dr. Robert L. Mills, led to the demolition of the beloved Rucker Hall. This period of growth amazed and delighted Georgetown, and it reflected the manner in which almost every aspect of the college excelled. For example, Georgetown at that time boasted more Fulbright Scholars than any other school in Kentucky except for the University of Kentucky.

The bust and boom of the 1960s naturally slowed down by the 1970s. However, new buildings continue to be erected, the college is still supported by the Southern Baptist Convention, and student life remains lively.

A unique feature of Georgetown College since its beginnings has been its religious life. At the Christian college, many Georgetonians attend chapel and religious services regularly. Over the past 30 years, religious activity has thrived and remains a highlight of the college today. Even now, a wide variety of spiritual activities are offered with high levels of student participation. To sum up, Georgetown College is not merely an NAIA (National Athletic Intercollegiate Association) three-time football championship winner, or even a good "teacher and preacher" school, but a community of educated and independent thinkers where students can feel the presence of God and His call for their lives.

One

Notable Georgetonians

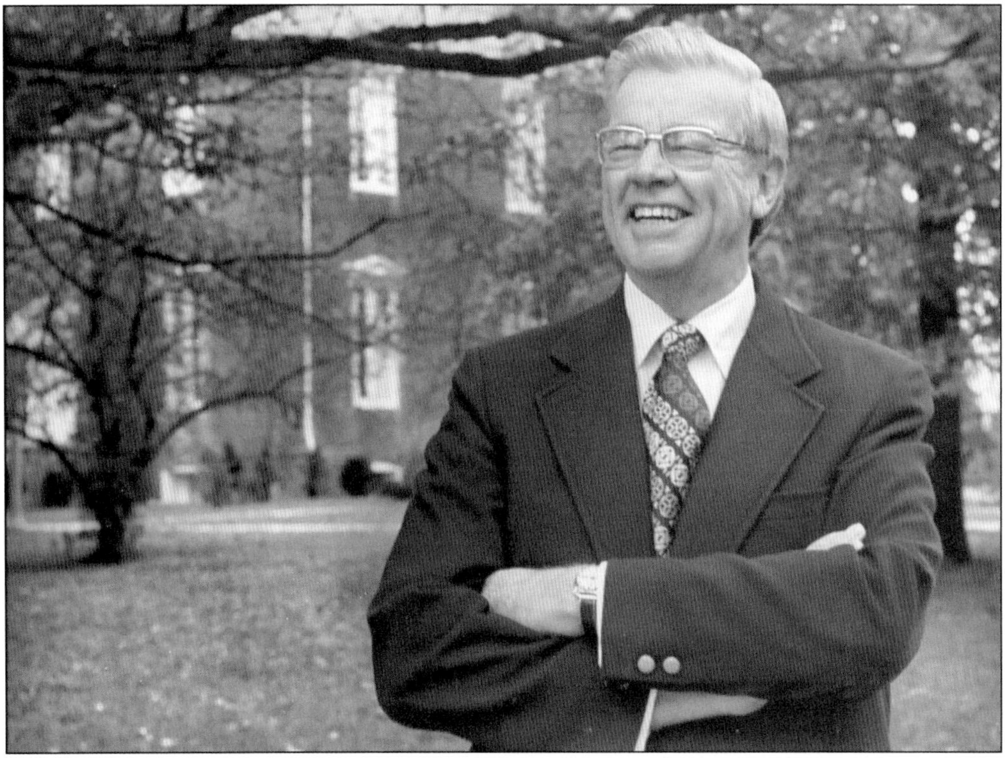

Dr. Robert L. Mills. Dr. Robert Lee Mills instigated vast changes during his 19-year term as president of Georgetown College from 1959 to 1978, the longest term held by a Georgetown College president. Dr. Mills initiated plans and authorized construction of a 12-dorm complex known as "south campus," and he also raised faculty salaries. The landmark leader presided over Georgetown during some of the college's most prosperous and developing years.

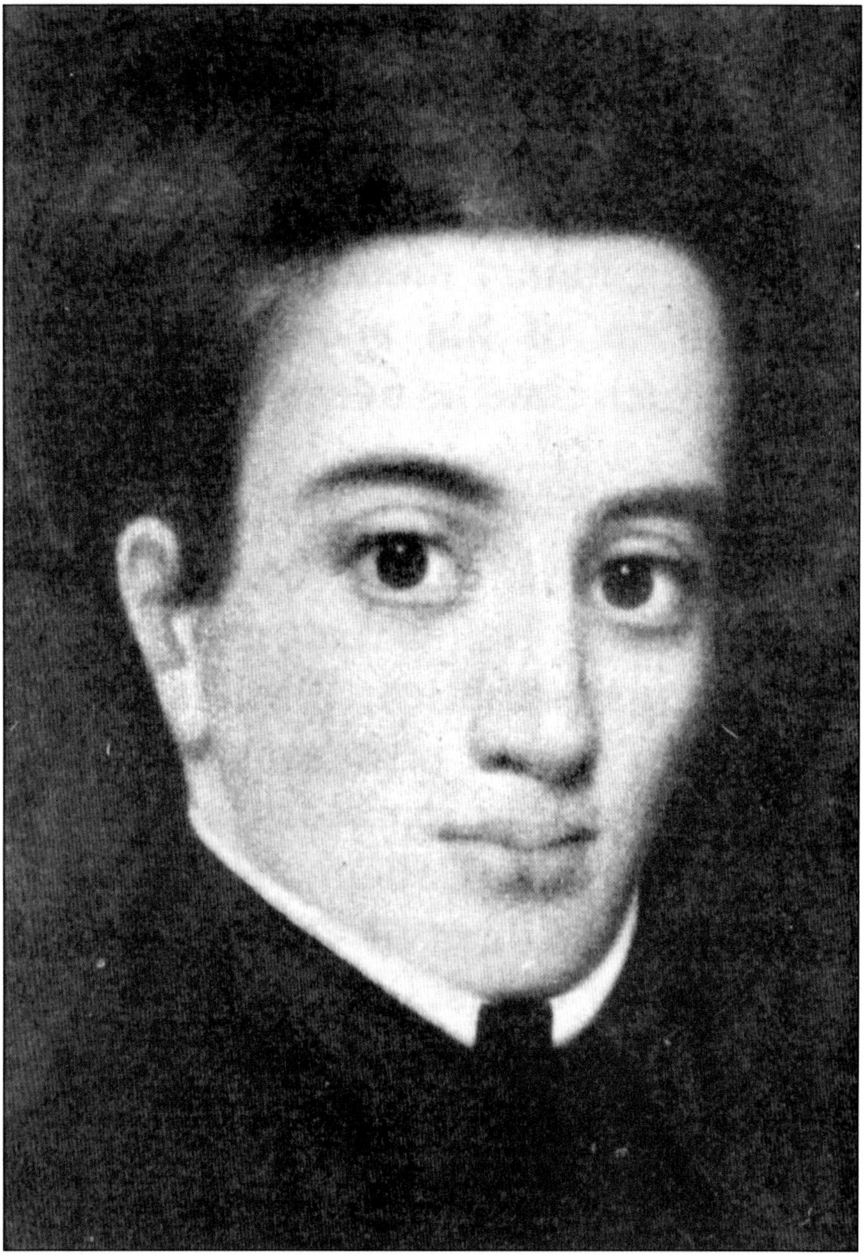

Rockwood Giddings. Rockwood Giddings, elected president in 1838, came to Georgetown College a born leader whose short time in office completely transformed the college. During his presidency, he raised an $80,000 endowment, an amazing achievement for a man in his late 20s. The replacement of one faction of the college's board with an organization much more harmonious benefited growth as well. In the 1905 *Belle of the Blue* annual, one of its writers comments on Giddings: "Frail of body, delicate, almost effeminate of countenance, he possessed a soul that seemed in some strange way to gain the ascendancy over all with whom he came in contact." In 1839, the college mourned the loss of their beloved leader—Giddings had died while preaching in the pulpit in Shelbyville, Kentucky.

HOWARD MALCOM. As successor to Rockwood Giddings, Howard Malcom assumed the presidency of Georgetown College in 1840. A well-known author of religious publications, Malcom expanded the curriculum and secured construction plans for the future Pawling Hall, which was designed originally to house ministerial students. Malcom also collected the college's first extensive library and established a museum. Unfortunately, Malcom's support for emancipation clashed with the views of the college community and he resigned in 1849.

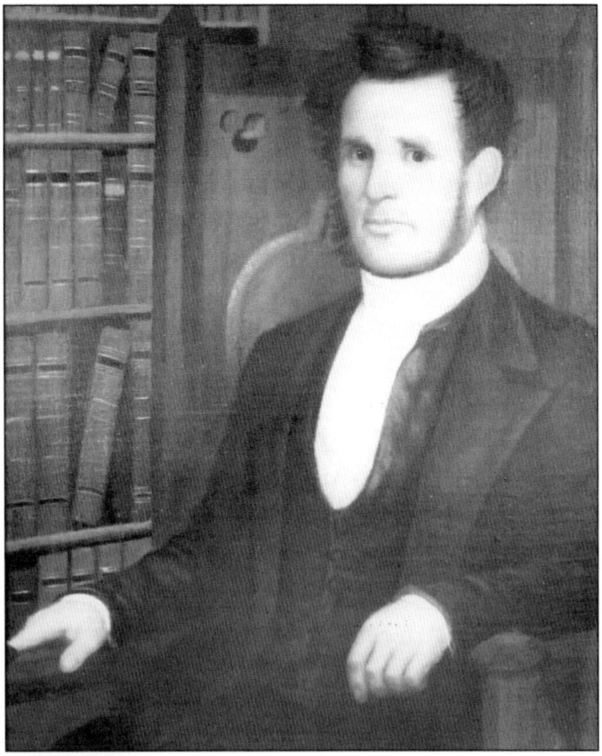

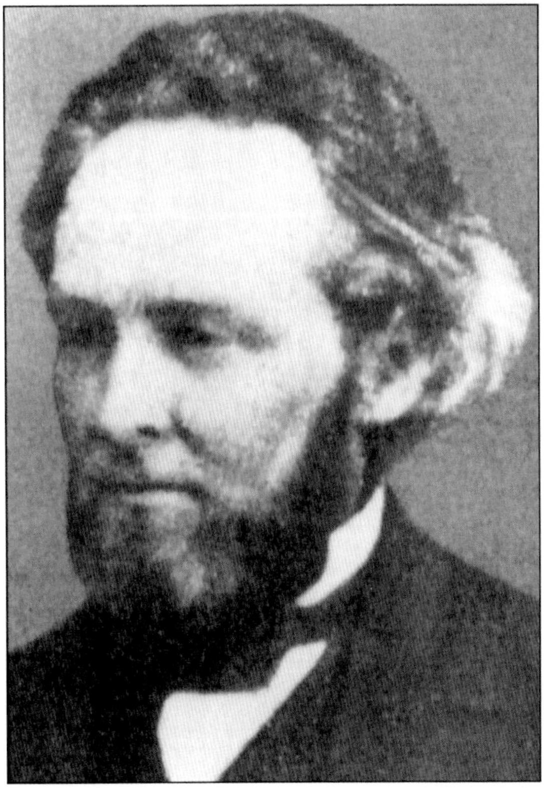

DR. BASIL MANLY. Dr. Basil Manly, president of Georgetown from 1871 to 1880, extended the college's education program to offer Bachelor of Arts and Bachelor of Science degrees. A major undertaking of Manly's was the enlargement of Pawling Hall, for which he asked individual churches to furnish its rooms. An Italianate-style structure, Pawling Hall housed mainly male ministerial students at the time. President Manly also implemented a decisive change in curriculum as he instigated the elective curriculum at Georgetown.

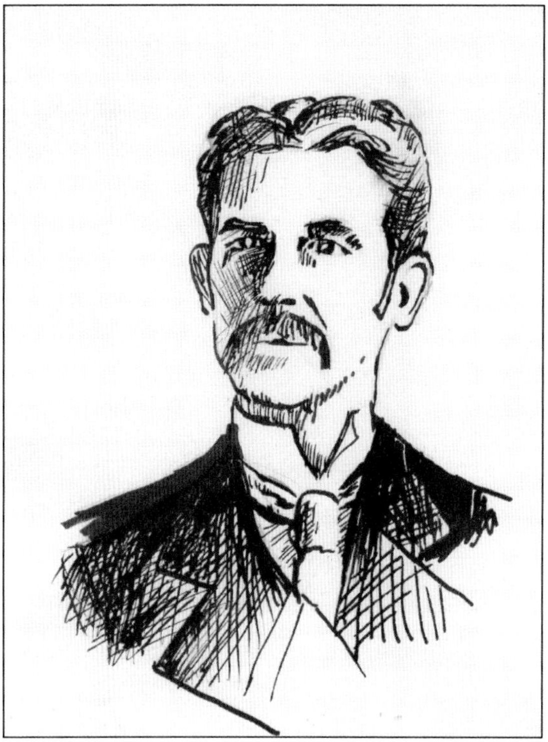

Dr. Arthur Yager. An 1882 Georgetown alumnus, Dr. Arthur Yager served as president of the college from 1908 to 1913. He returned to the area in 1884 after obtaining his Ph.D. from John Hopkins University, where he was in the same class as Woodrow Wilson. This connection proved to be instrumental to Yager's career, for in 1914 President Wilson appointed Dr. Yager as the governor of Puerto Rico.

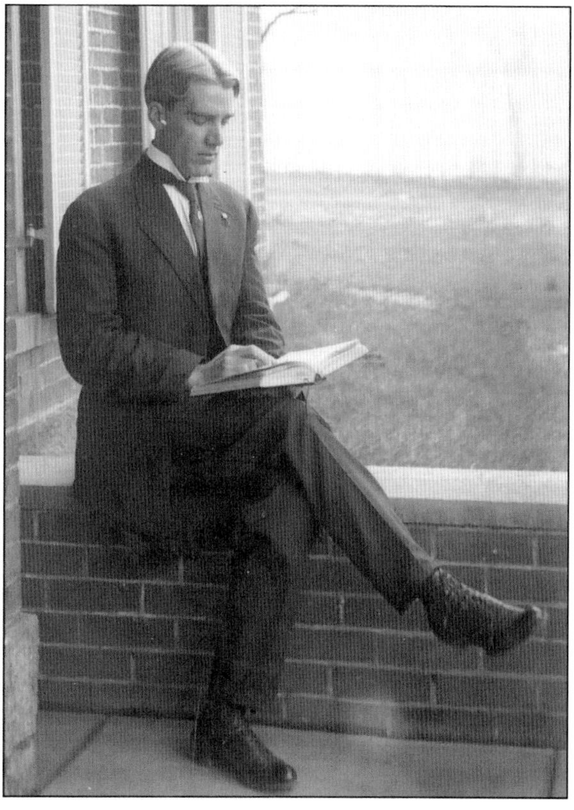

John L. Hill. As dean of the college as well as professor of history, economics, and political science, John L. Hill deeply imprinted a lasting mark on the history of Georgetown College. He proved to be so influential that the rebuilt chapel in 1948 was named after the former dean. Hill was an 1899 graduate of Georgetown College but left Georgetown after serving as dean to work for the Sunday School Board of the Southern Baptist Convention.

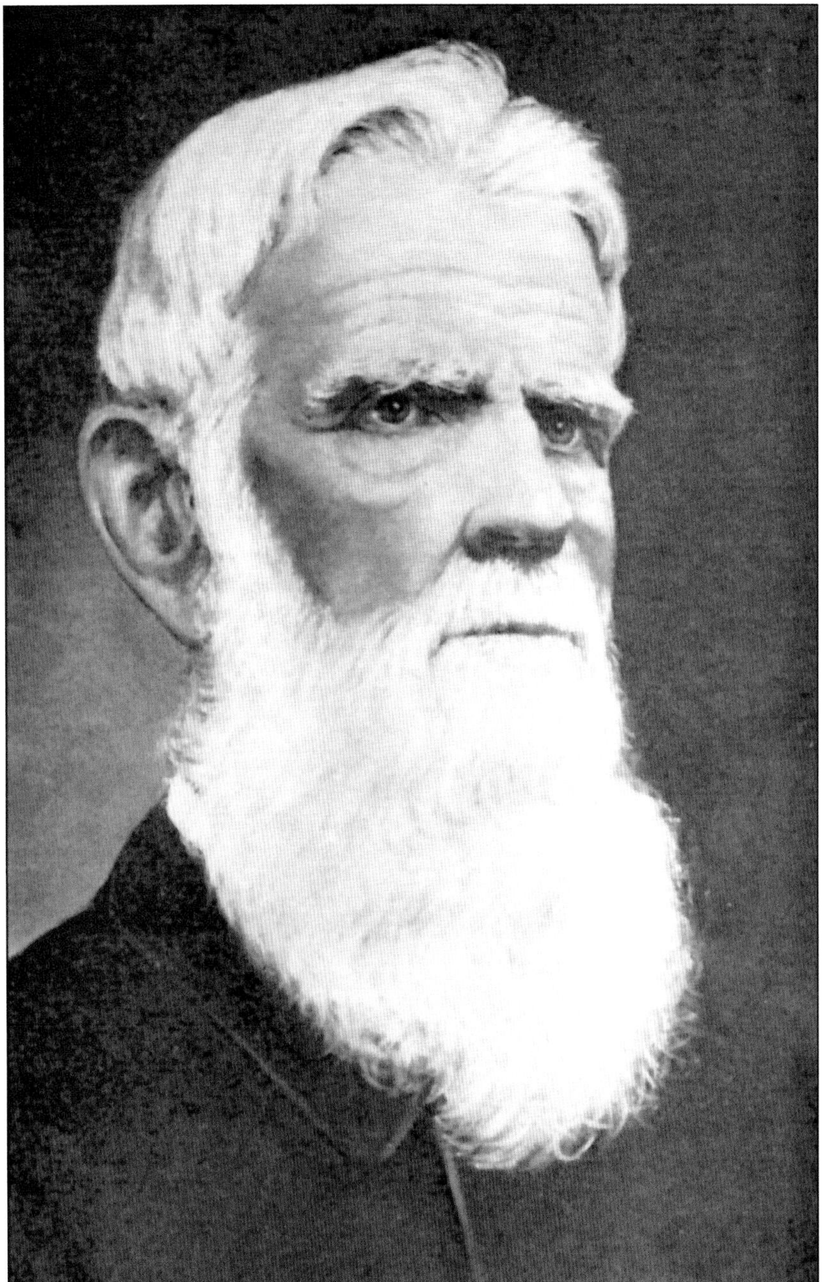

J. J. RUCKER. Pioneer of co-education, Prof. James Jefferson Rucker assumed leadership of the Georgetown Female Seminary by teaching at his home after the seminary building was consumed by a fire. A new seminary building was constructed in 1869; because coeducation was permanently adopted in 1892, and the institute eventually merged with Georgetown College, the building was called "Old Sem" after 1894. J. J. Rucker also was known as the "Father of the Euepian," a literary society for women. In 1895, an architecturally exquisite women's dormitory was built in an American Gothic style and named in his honor.

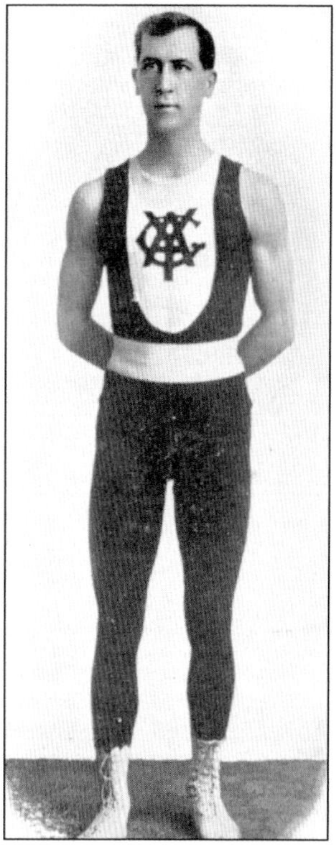

Robert T. Hinton. A graduate of Georgetown College, Robert T. Hinton proved to be an extremely gifted individual in the field of athletics. He furthered his education by attending Yale University as a graduate student and excelled athletically by winning the Intercollegiate Gymnastic Individual Championship at Philadelphia in 1902. His extended experience in athletics enabled him to be the perfect man for the position of associate professor and director of athletics at Georgetown, coaching all sports teams at one time.

Corts Brothers. Brothers Dr. Paul E. Corts (left) and Dr. Thomas E. Corts (right), both graduates of Georgetown, went on to both become presidents of higher institutions of learning. Paul Corts serves as president of Wingate College and Thomas Corts is president of Samford University.

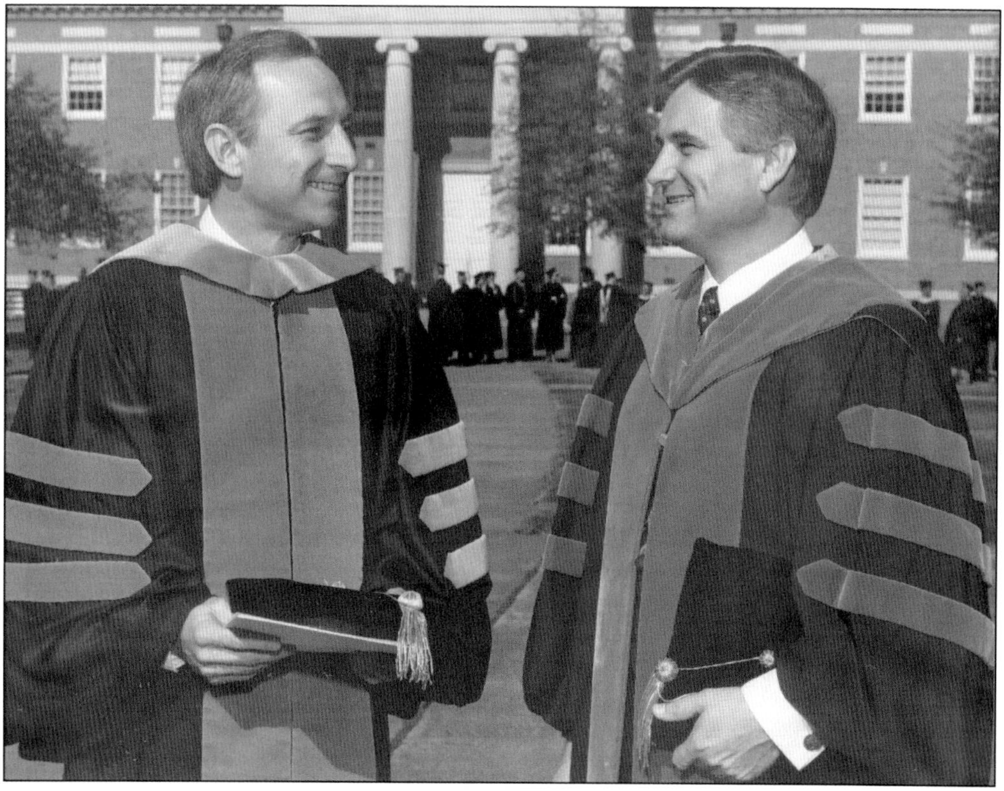

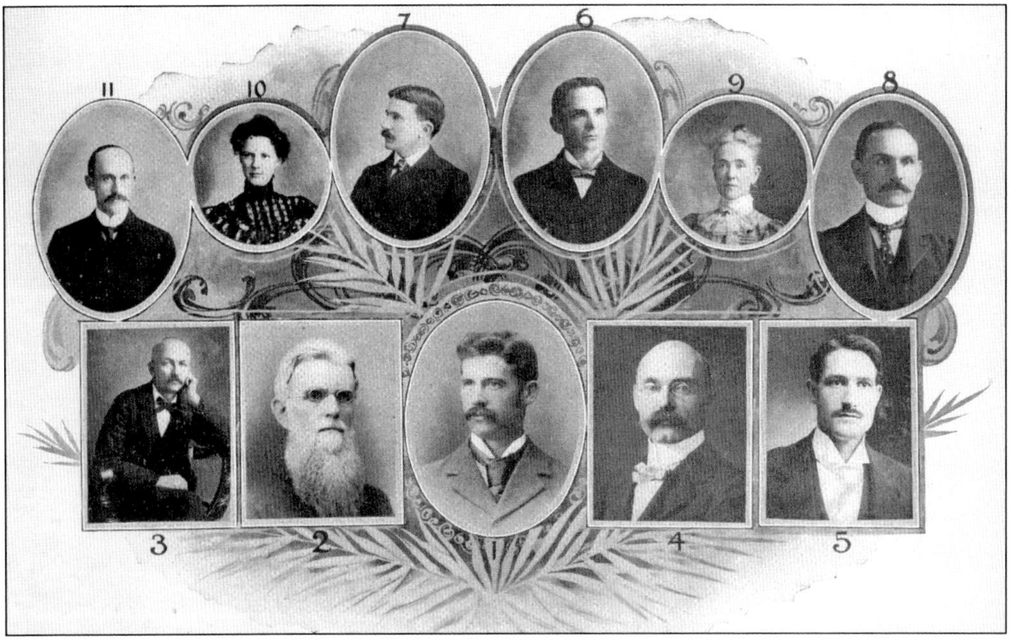

Faculty. This group of faculty from 1901 represents one of the early years of co-education. That year's yearbook, published by the senior class, was in fact called *The Co-ed.* Pictured from left to right are (top row) W. M. Smith, Miss Elizabeth Gatton, J. C. Metcalf, E. E. Ayres, Miss Rowena Pollard, and S. J. Pulliam; (bottom row) J. F. Eastwood, J. J. Rucker, Arthur Yager, Glanville Terrell, and D. E. Fogle.

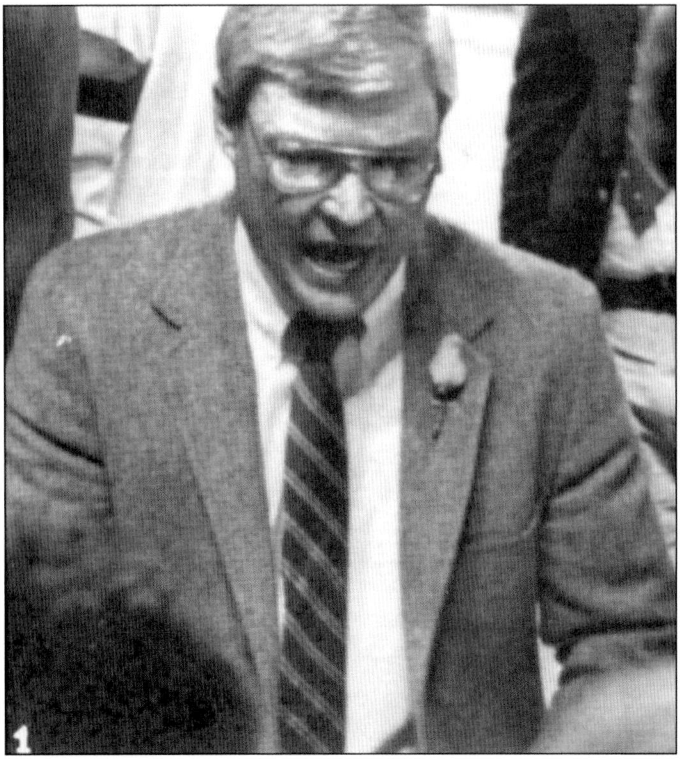

Jim Reid. A remarkable figure in the athletic history of Georgetown College, Jim Reid coached basketball for 23 years at the college, beginning as a graduate assistant to Bob Davis's coaching staff. In 1981, he was named Georgetown's athletic director, and he achieved NAIA Coach of the Year in 1994 and 1996. A mentor to his successor, Happy Osborne, Reid was elected to the NAIA Hall of Fame three weeks before he died of cancer.

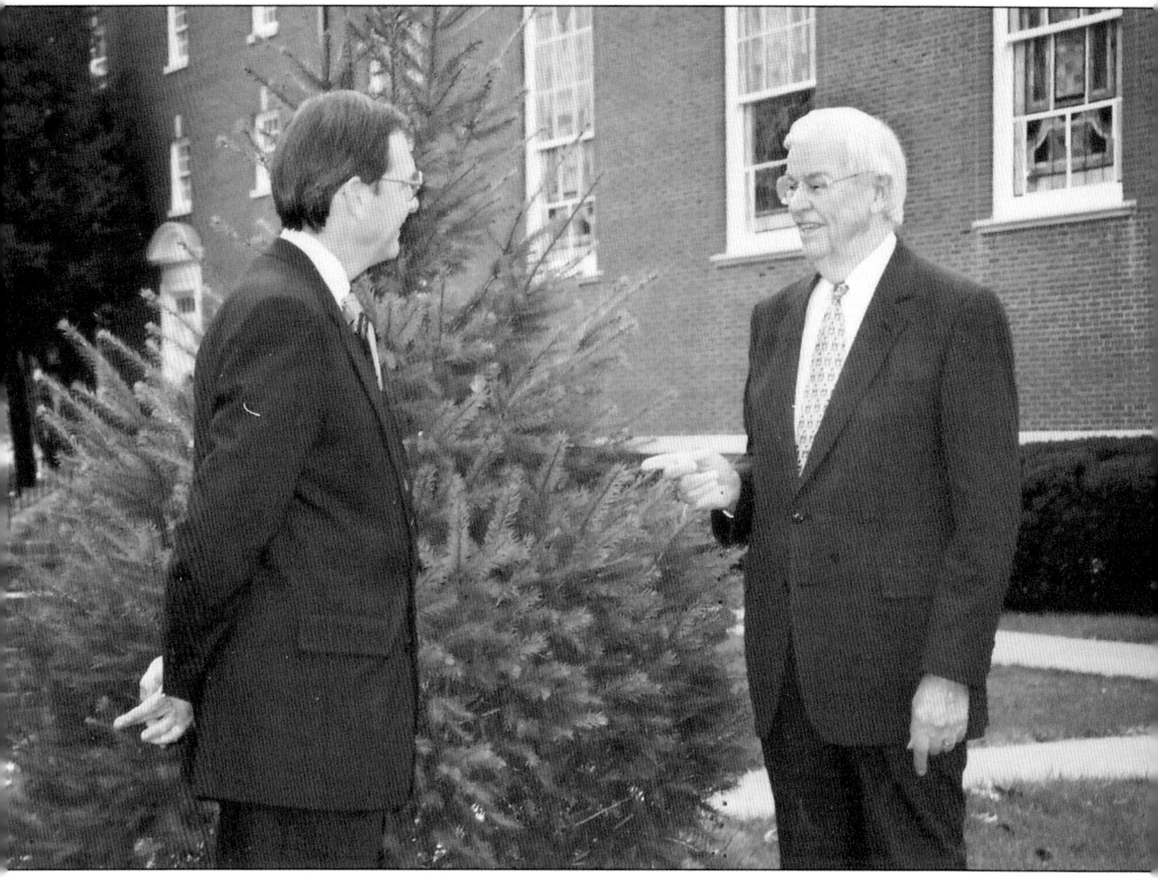

Dr. Crouch and Dr. Mills. Two very prominent figures in Georgetown's history, Dr. William H. Crouch Jr. (left) and Dr. Robert L. Mills (right) both promoted enormous building campaigns. Dr. Mills, president from 1959 to 1978, facilitated the construction of what is now known as "south campus" as well as the science center and student center. Dr. Crouch organized the building of the new learning resource center, a recreational center, and a fine arts building while also strengthening Georgetown College's international ties. Both phenomenal leaders saw increased enrollment and the sprouting of innovative programs during their terms.

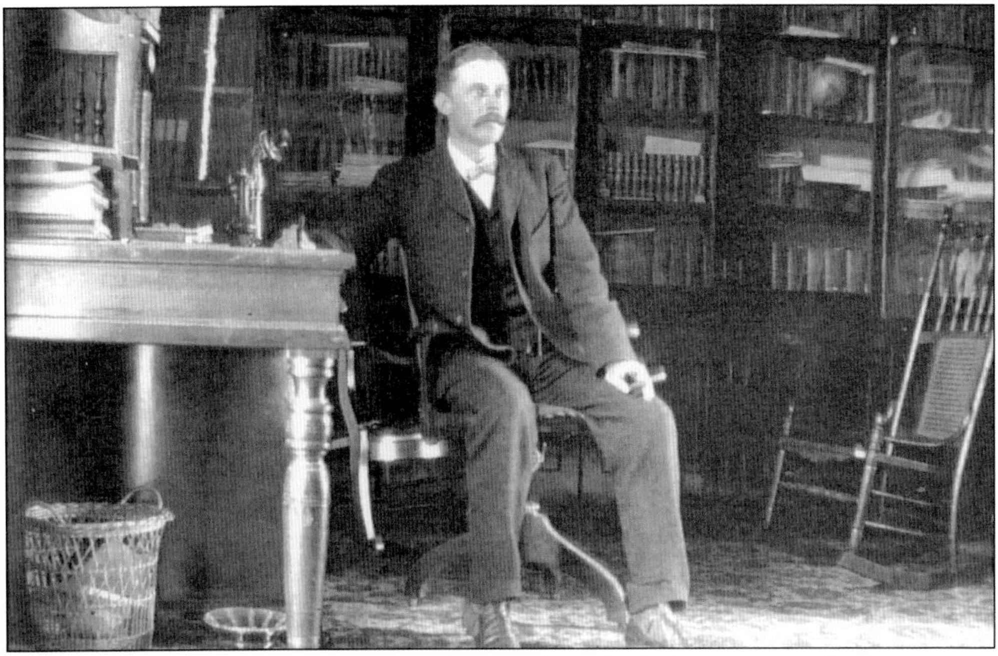

Rhodes Thomas. Rhodes Thomas was the son of Danford Thomas, an early Georgetown College professor who arrived in 1839 on horseback from Maine. Rhodes graduated from Georgetown in 1882. Danford passed away only a month before Rhodes's graduation, at which Rhodes gave the valedictorian speech next to the chair, draped in black, where his father always sat. Rhodes went on to become chairman of the board of trustees at Georgetown. (Photograph courtesy of Horace Hambrick, grandson of Rhodes Thomas.)

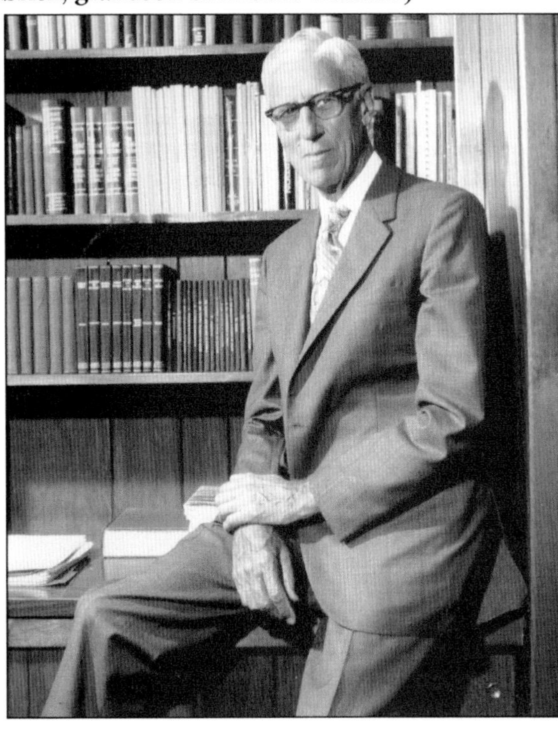

Ira J. Porter. A Georgetown College trustee from 1924 to 1982, Ira J. Porter was nominated "Mr. Georgetown" upon his retirement from the college. Not only did he serve as president of the board of trustees, but he also displayed excellent fund-raising skills, an attitude of a devoted alumnus, and the embodiment of the spirit of Georgetown College. (Photograph courtesy of Maribeth Hambrick, daughter of Ira J. Porter.)

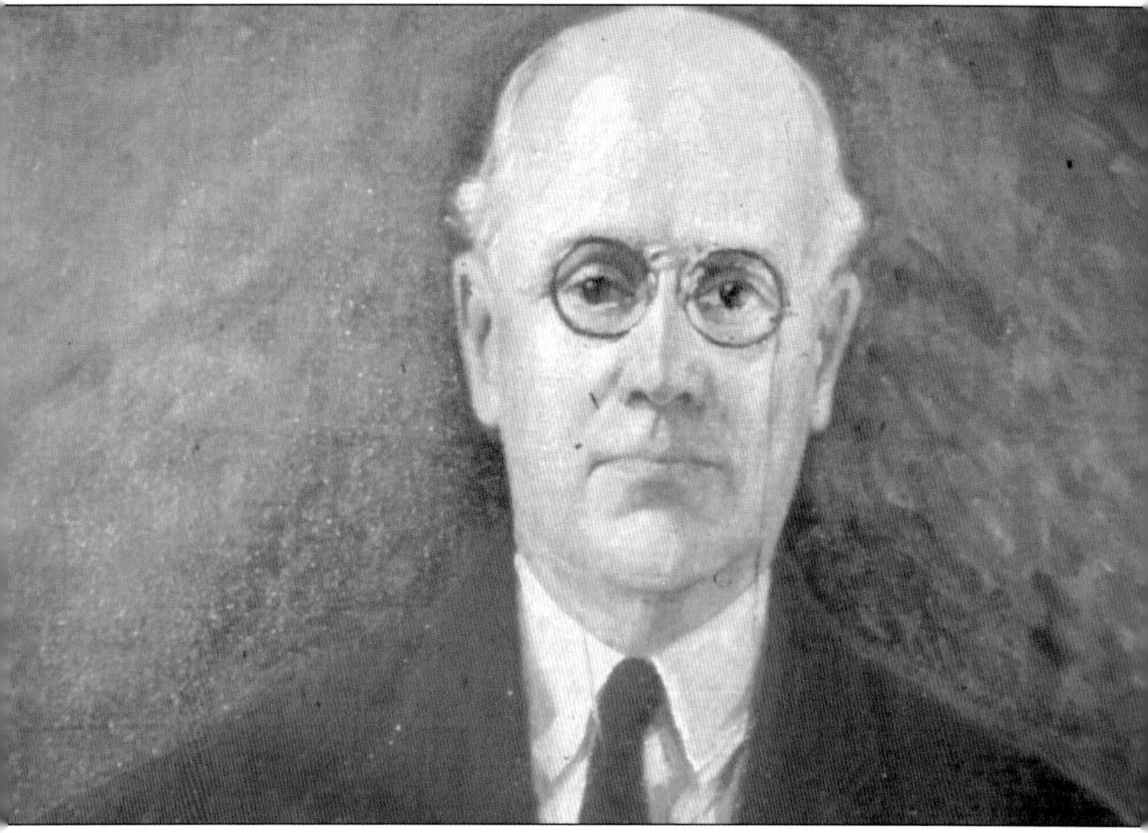

Dr. Adams. Dr. Maldon Browning Adams served the college as president for 17 years, resigning in 1930. With 400 students and 31 faculty, Dr. Adams facilitated and strengthened Georgetown's financial status. In 1926, a new gymnasium was built to the delight of the students, whose efforts in raising $25,000 for the building paid off. Citizens of Georgetown raised another $75,000, contributing to the growth and development of the college. However, the economic progression wilted not long after it had blossomed when the Great Depression started in 1929.

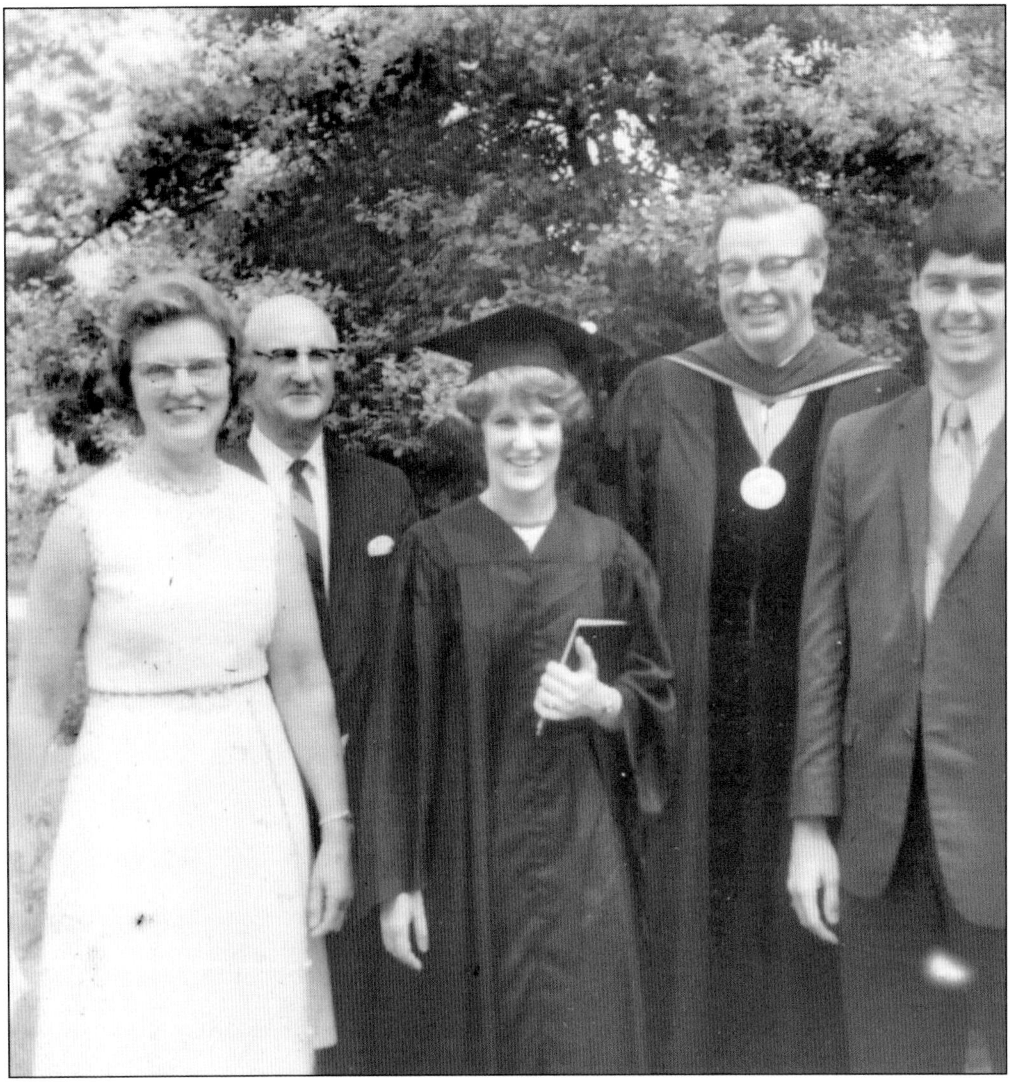

GEORGETOWN FAMILY STRAINS—GRIESSER FAMILY. Many families send scores of their descendants to Georgetown, and soon the school becomes a traditional part of their family heritage. This tendency was strong in the Griesser family, pictured here with Dr. Mills (second from right) at the 1970 graduation ceremony. Dorotha and Carl Griesser (at left), both Georgetown graduates, pose with their daughter and son-in law, Peggy Griesser Roberts and Howard Roberts, also graduates of Georgetown. The proud Griesser parents sent to Georgetown all three of their children, Peggy being the youngest, who in turn all met their spouses at the college. The Griesser children married and a total of six of their combined children also sought education at Georgetown. Another family that traces its roots back to Georgetown is the Snyder family, which totals an impressive 36 family members who have attended Georgetown College. (Photograph courtesy of Carla Cook.)

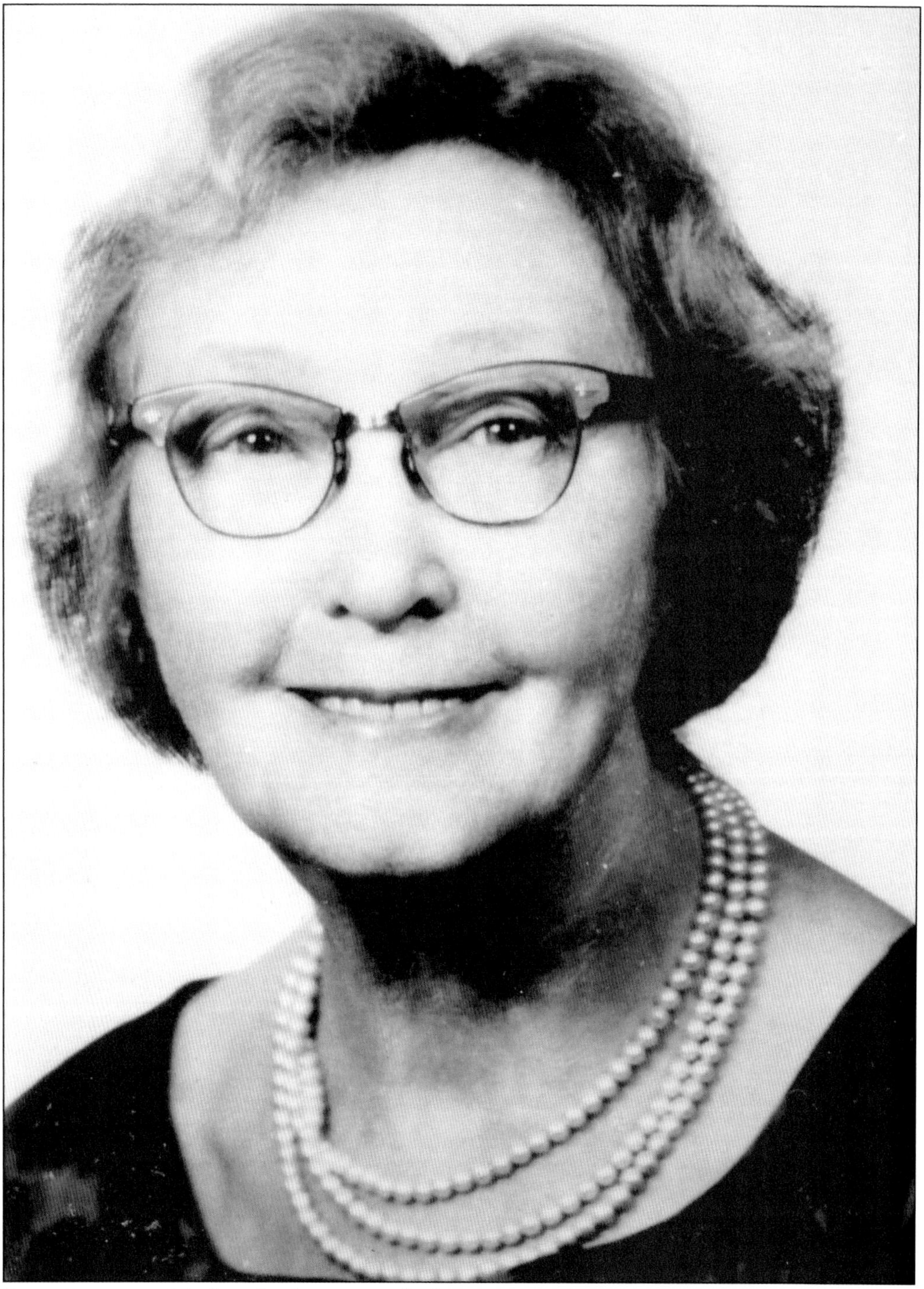

Rena Calhoun. A beloved educator and advisor to students, Rena Calhoun served as the dean of women as well as the sponsor and director of Maskrafters, the college theater club. Living in Rucker Hall, she taught drama and speech in the elocution department and advised the Greek organizations. Dr. Horace Hambrick says of Miss Calhoun, "When girls had a problem, she settled it quickly. . . . She was very well respected."

Two

Building Booms

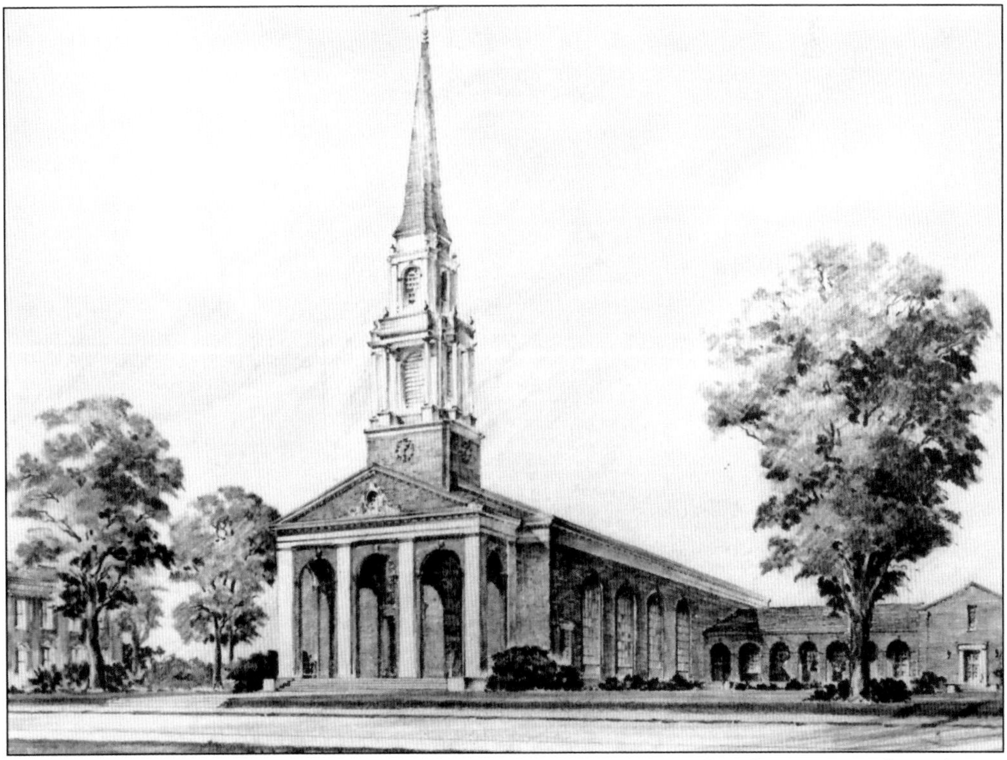

Architectural Drawing of the Chapel. The desperate plea for a new chapel was finally satisfied in 1949 under the administration of Dr. Samuel S. Hill. The new John L. Hill Chapel, named for former dean of the college, seated around 1,000 people. The architectural plans expanded as the student body grew rapidly after World War II. The final size of the chapel included six classrooms on the ground floor and three floors of offices at the rear of the building.

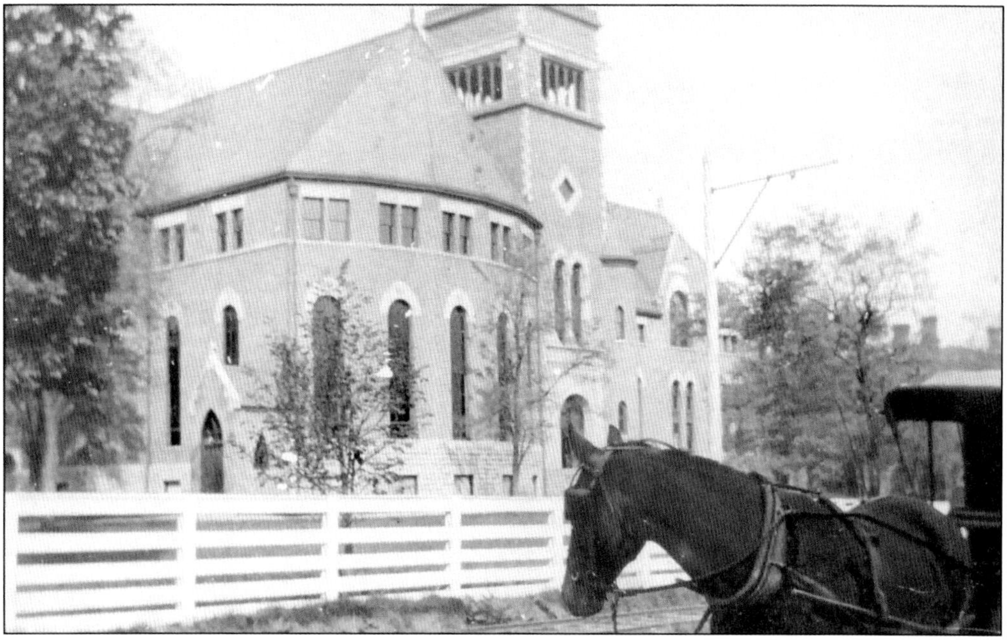

Chapel with Horse and Buggy. The front of the chapel-library building, dedicated in 1894, encapsulated much of Georgetown's student activity within its walls. Its front façade faced Jackson Street, the avenue on which this horse and buggy are traveling. The multi-purpose chapel building, built at a cost of $40,000, included extra cavities to provide halls for the literary societies, space for a swimming pool on the ground floor, as well as a museum in the north wing. It also housed the college's second gymnasium and included a bell tower that called students to classes and chapel.

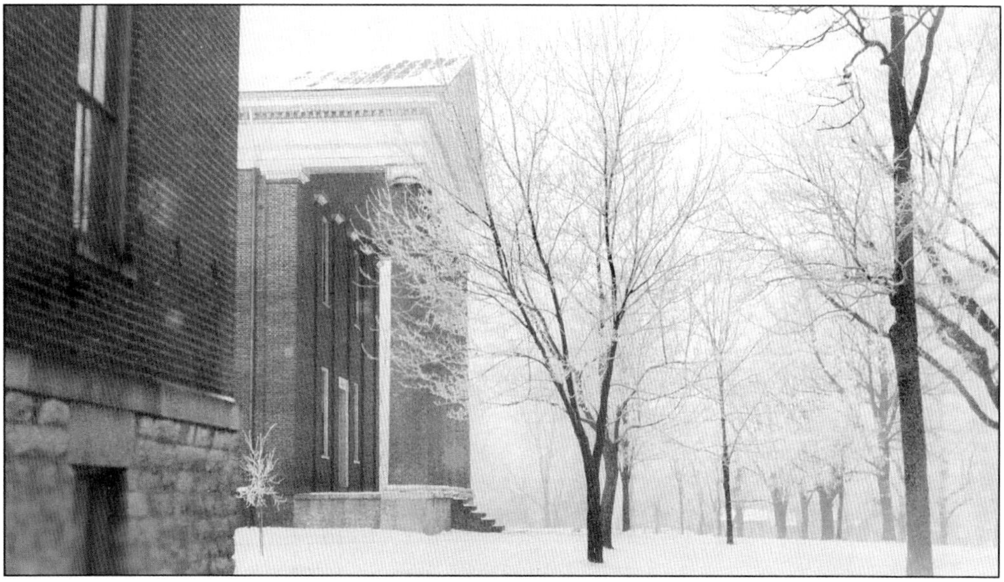

Georgetown in Snow. The serene campus of the college during a peaceful snowfall is a stunning scene. Snowball fights are a favorite pastime among students during the winter season. After the fun ends when noses and fingers become numb, students venture inside to anticipate the canceling of classes for the following day.

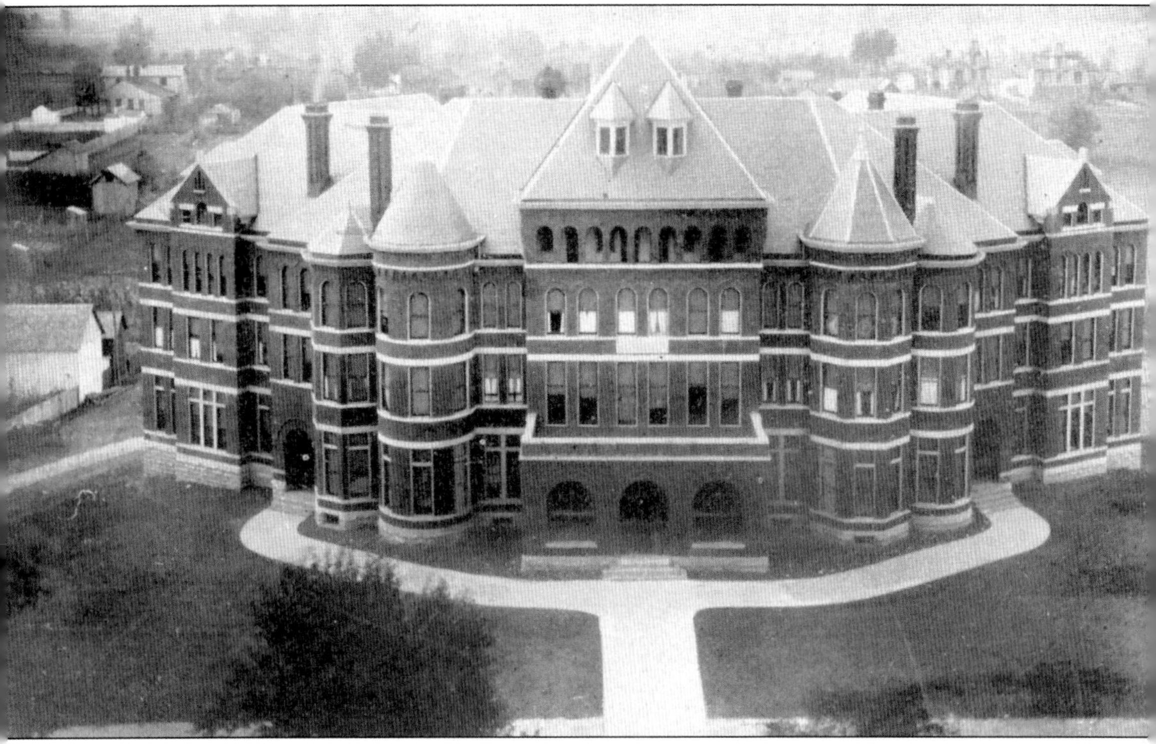

Rucker Hall. The women's dormitory, Rucker Hall, was built during the presidency of Dr. Richard M. Dudley and was completed in 1896. The building of the new dorm thrived under the financial leadership of James J. Rucker, who helped to raise $50,000 for the massive structure. A native of Missouri and a graduate of Georgetown College in 1854, J. J. Rucker returned to the college as a faculty member teaching mathematics and directing the academy. In 1943, during Dr. Samuel S. Hill's term, Rucker Hall received a face-lift. In 1971, the college sadly demolished the grand feat of architecture in order to build a "mall-like" complex and provide students with adequate housing on campus.

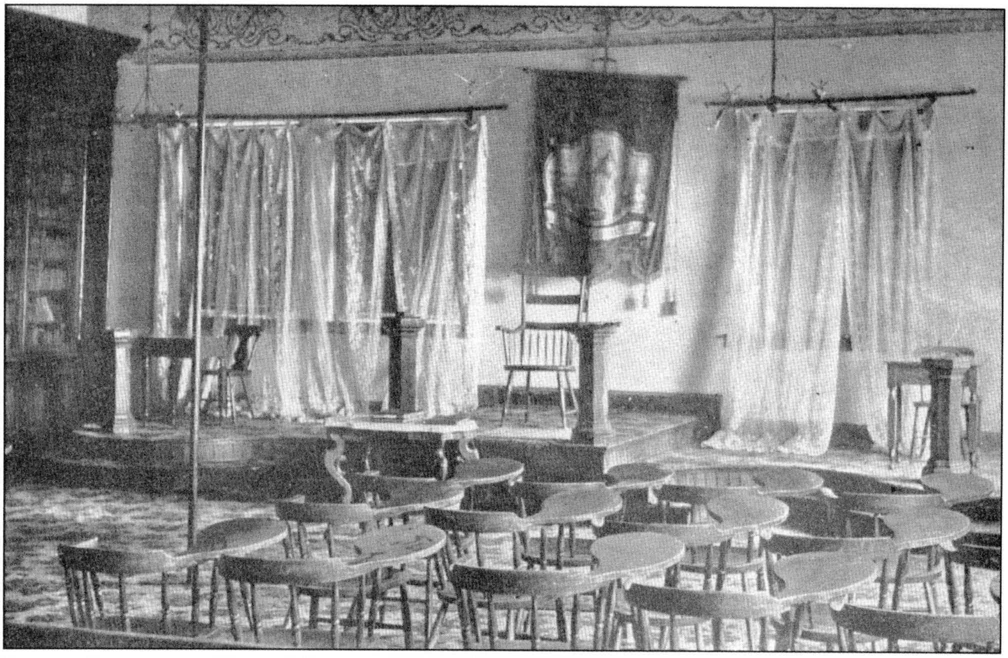

INSIDE CICERONIAN HALL. The ornamental halls of the Ciceronian and Tau Theta Kappa Societies evoked a serious aura for oration and debates. Located originally in the upstairs of the old academy building and then in the chapel-library building, the literary societies were so adverse to each other that they used separate entrances to their halls.

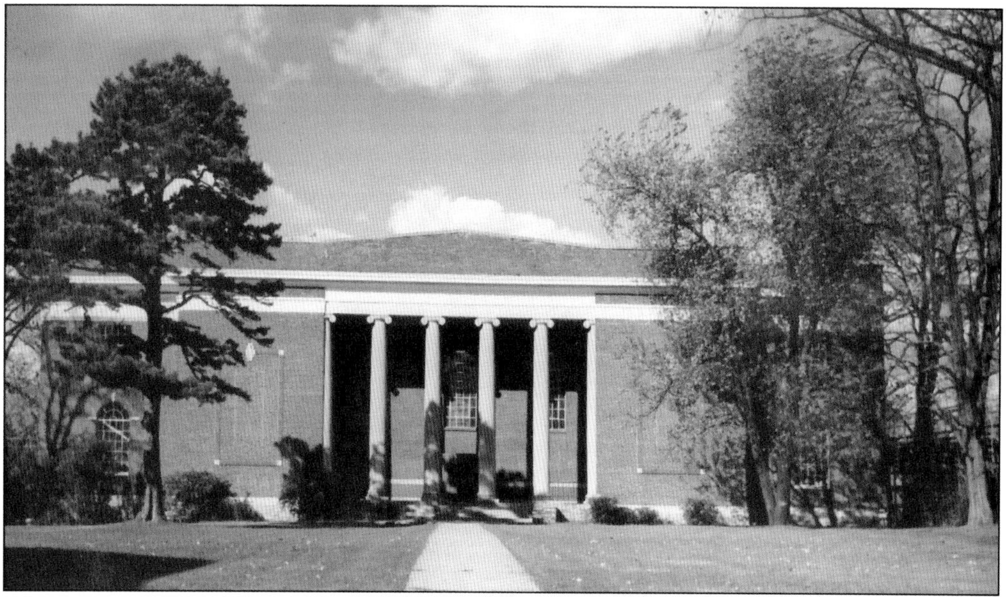

ALUMNI GYMNASIUM. Now used for only intercollegiate athletic practice and competition, Alumni Gym was once a facility with a tightly packed schedule, since it provided a recreational outlet for intramural sports as well. Scores of notable athletes have sported the orange and black uniforms, including Kenny Davis, an All-American basketball player and member of the 1972 Olympic team. At one point, living quarters were so scarce that the balcony of the gymnasium was sectioned and converted into living spaces for students.

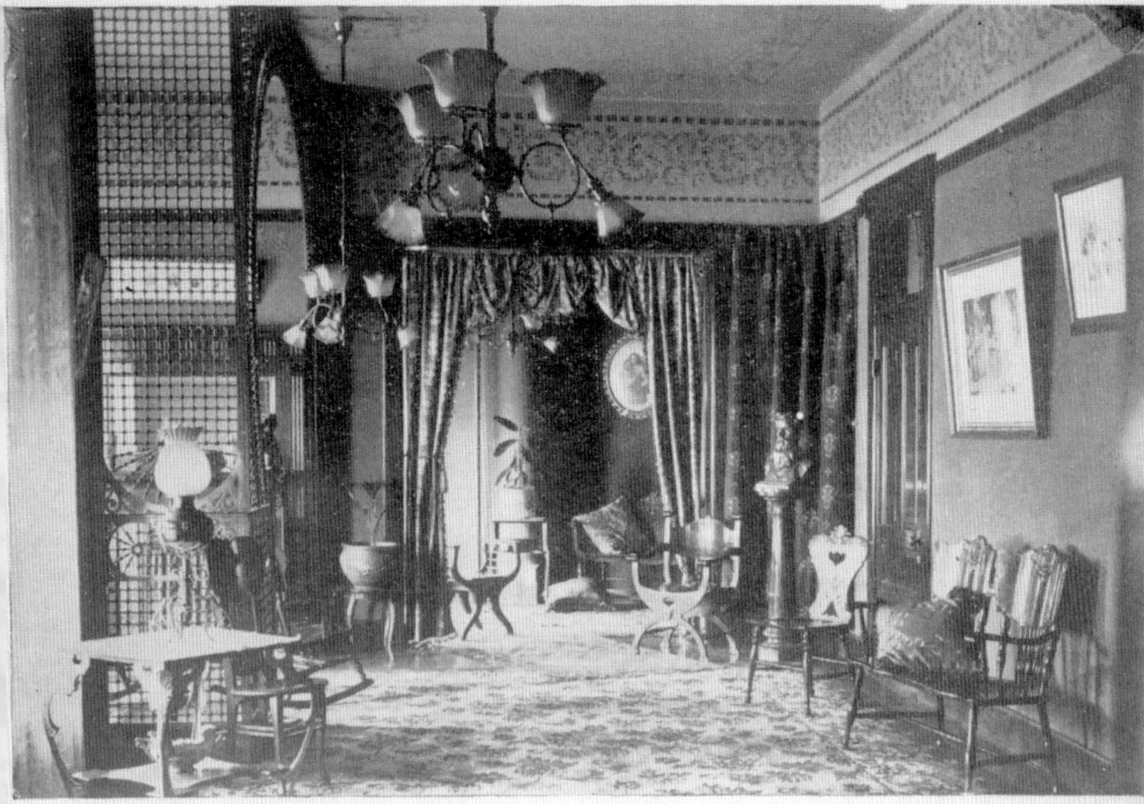

THE FANNIE T. SUMMERS PARLOR IN RUCKER HALL.

Photo by Wahdling

PARLOR OF RUCKER HALL. Rucker Hall was the core of social activity for 70 years. Housing much more than dorm rooms, women in Rucker Hall did not have to leave the premises to dine or participate in a game of bowling. This photograph captures the Victorian parlor of Rucker Hall, where women were required to sign in and out. One telephone for the entire dorm was located in the lovely parlor, and women made sure to return to their dorm by the installed curfew time. Males, however, were deemed responsible enough to have no curfew.

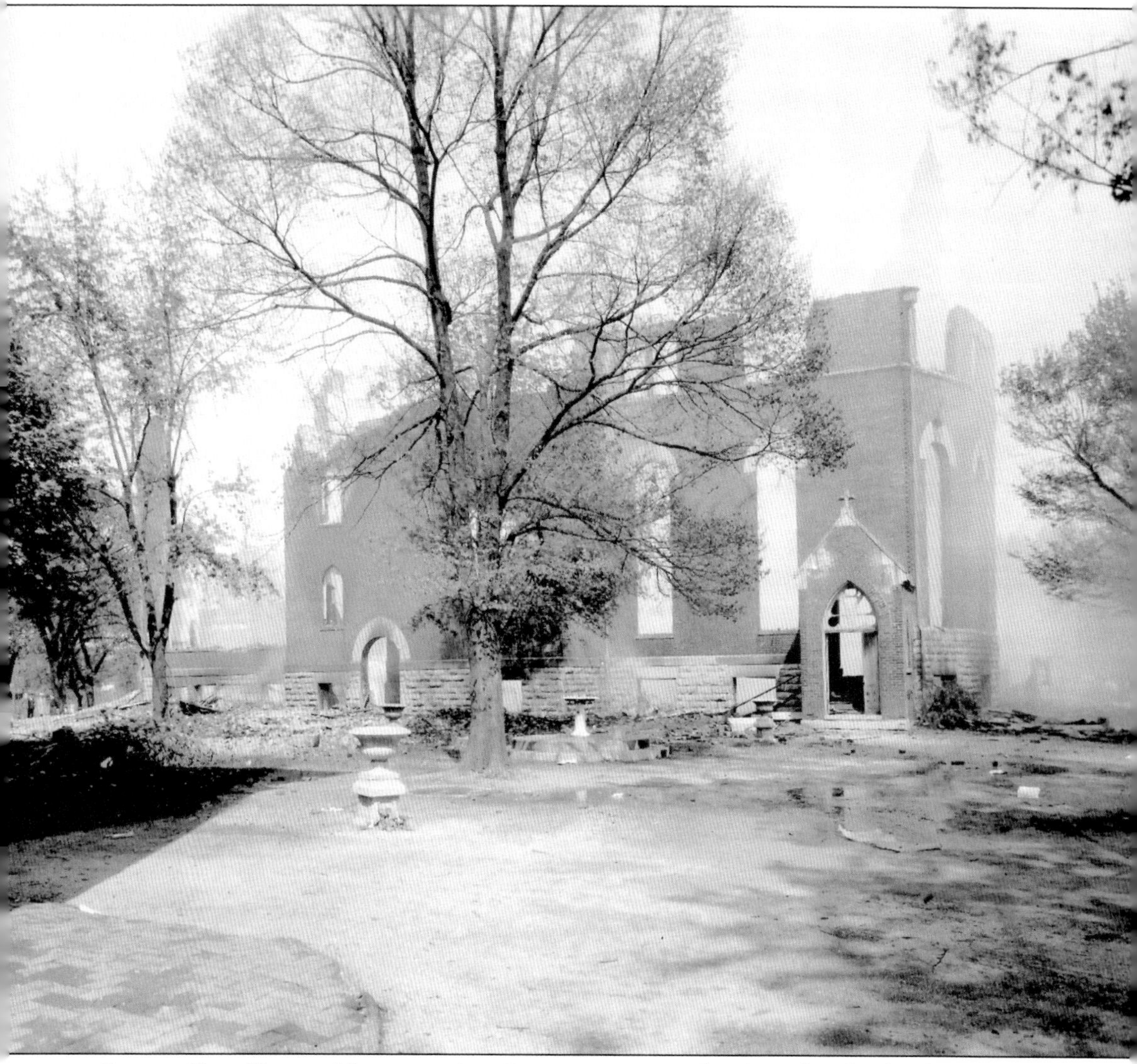

CHAPEL FIRE RUINS. The stunning Romanesque-style chapel, which also housed a gymnasium, library, museum, swimming pool, literary society halls, and additional classrooms, was swept away in flames in 1930. The college mourned their $450,000 loss, especially as even more difficulties arose when braced with the question of rebuilding during the Great Depression. The succeeding new chapel, named for John L. Hill, former dean of the college, was constructed and dedicated in 1948.

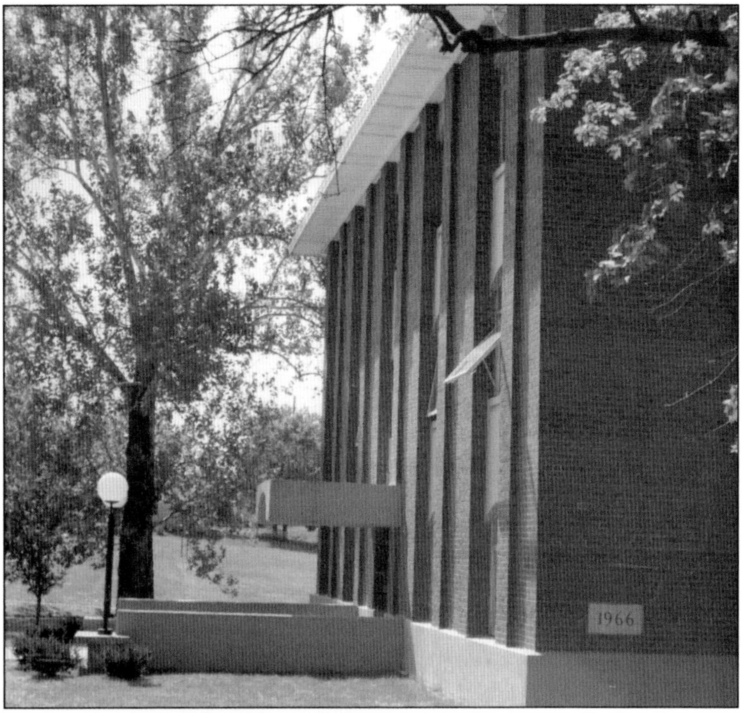

Side View of Pierce Hall. Pierce Hall opened in 1966 as part of the "mall plan" on south campus, along with the other "independent" dormitories: Collier Hall, Flowers Hall, and Allen Hall. Each dorm houses around 86 students at three stories high. As a result, Rucker Hall was demolished in order to construct the last of the 12-dorm complex and necessary recreational space.

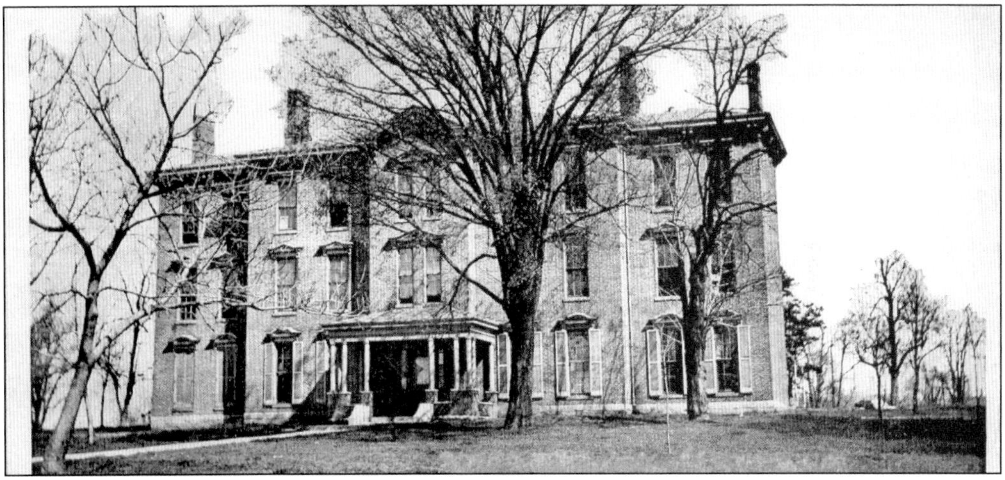

Pawling Hall Postcard. The second building constructed on campus, Pawling Hall, was named for Isachar Pawling, who provided a portion of the college's early endowment. Originally created as a male dormitory for ministerial students, Pawling Hall now houses classrooms and offices for students and professors of English, history, philosophy, psychology, and religion. Pawling Hall was constructed under the administration of Pres. Howard Malcom, who stated the following about the building: "The most important fact since my last report, is the opening of Paulding Hall, for the reception of students preparing for the ministry. . . . The whole of this beautiful and profitable arrangement has been accomplished by the personal labor of the young bretheren of the Hall. . . . The expenses of each student in Paulding Hall, for board and washing have amounted to only *eighty cents* per week! A room double the size of the others forms a convenient chapel where family worship is held daily, and a prayer meeting on Wednesday evening."

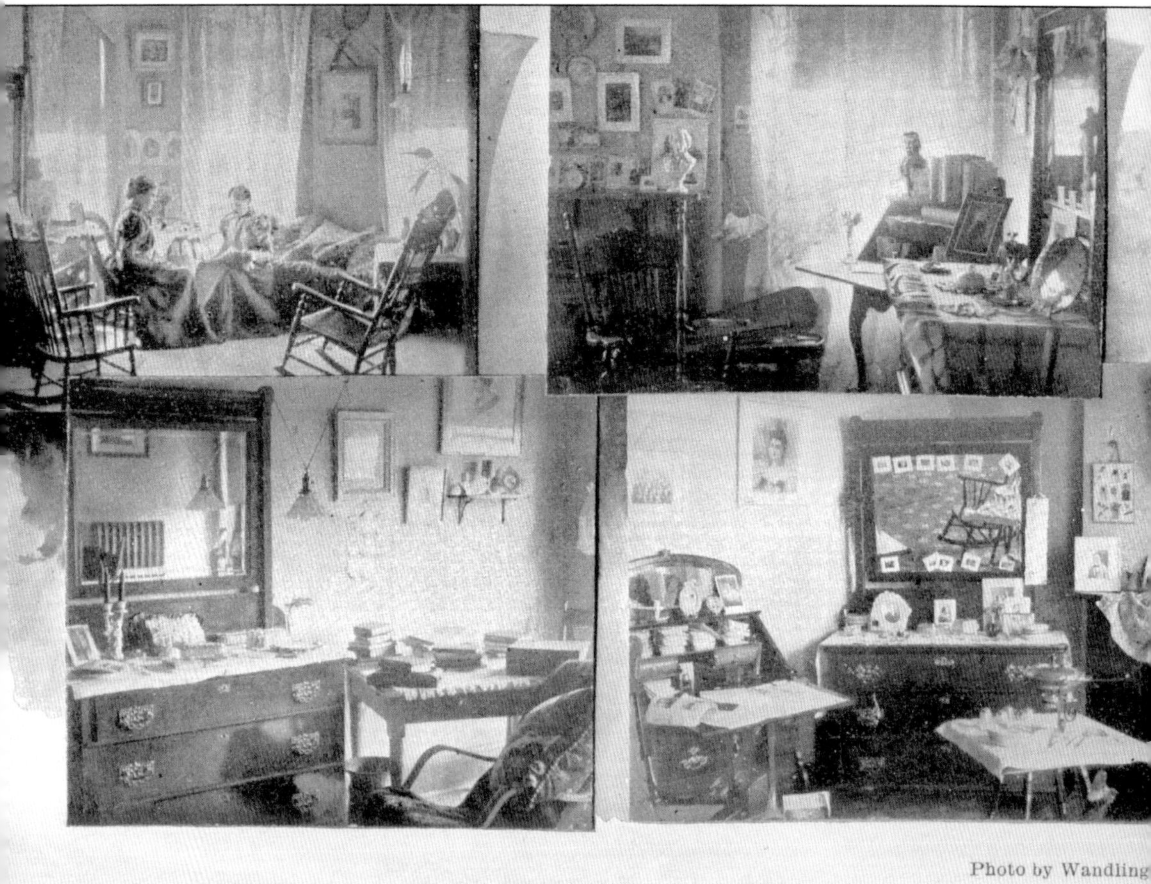

RUCKER HALL BED-ROOMS.

Rucker Hall Bedrooms. The spacious and well-illuminated bedrooms in Rucker Hall made dorm life pleasant and comfortable. The furniture featured in this photograph is now of a state one would call "antique." When this architectural gem was demolished, the furniture in the newer dorms replaced the older furniture in Rucker Hall with a more modern style. Rucker Hall, built in 1895, functioned primarily as the women's dormitory. Later, as the campus population increased and more dorms were erected, it became home to mainly freshmen and independent women (not affiliated with a sorority).

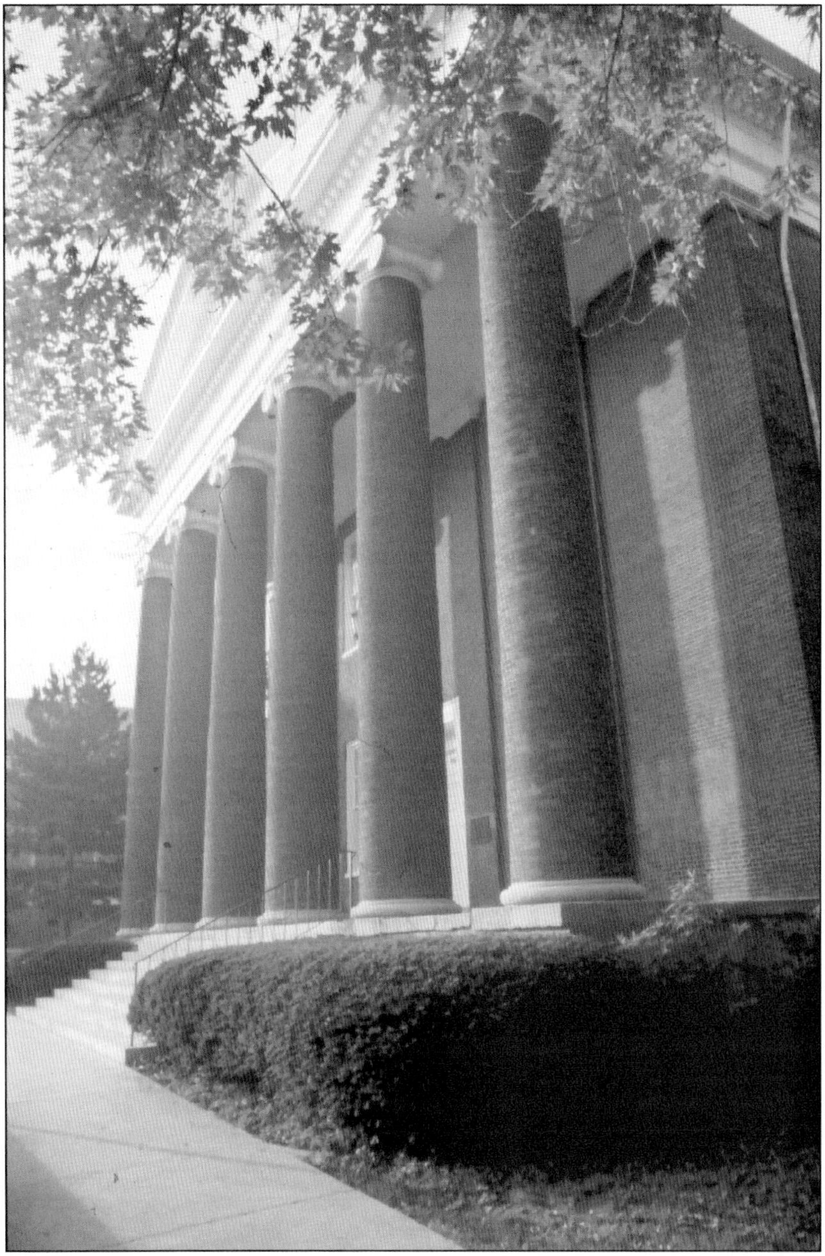

GIDDINGS HALL. This photograph of Giddings Hall, taken in the 1960s, highlights the building's most prominent feature: its colossal and domineering columns. Giddings Hall, earlier known as Recitation Hall, set an architectural standard when it was constructed in 1841 as the first building on campus. Giddings was utilized for a wide spectrum of purposes. It housed science classrooms and provided space for a theater and oratorical hall. A long-sustained legend about Giddings supposedly hides in its stately columns: a keg of whiskey belonging to Elijah Craig, the Baptist preacher who established the school that was to become Georgetown College, is supposedly hidden inside one of the brick columns. As students daily pass the monumental structure, they are reminded of past traditions while looking forward to the future.

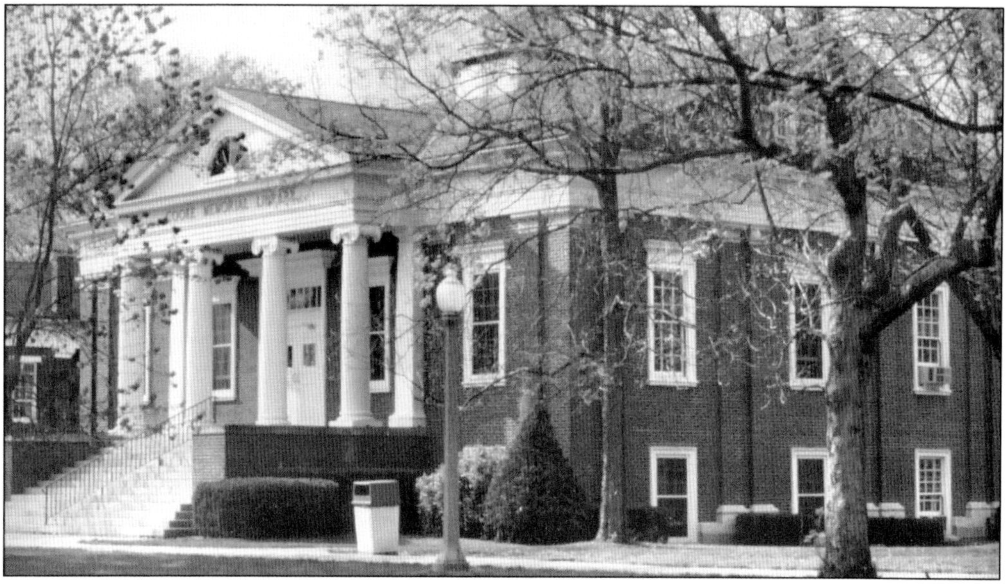

COOKE MEMORIAL LIBRARY. Constructed in 1954, Cooke Memorial Library fulfilled a great need on campus that had existed since 1930, when the old library burned in the chapel-building blaze. Located in the basement of Cooke was a grill enjoyed by students and professors. In 1998, the new grand Learning Resource Center opened and Cooke Memorial Library was modified into classrooms, an information technology services center, and office space for professors.

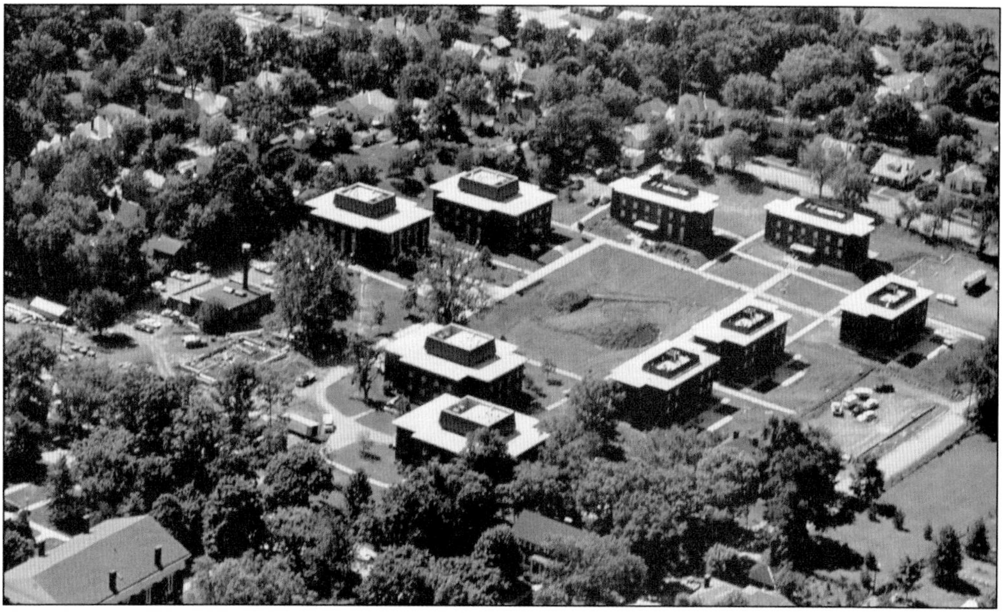

MINI-DORM COMPLEX. Constructed in 1965 and opened for living space in 1966, the new dorms provided the much-needed space for students that the college previously did not possess. Smaller, 40-bed dorms were built for fraternities and sororities while larger, 80-bed dorms housed "independent" students in Flowers, Pierce, and Collier Halls. In the center of the mall-like plan is the quad, which has become the core of student outdoor leisure activity.

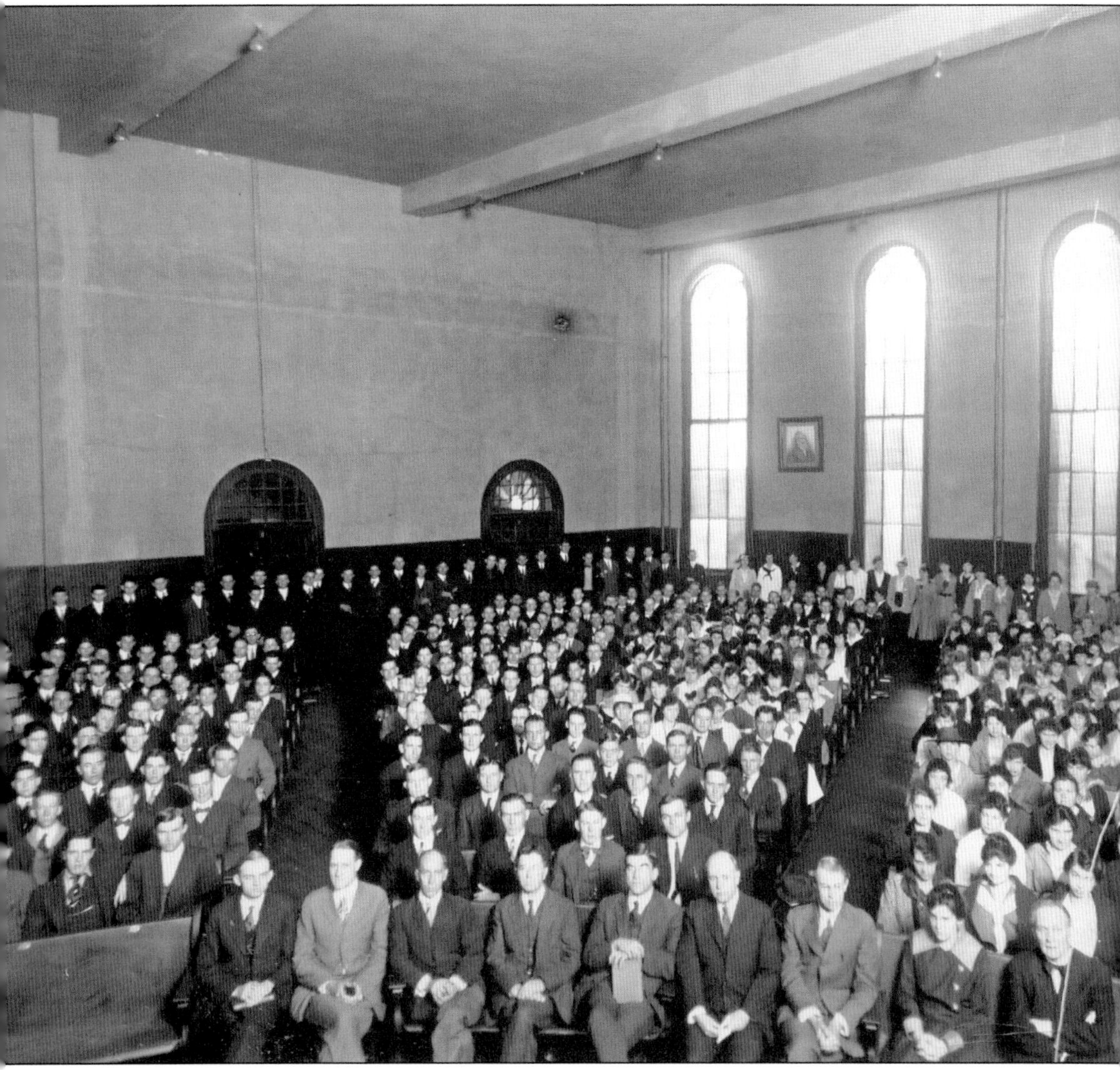

OLD CHAPEL. Truly the heartbeat of campus, the original chapel building not only housed the majority of religious activity, but also a library, gymnasium, museum, lecture halls, and classrooms. The inside of the stunning structure is shown in this photograph, where walls were quite plain but the structure was Gothic in design. Notice that all the females were seated to one side and the male students on the other so as not to cause distraction. The chapel tragically burned in 1930 as students exited in an orderly fashion from the blazing building.

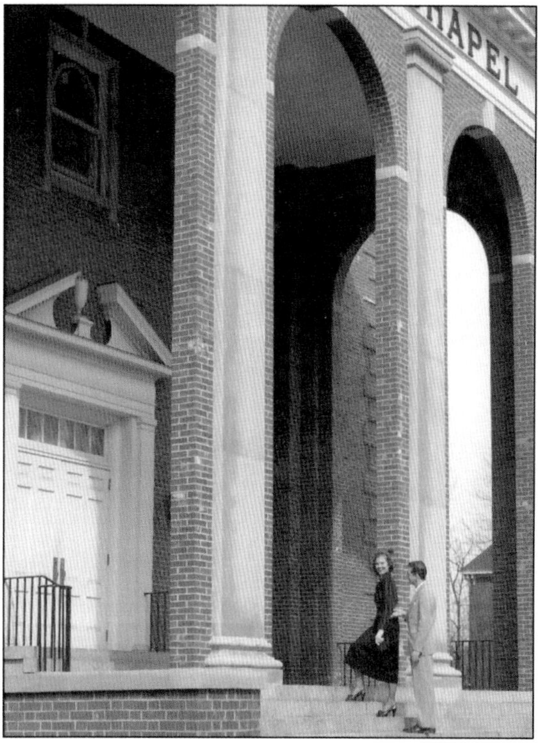

CLOSE-UP OF JOHN L. HILL CHAPEL. This close-up frontal view of the John L. Hill Chapel, shown not long after its completion in 1949, highlights the structure's domineering arched columns.

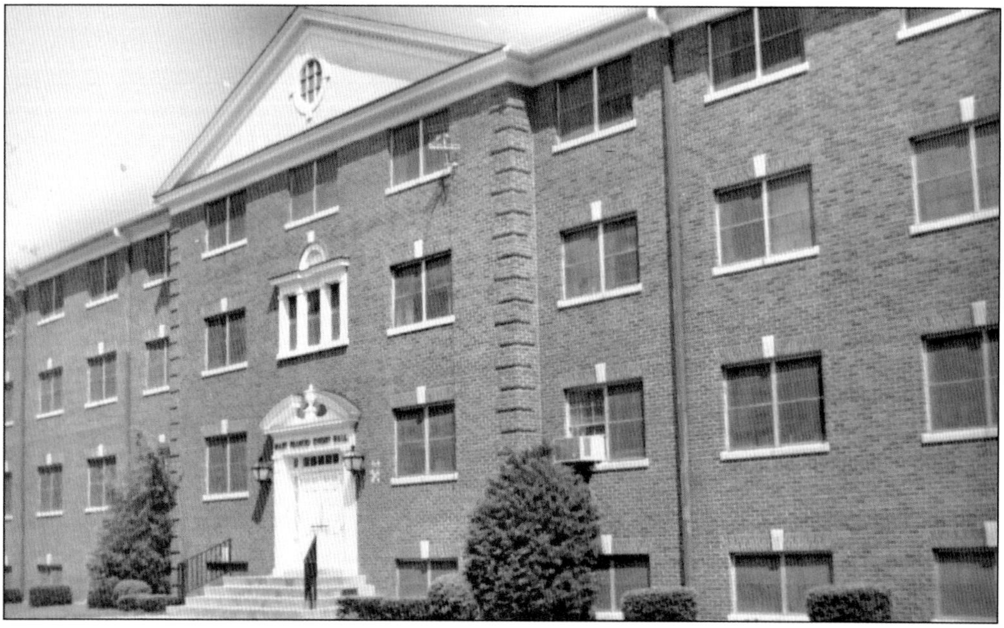

KNIGHT HALL. Built around 1957 as a dormitory for women, Mary Francis Knight Hall still serves today as a women's dorm, housing mostly freshman students. Today Knight Hall is equipped with a full kitchen and a "tiger den," in which students can choose to recreate or study. Knight Hall was named in memory of Dr. L. B. Knight's mother. Dr. Knight donated funds to the building of the chapel, and its basement is also named Knight Hall.

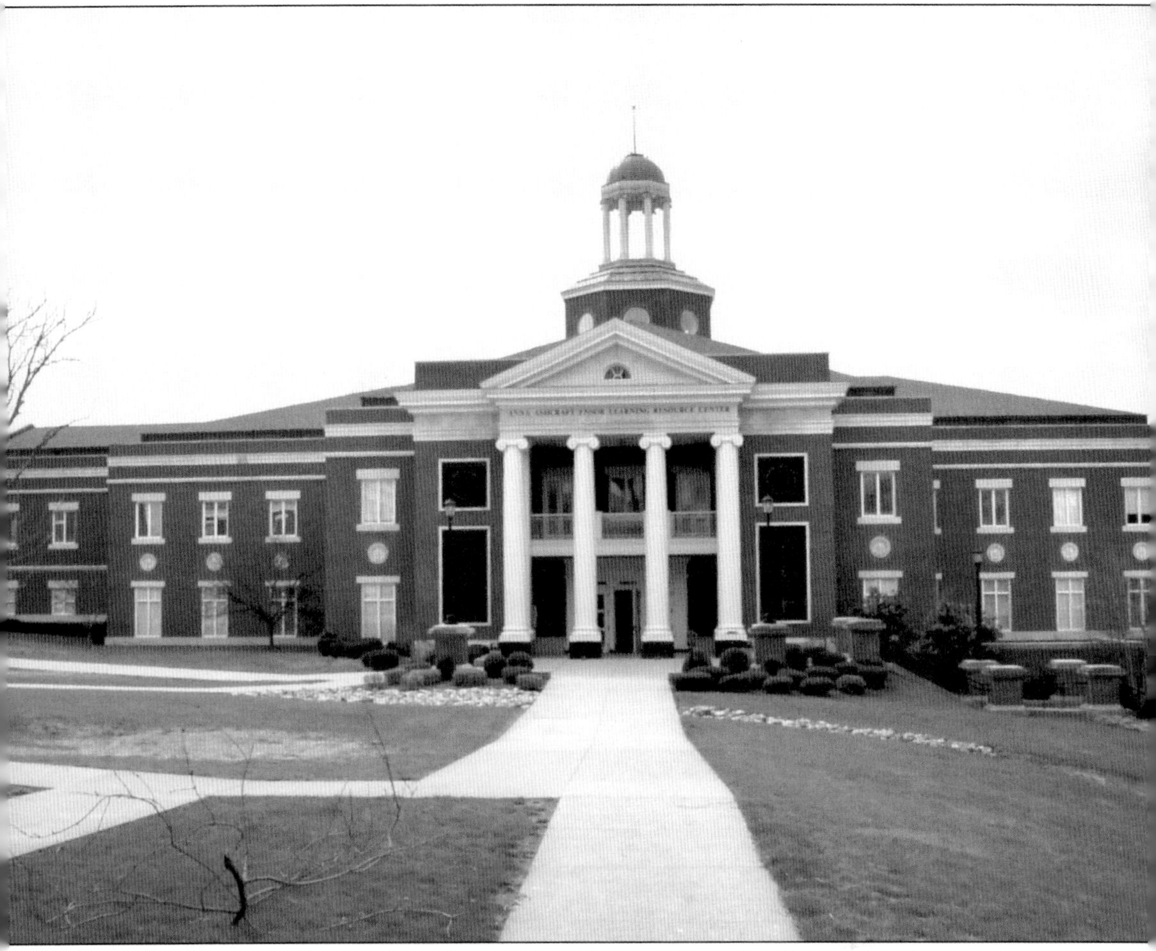

LEARNING RESOURCE CENTER. The Anna Ashcraft Ensor Learning Resource Center, or LRC, was completed in 1998. It now stands on what used to be the site of the arts and crafts building. The magnificent Greek Revival structure is elegant both inside and out, furnished with cherrywood tables and fine leather armchairs. A double-staircase leads students to the second floor, where books and study rooms are available. Students venturing to the third floor will encounter microfilm, periodicals, journals, and magazines. The first floor is equipped with a computer lab called the "T-3" center and a large reference wing that houses reference materials and computers, study areas, and the archives/special collections room. Attached to the rear of the LRC is the Mulberry Café, and located in the basement are offices, two computer labs, the Writing Center, and storage. The LRC is not only a retreat from the distractions of the dorm room, but it is also the academic heart of Georgetown. (Photograph courtesy of Jessica Ehleben.)

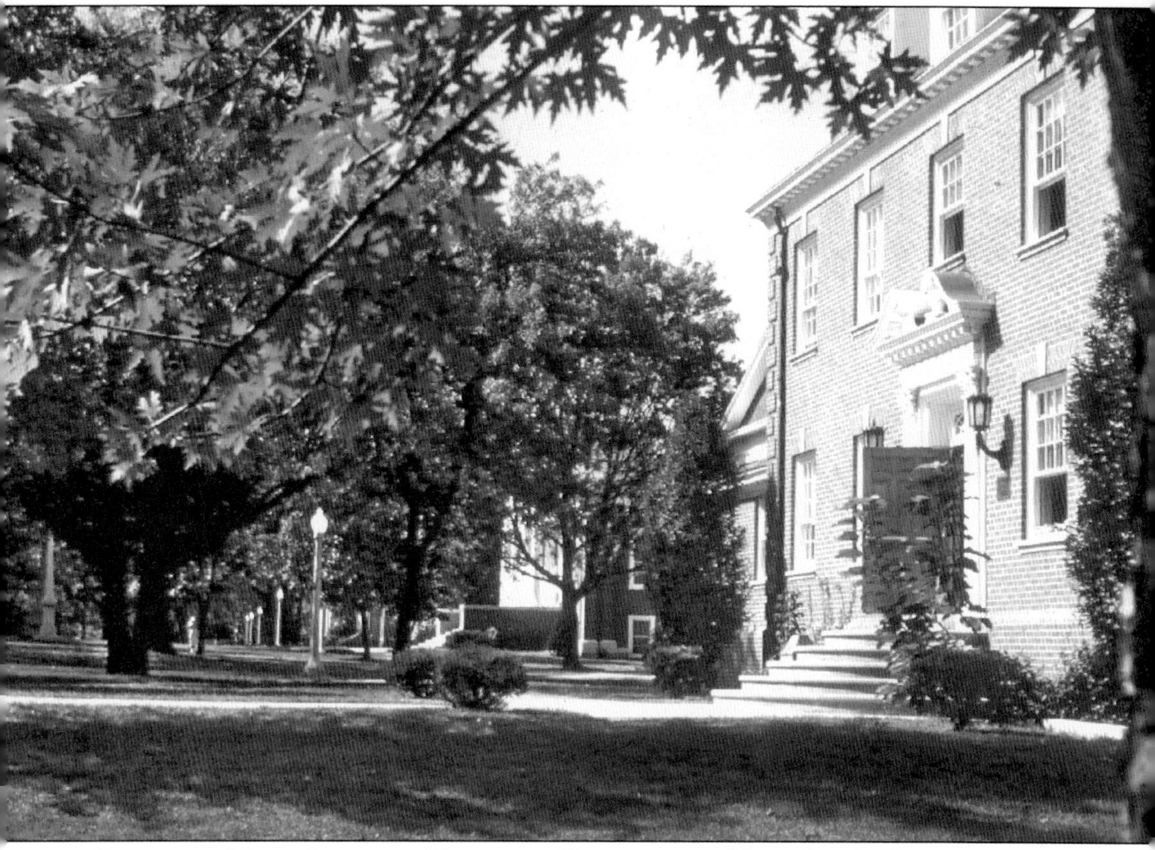

Nunnelley Music Building. The Nunnelley Music Building, finished in 1952, houses practice rooms and classrooms for students engaged in all forms of music. Gilmore Hays Nunnelley, a prominent businessman, held the position of president of the college's board of trustees in 1919, and during his life, he generously granted financial gifts to Georgetown College and the city of Georgetown. The building rings with harmonious sounds such as cheerful piano tunes and the energetic Tiger Band.

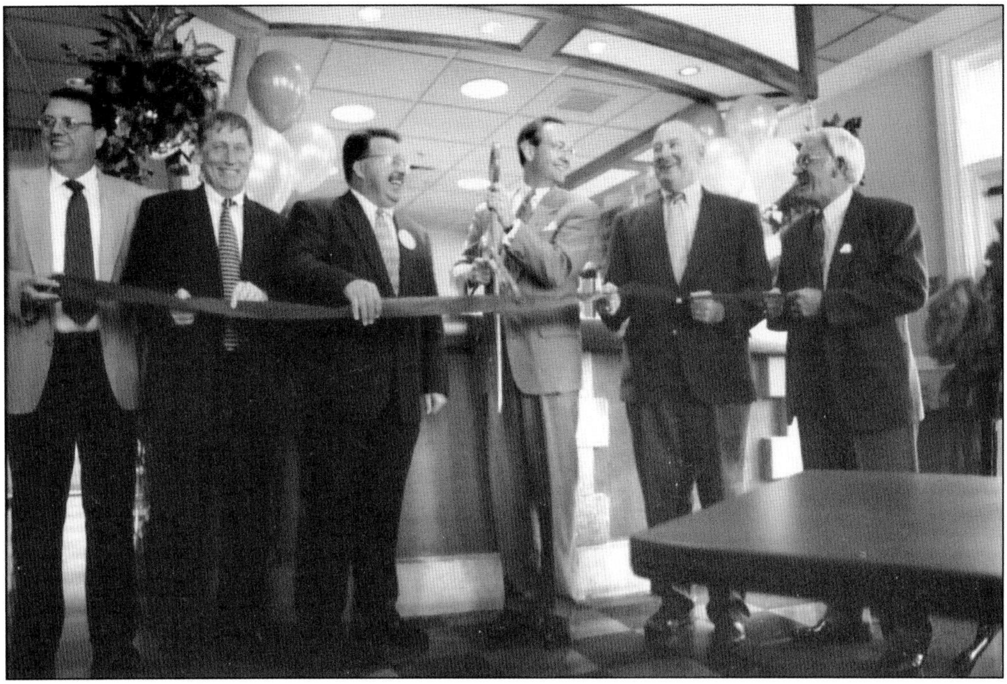

Opening of Mulberry Café. One of the Ensor Learning Resource Center's many gems, the Mulberry Café offers Starbucks Coffee, pastries, and a selection of light fare. President Crouch cuts the ribbon in this photograph, signaling the opening of the café in 1998. The Mulberry Café provides students with that late-night latté or the pick-me-up brew in the morning and creates a cozy atmosphere in which to read.

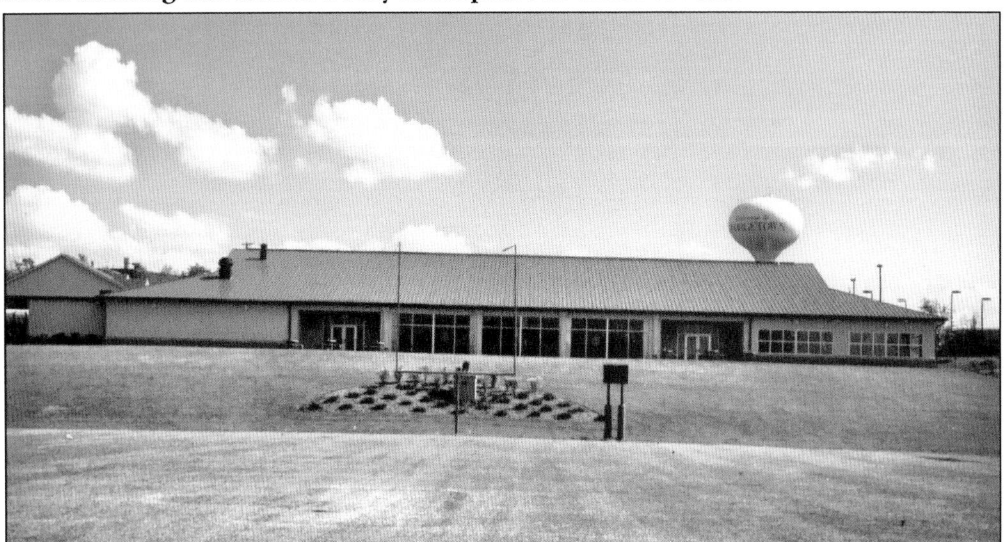

Conference Center. The Conference Center, located on east campus, was constructed as part of Rawlings Stadium for the NFL's Cincinnati Bengals training camp during the summer. The Georgetown College football team trains at the building during the year. The conference center also serves as a prime location for events such as banquets and business meetings.

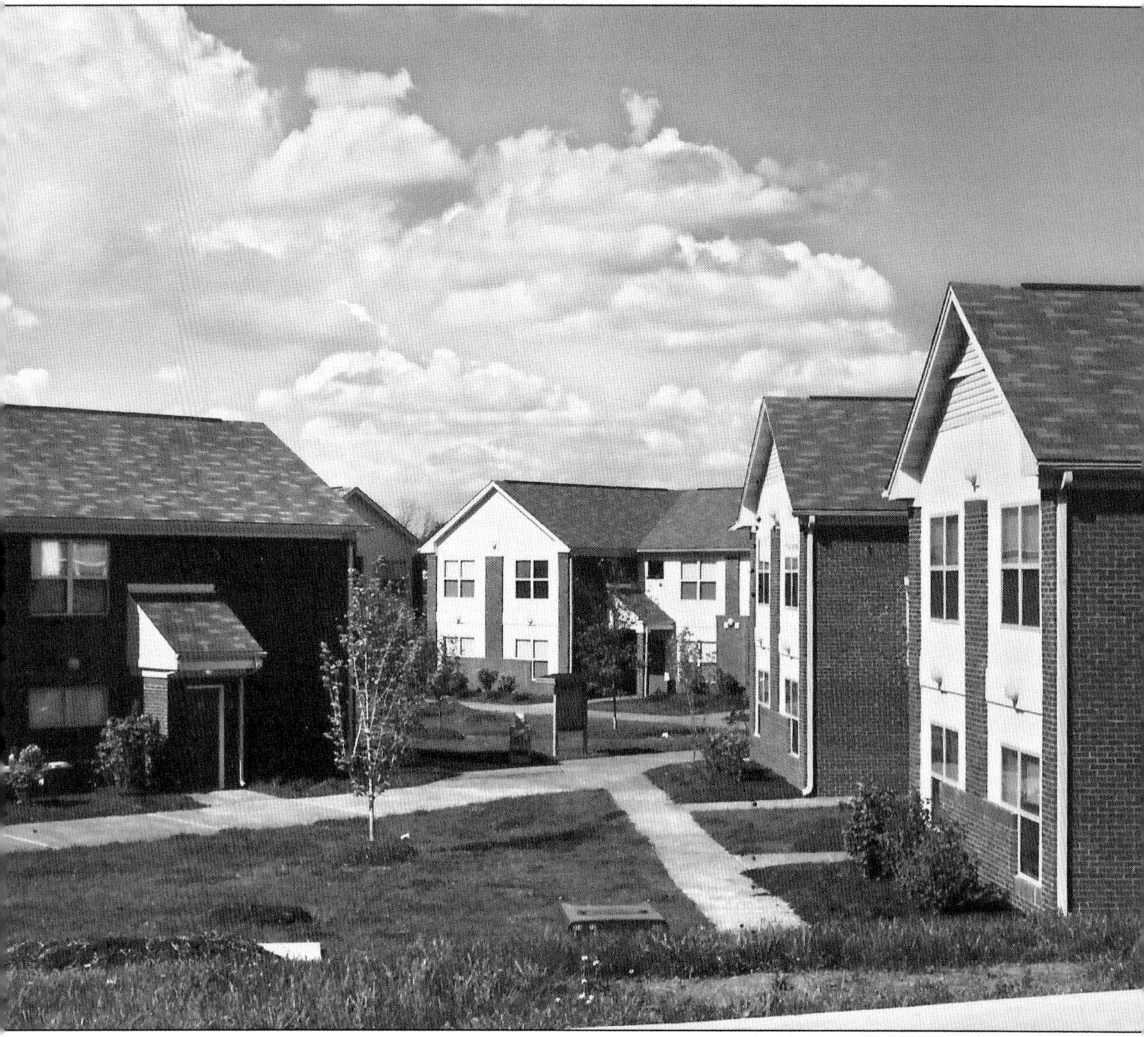

EAST CAMPUS APARTMENTS. Built as a piece of the Bengals training facility, East Campus Apartments offer students an alternative to dorm life. Originally erected to house the NFL Cincinnati Bengals football team during their training camp in the summer, the apartments are occupied by students who seek a more secluded retreat from the central campus.

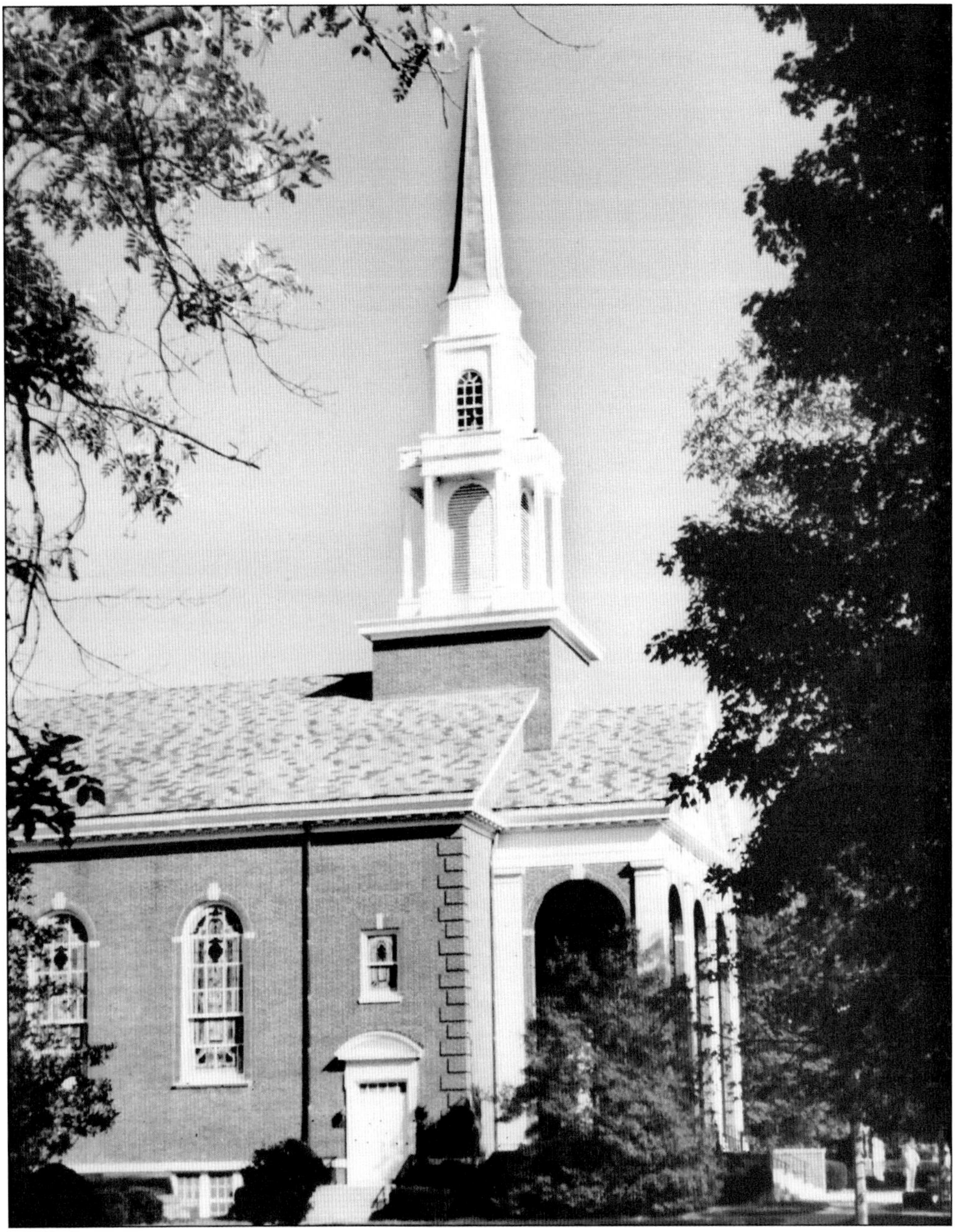

JOHN L. HILL CHAPEL, SIDE VIEW. The John L. Hill Chapel, named for an alumnus and former dean of the college, was constructed to the delight of anxious students and faculty in 1948 and was dedicated in 1949. The main floor plus balcony seating was designed to seat approximately 1,000 people. Colorful stained-glass windows were donated by philanthropic community members and families of Georgetown College students, many given in honor of soldiers who died during World War II. Renovated in 2002, the chapel plays a vital role in the spiritual life of Georgetown College.

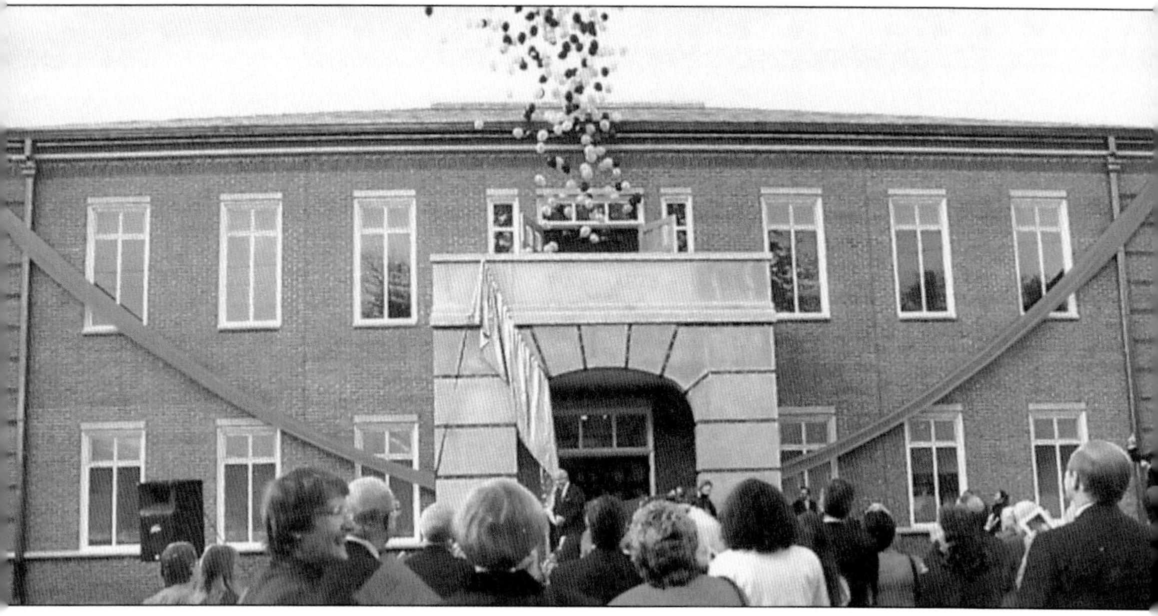

Fine Arts Building. The Anne Wright Wilson Fine Arts Building, opened in 1997, provides students with a facility for several medias of art. The building features a computer lab for digital imaging classes, a darkroom and photography lab, a large drawing room, a ceramics studio, and an industrial arts studio.

Three

Women in Co-Education

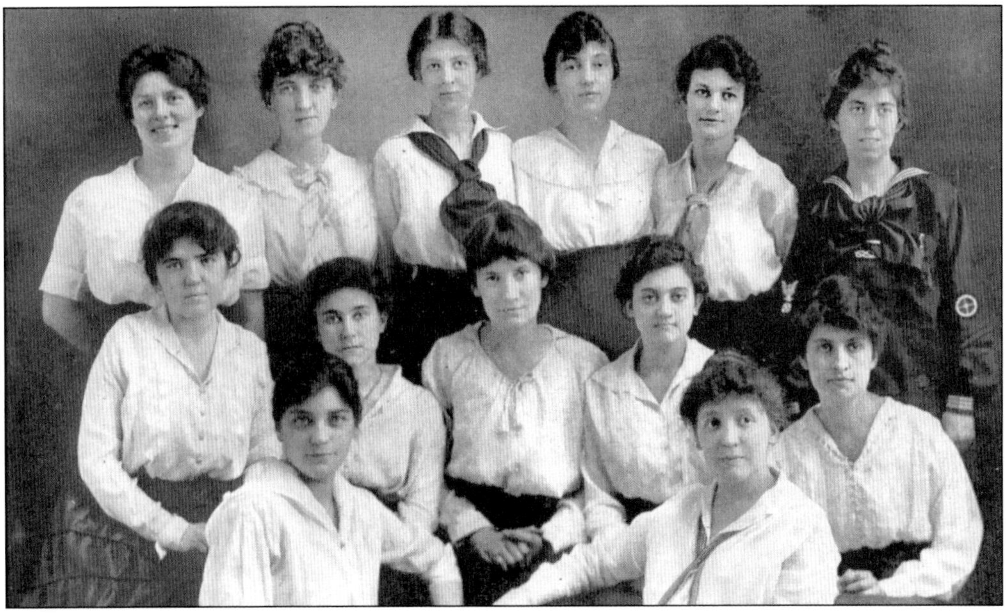

YWCA Officers. Organized in 1892, the Young Women's Christian Association of Georgetown College specialized in winning young women over to Christ, deepening the spiritual life of Christian students, and preparing women for mission work and active Christian service. The regular schedule of the YWCA consisted of devotionals, missionary meetings, prayer circles, and Bible studies. It offered an outlet for young Christian women who were not able to be closely involved with a church because of their studies and campus life, thus linking the young women's earlier Christian lives to the lives they would carry on after the school term ended.

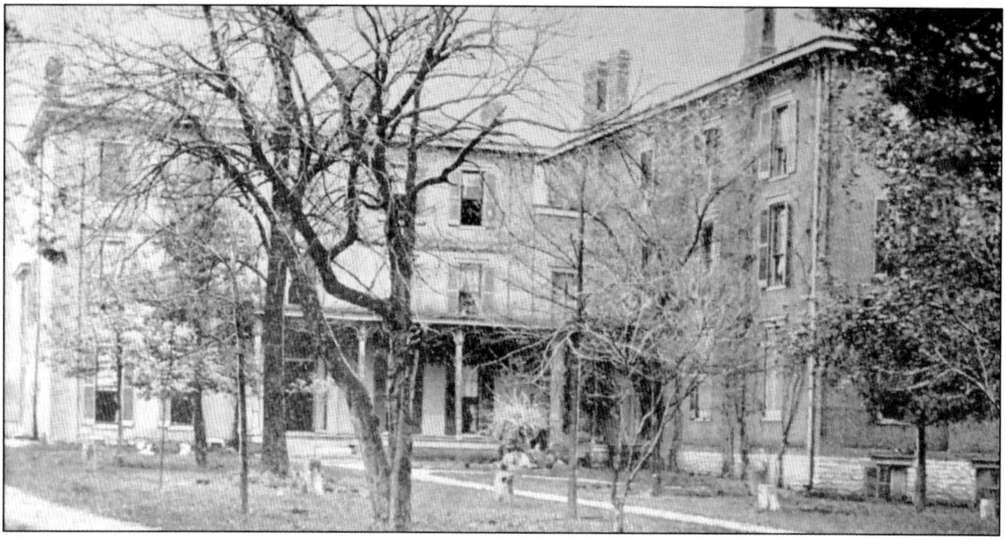

"Old Sem" Building. Before women were admitted to Georgetown College, Georgetown Female Seminary offered an option for further study beyond the basic female education. College boys attempted to serenade the young women despite strict prohibition from J. J. Rucker, leader of the seminary and figurehead of co-education. A new building built after the former building burned was later dubbed "Old Sem" when a co-education program was permanently installed at the college in 1892. The decision to incorporate women in the student body at Georgetown was determined by the performance of women as they undertook the same class work as men for a year. The girls of 1890–1891 diligently did their homework and secured opportunities for waves of young women to come.

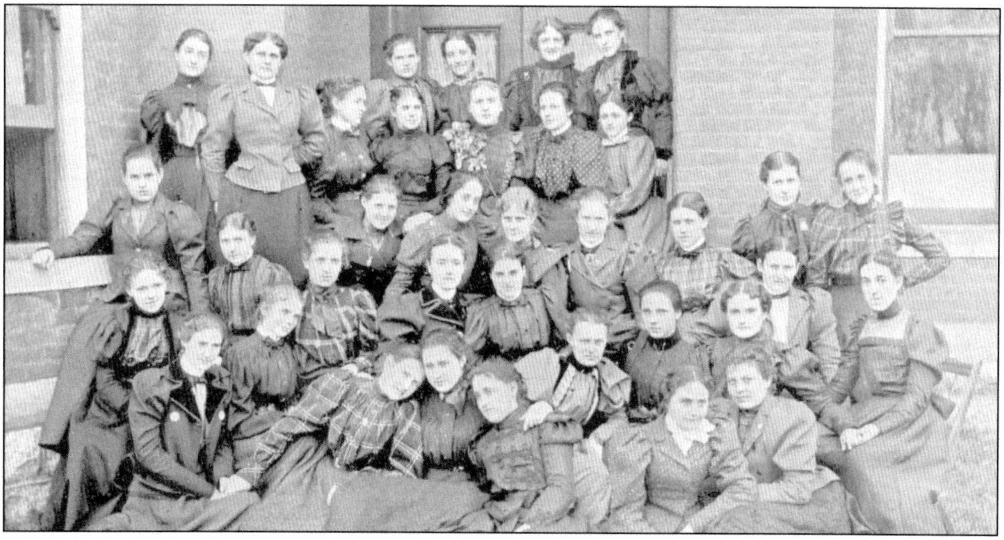

Euepian Society. Pupils from the Georgetown Female Seminary organized a female literary society in 1871, called the Euepian Society. The society first engaged in debate, recitations, essays, and music at the old seminary building and later relocated in 1896 to Rucker Hall. Known as the "Father of the Euepian," James J. Rucker was responsible for its formation and guided and sustained the society through its first few struggling years. The Euepian Society was later divided into Alpha Euepian and Zeta Euepian to encourage and ignite competition.

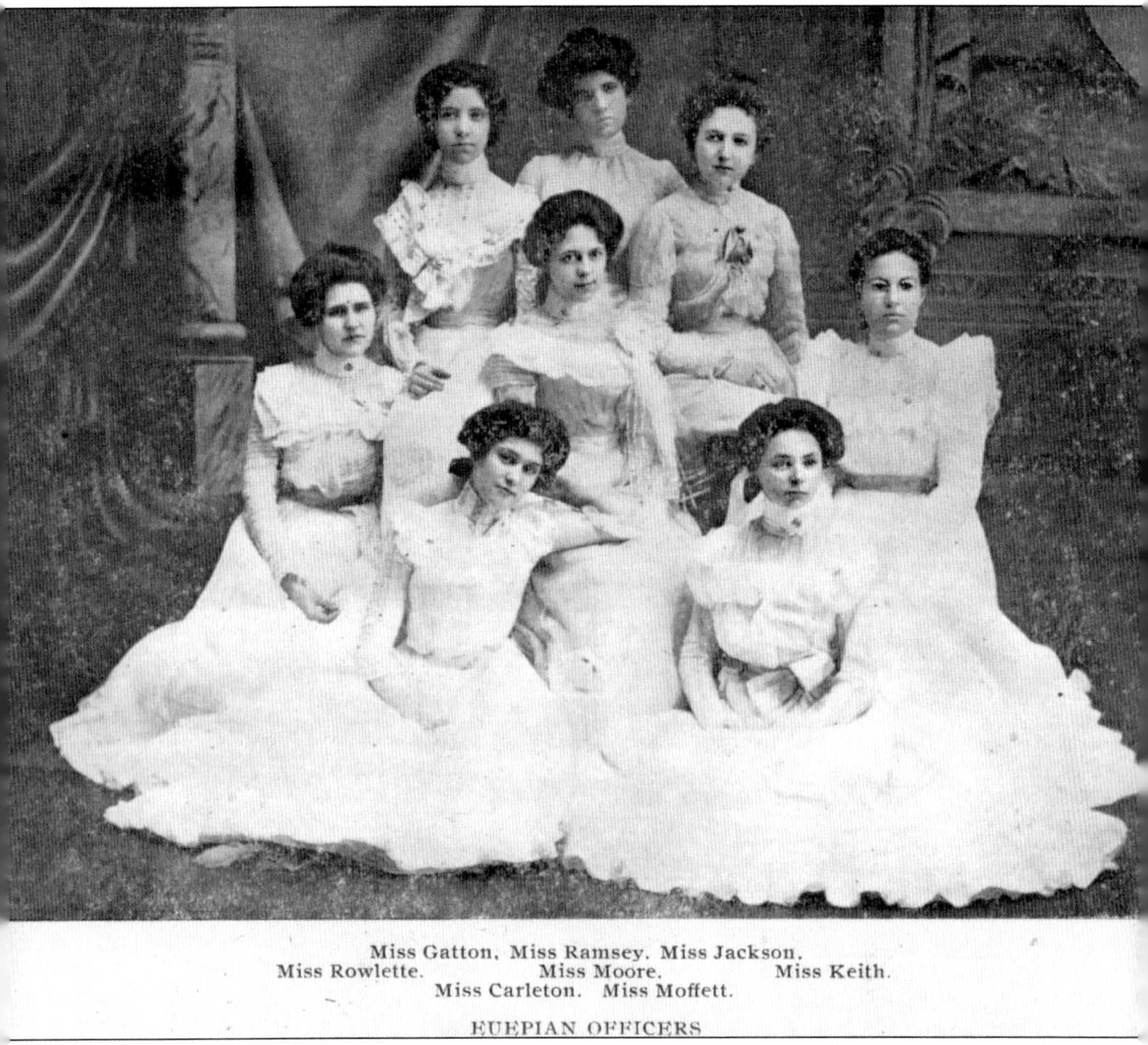

EUEPIAN OFFICERS. The Euepian Society met in Euepian Hall, located within Rucker Hall. The officers in the photograph are Miriam Moore, Gayle Jackson, Mary Keith, Juilia Ramsey, Rachel Gatton, May Moffett, May Carleton, and Mabel Bagby. The Women's Association of Georgetown College was also founded in the late 19th century and met in Euepian Hall. Miss Rowena Pollard was the second president of the Women's Association, which was designed to encourage female education and scholarship. Originating in 1897, today the Women's Association remains active, providing scholarship opportunities for aspiring young women.

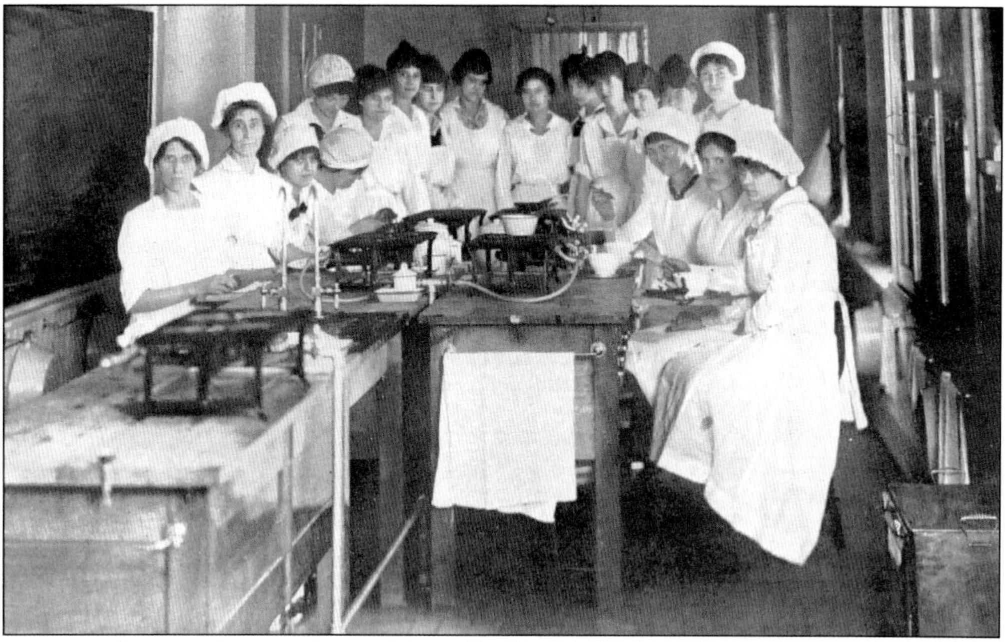

Domestic Science Class. A class solely created for and taken advantage of by women, this domestic science class is an example of the marked separation of men's and women's education that existed in the year 1916. The women in this photograph appear to be engaged in a cooking project.

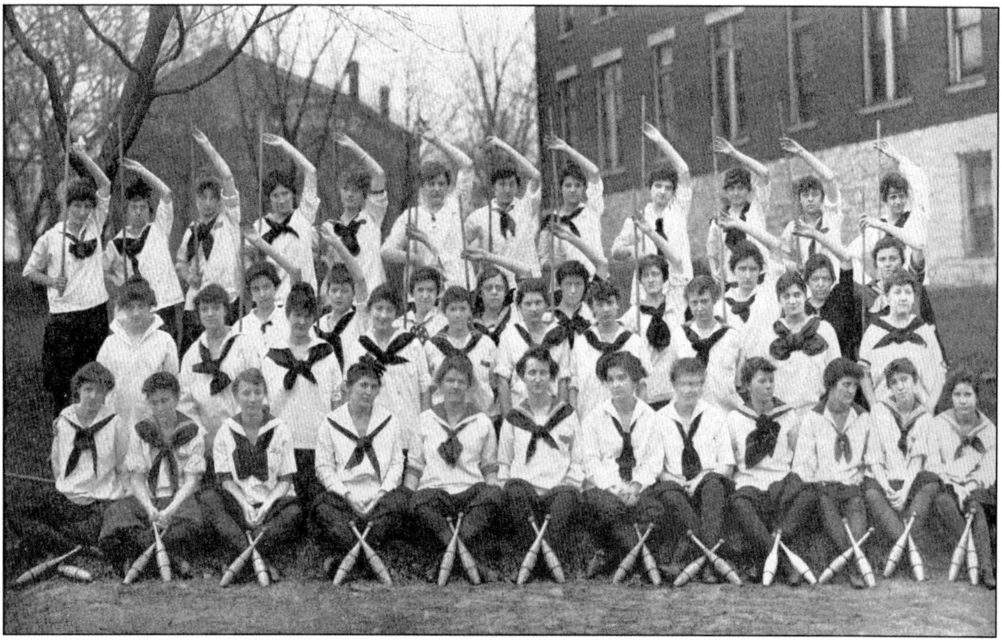

Women's Gym. The department of physical training for young women opened in 1911. Women exercised to improve deformities and to offer the gifts of grace, coordination, and endurance of the lungs. Notice the young women in front hold juggling pins and those in the back hold long batons.

COED CHARACTER. In 1891, Georgetown College admitted female students for a trial year. If these women performed well in their studies, then co-education would become permanent the following year. Thus just a few years later, the 1901 yearbook was called *The Coed* instead of its traditional name, *Belle of the Blue*. This amusing character embellished the outside and inside of the cover.

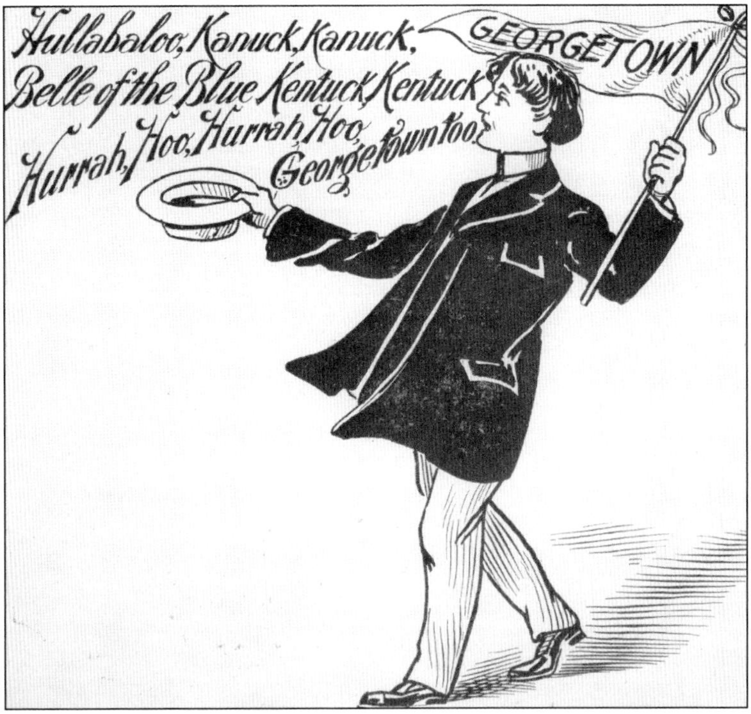

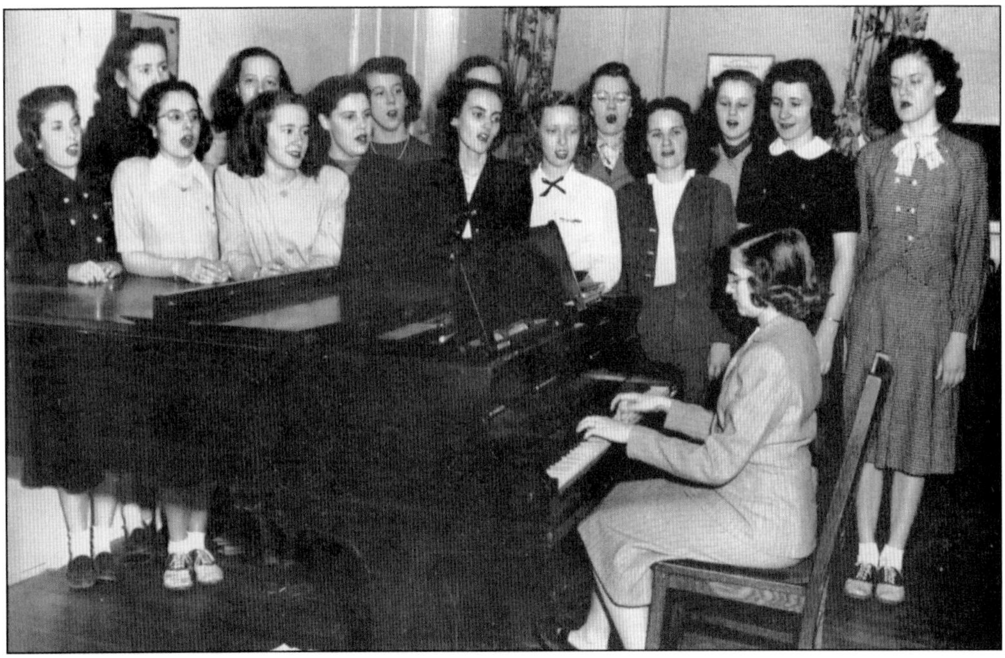

DELTA OMICRON. Delta Omicron was established as a women's music honorary society in 1933 at Georgetown. The 1948 class of initiates, pictured here from left to right, includes Lois Jean Buky, Bobbie Blaine Burke, Ruth Widick, Louise Bowman, Faye Anderson, Linda Overall, Lois Chism, Carol Zimmerman, Josephine Widick, Marjorie Adams, Lou Emma Taylor, Martha Jane Robinson, Helen English, Roberta Carter, Sarah Dean, and Clara Lee.

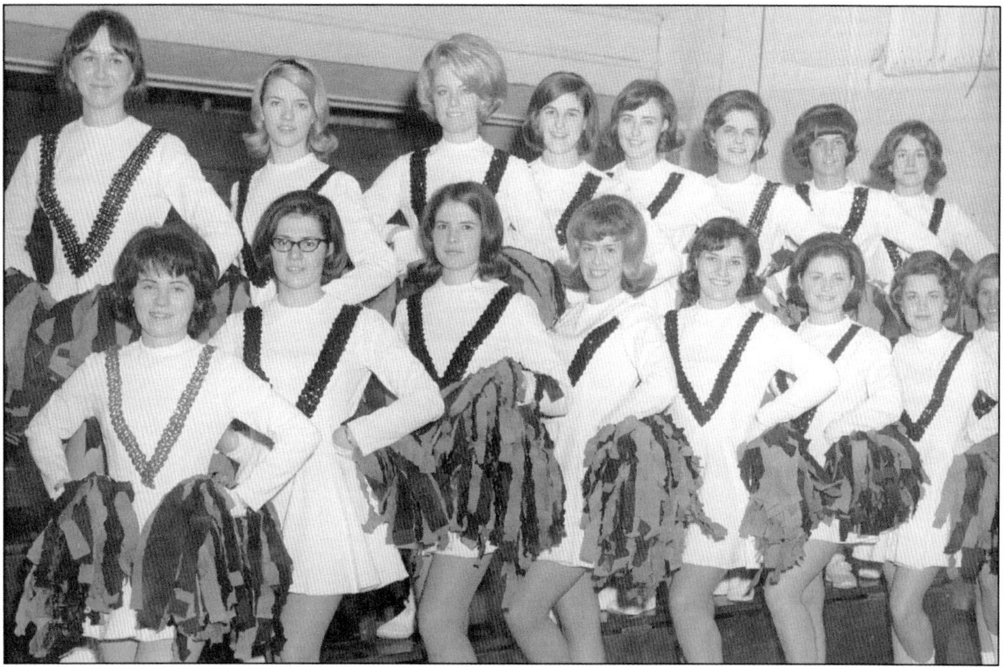

Majorettes. These ladies comprised the Georgetown majorette squad that performed with the marching band, both of which no longer exist at Georgetown today. Though not pictured with their batons in this photograph, majorettes also performed with streamers, wings, fire, and various props relating to the band's show theme. Now a dying art in the state of Kentucky, twirling was highly popular in the 1950s and 1960s.

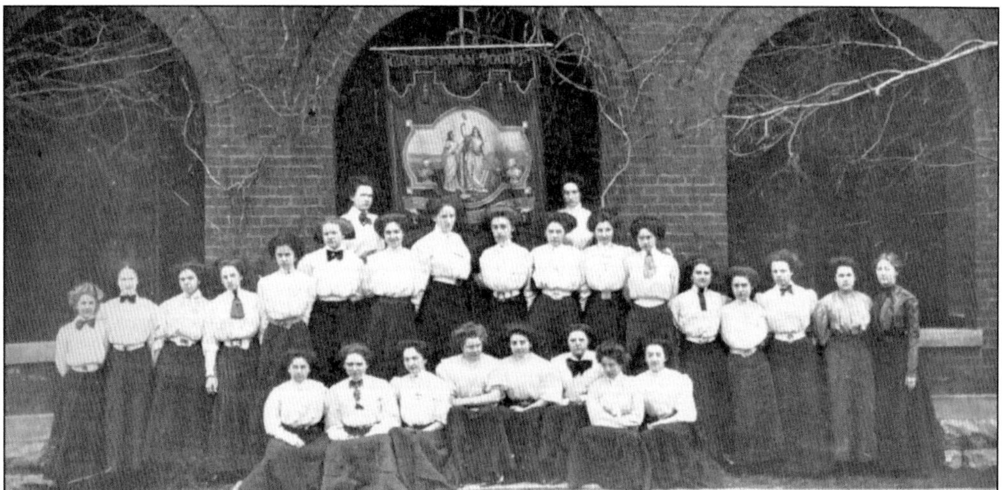

Literary Society Sympathizers. The two dominant men's literary societies were such an integral part of campus life that they even drew loyalty from the female supporters. These "sympathizers" would proudly wear the societies' colors and zealously cheer for their choice group during contests and regular debates. Female student loyalty to male organizations is still practiced today at Georgetown. For example, fraternities elect "Little Sis" candidates, "Crescent Girls," "Diamonds," "Roses," and "Ladies of the Laurell" to represent and support their endeavors.

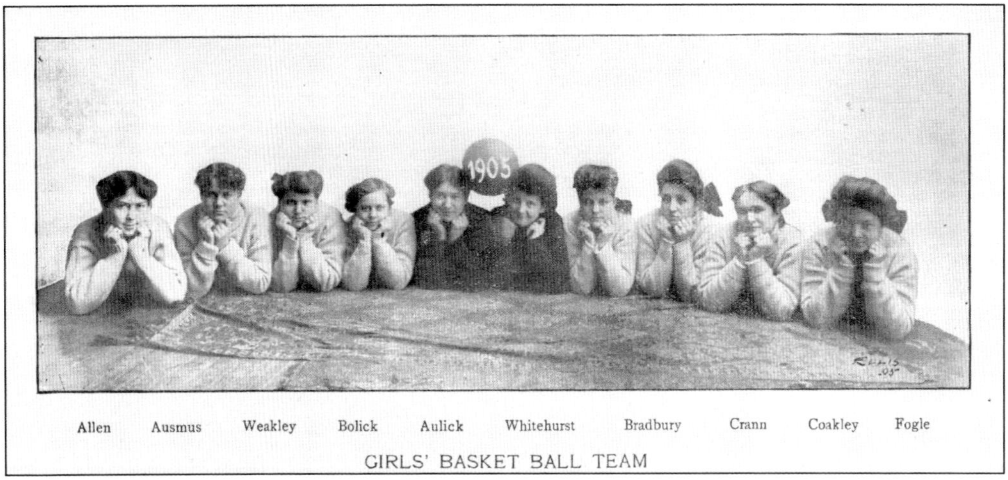

Girls' Basketball Team. The Georgetown College girls' basketball team of 1905 was still a revolutionary concept, considering that basketball for women did not officially develop until 1892. The first intercollegiate game of women's basketball was played in 1896. At a small Baptist school like Georgetown, the sport was probably discouraged to women because of its aggressiveness. Boys were not permitted to attend women's games in the early years of the sport because the girls wore skirts of shorter-than-usual length with bloomers underneath. The last names of the women pictured here on the 1905 team are, from left to right, Allen, Ausmus, Weakley, Bolick, Aulick, Whitehurts, Bradbury, Crann, Coackley, and Fogle.

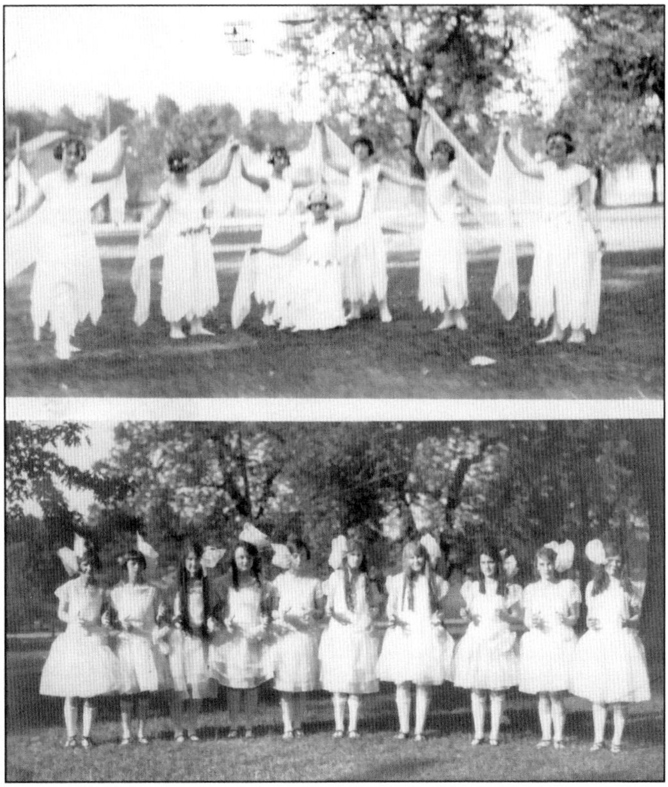

May Day Girls. Celebrating the arrival of spring, May Day festivities provided excitement for both the students of Georgetown College and citizens of Scott County. Families would bring food and picnic outside, while other students dined inside if their family members were unable to attend. During Dr. Samuel S. Hill's term as president from 1942 to 1953, the meal transitioned into a burgoo. The May Day girls, all dressed alike in this photograph, are most likely performing a traditional dance called the "Doll Dance."

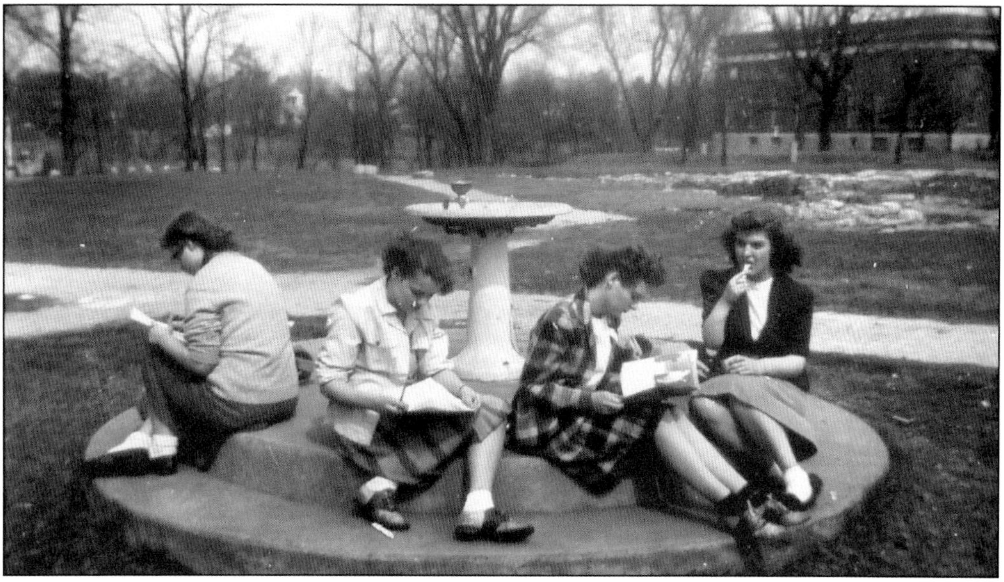

Kappa Deltas Around a Fountain. These four Kappa Delta ladies sit around the fountain in front of Giddings Hall. During the 1920s, sororities and fraternities were abolished at Georgetown due to their off-campus living arrangements and exclusiveness. However, about four years after the ban, Greek organizations were allowed back on campus but with new regulations. During this time, Greeks comprised approximately 40 percent of the student body.

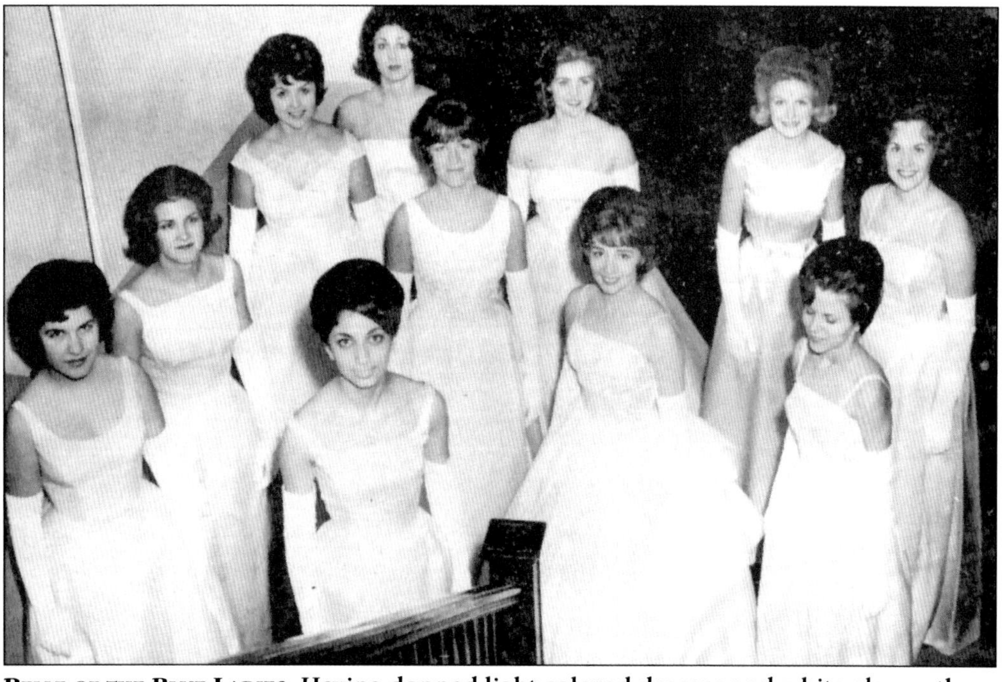

Belle of the Blue Ladies. Having donned light-colored dresses and white gloves, these young women are shown competing for the title of Georgetown's "Miss Belle of the Blue." Currently in the Belle of the Blue pageant, women are required to perform a talent, participate in an interview, and are also judged on their grade point average.

Four

Athletics

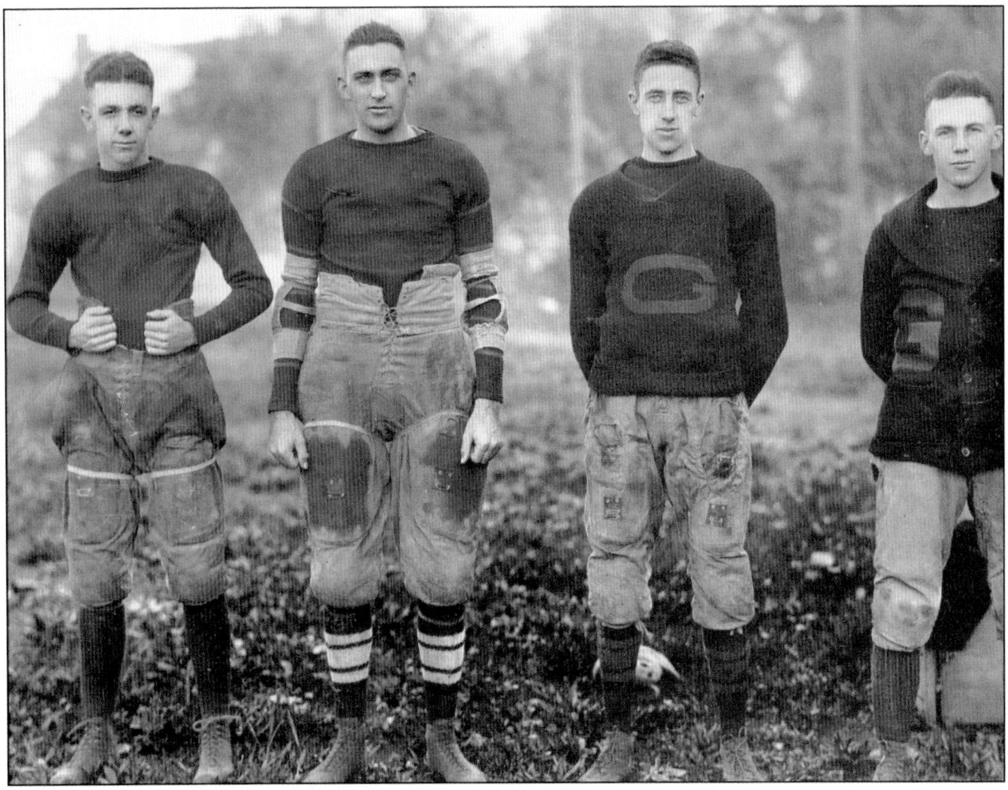

Four Football Players. During 1919, the football team played its last season with Coach Robert Hinton with about 30 players. Georgetown's new coach, J. W. Coleman, set new strict rules, including a prohibition of tobacco use, large meals on Sundays, and even dating during the football season. However, it was also Coleman who instituted the tradition of homecoming at Georgetown, during which alumni would return to view the campus and watch the football game.

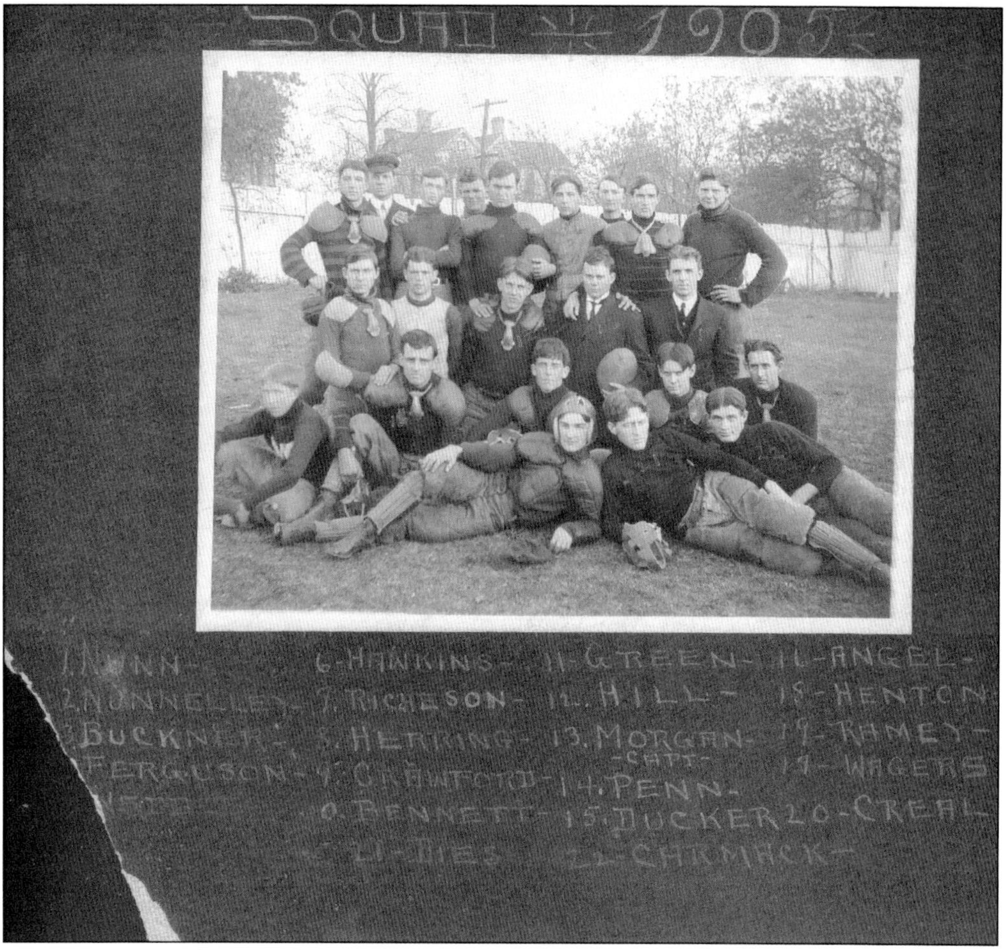

Football Team. The 1905 football team played under the Kentucky Intercollegiate Athletic Association and steadily grew in size and stamina from their previous years. Before 1893, Georgetown's team was lacking in strength and training, since their strongest player only weighed 135 pounds. The last names of players in this photograph, from right to left, are the following: (first row) Ducker, Angel, Henton, Wagers, Dies, Ramey, Carmack, and Creal; (second row) Bennett, Green, Hill, Morgan, and Penn; (third row) Nunn, Nunnelley, Buckner, Ferguson, Neddle, Hawkins, Richeson, Herring, and Grawford.

Richard Hays. This photograph features Richard Hays, a basketball player under Coach Bob Davis. Coach Davis not only coached basketball but also football, and in 1959, he was named NAIA Coach of the Year, the same year Georgetown was victorious over the University of Louisville.

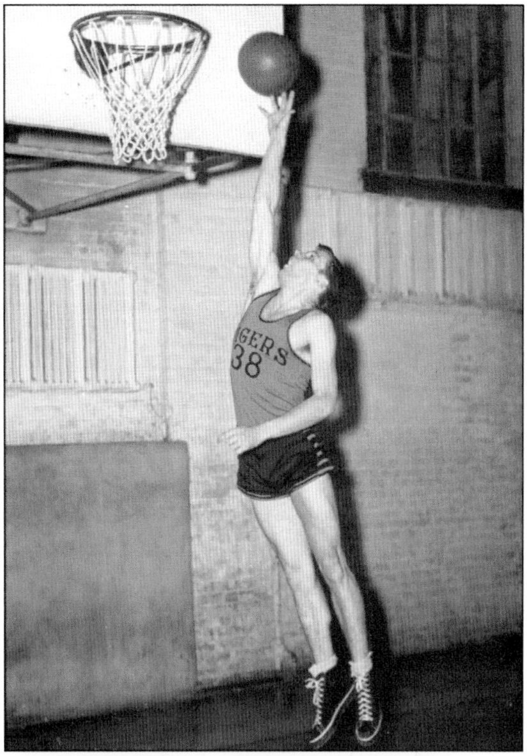

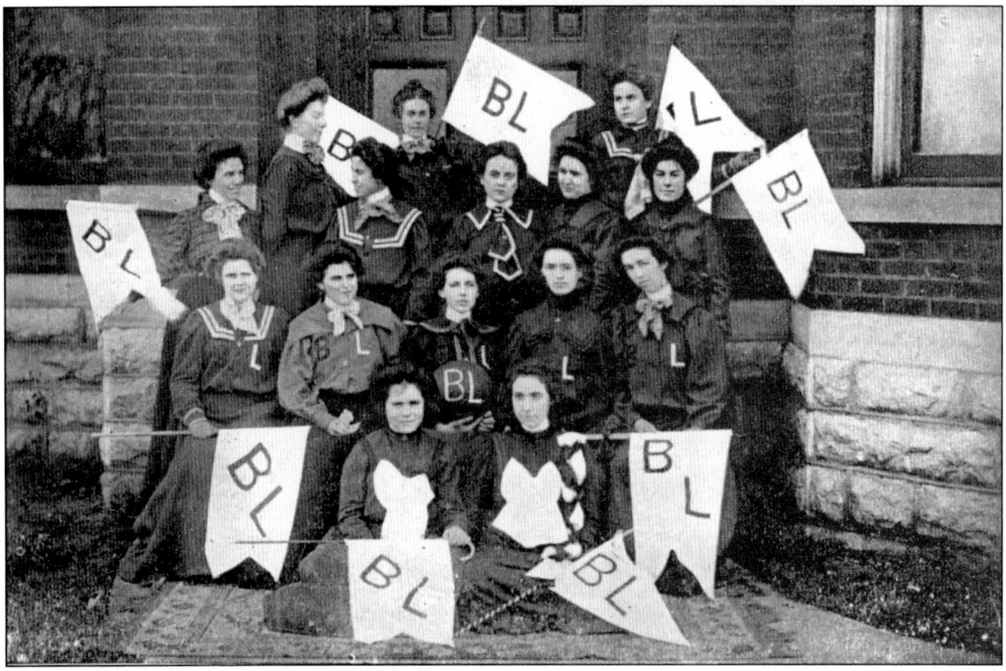

Bistro 'Leven. The Georgetown College women's basketball team, named "Bistro 'Leven," proved to be quite successful and displayed a wealth of enthusiasm for their team. In their spirit, the team members have embroidered a "B" and an "L" on either side of their uniforms and wave "BL" flags to show their pride.

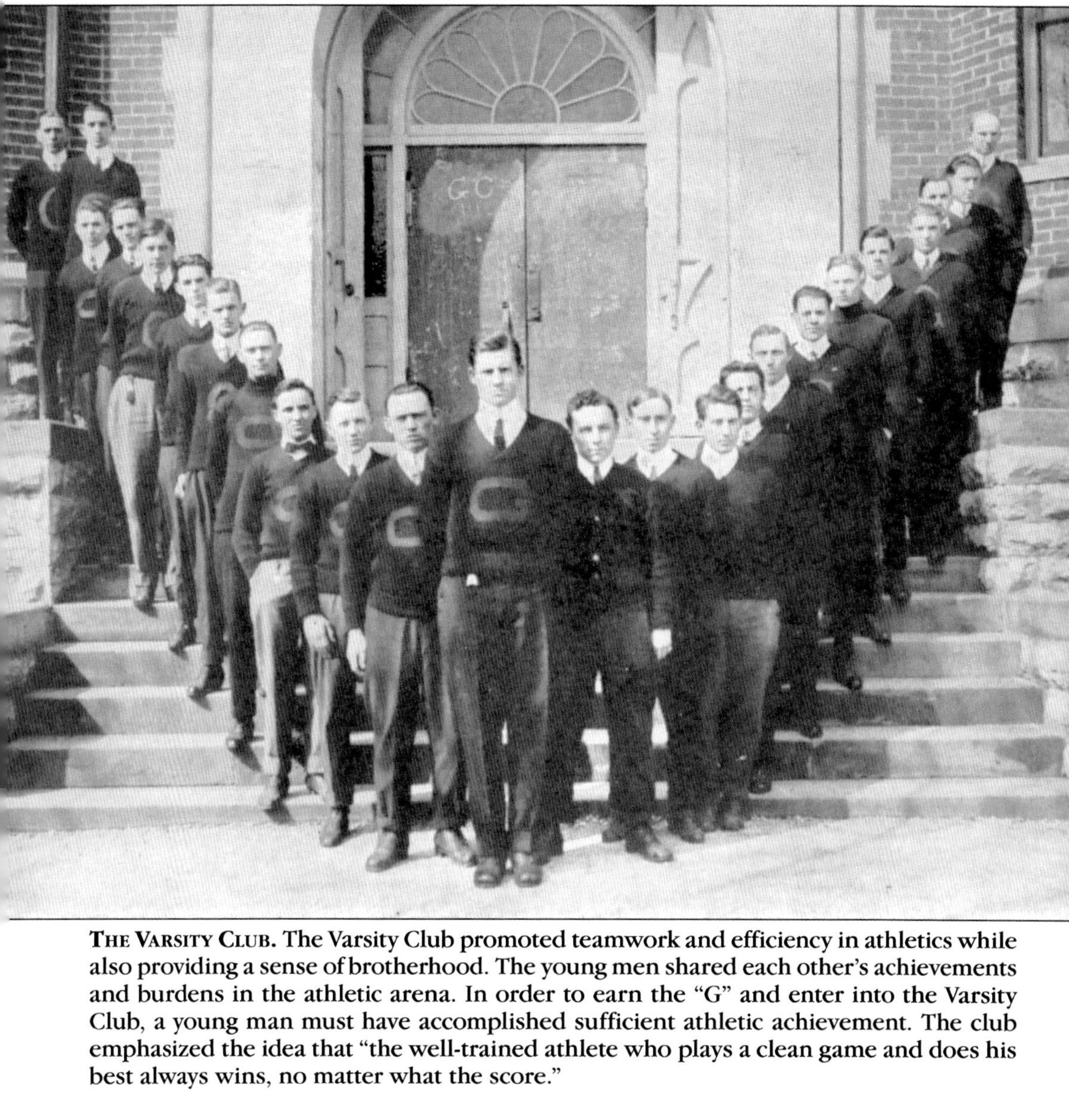

The Varsity Club. The Varsity Club promoted teamwork and efficiency in athletics while also providing a sense of brotherhood. The young men shared each other's achievements and burdens in the athletic arena. In order to earn the "G" and enter into the Varsity Club, a young man must have accomplished sufficient athletic achievement. The club emphasized the idea that "the well-trained athlete who plays a clean game and does his best always wins, no matter what the score."

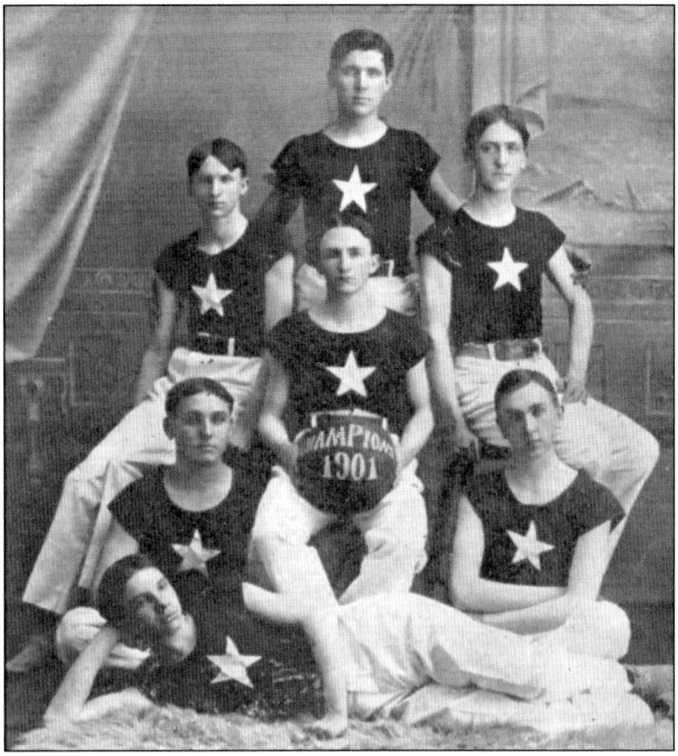

The "Stars" Basketball Team. The 1901 basketball team, perhaps the earliest team at Georgetown, was quite successful considering basketball did not develop until 1891. As conference champions from 1903 to 1907, Georgetown defeated Transylvania University and the Lexington schools that would become the University of Kentucky. In 1922, Georgetown defeated the University of Kentucky for the final time. These "stars" of the 1901 basketball squad include L. G. Anderson, G. B. Hawes, J. A. Baker, R. H. Towles, J. C. Bronough, J. H. Walker, and R. E. Barham (captain).

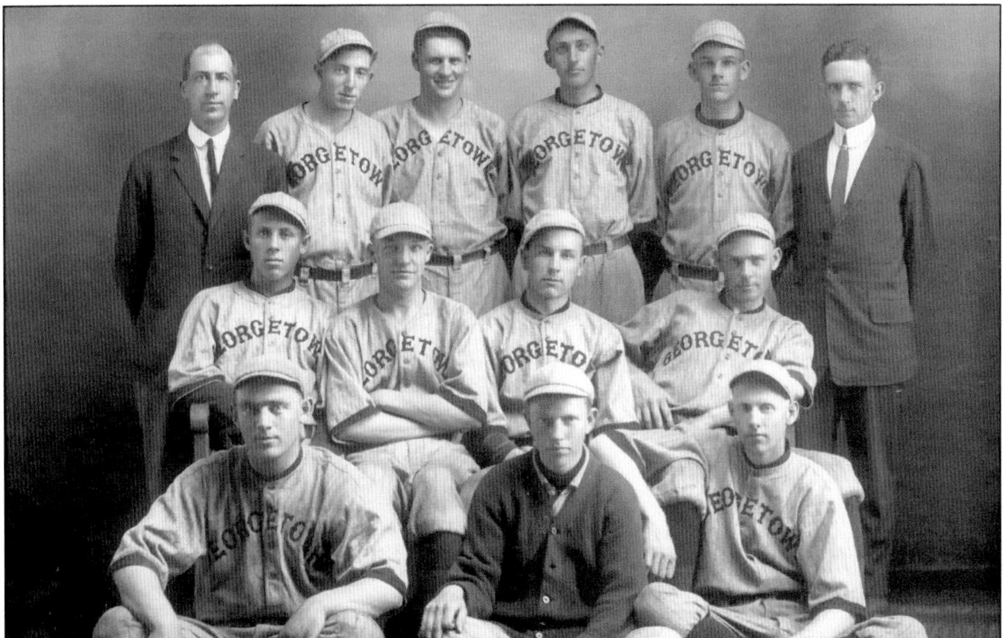

Georgetown Baseball. America's favorite pastime, baseball, was alive and well at Georgetown. In 1915, the baseball team won the conference championship, and the 1921 team played another winning season under the leadership of Courtlan Pollard, team captain. The 1921 Tiger baseball team won seven games, lost five, and tied one game.

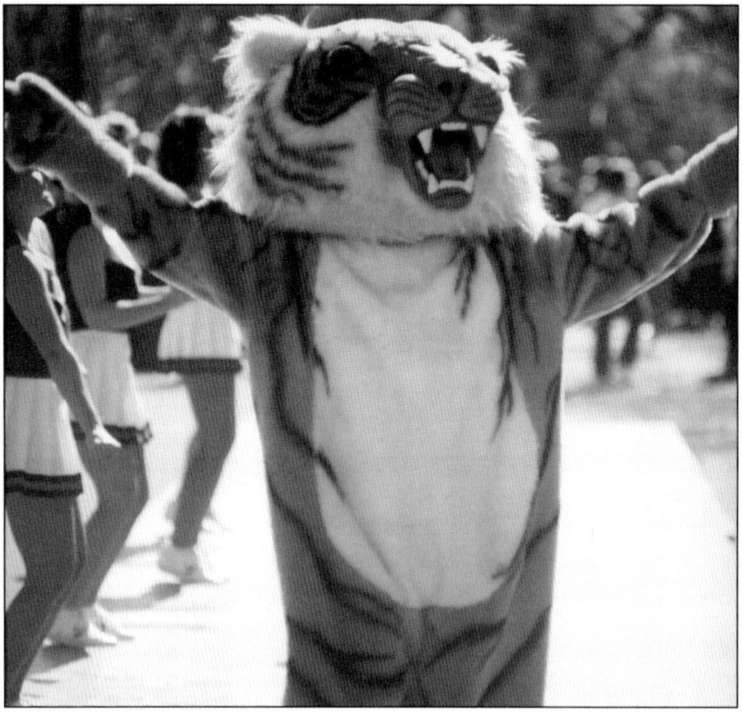

TIGER MASCOT. The Tiger mascot energizes crowds and excites school spirit at Georgetown athletic events. Here the enthusiastic figure sports its orange and black stripes in support for the school colors.

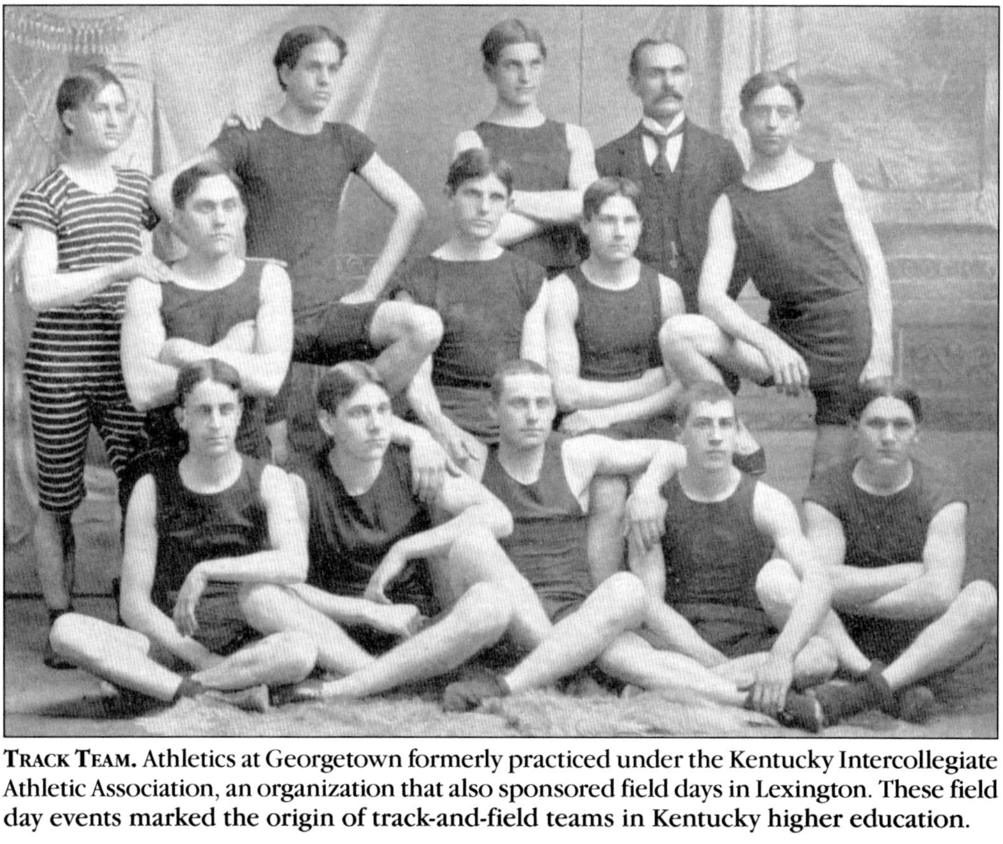

TRACK TEAM. Athletics at Georgetown formerly practiced under the Kentucky Intercollegiate Athletic Association, an organization that also sponsored field days in Lexington. These field day events marked the origin of track-and-field teams in Kentucky higher education.

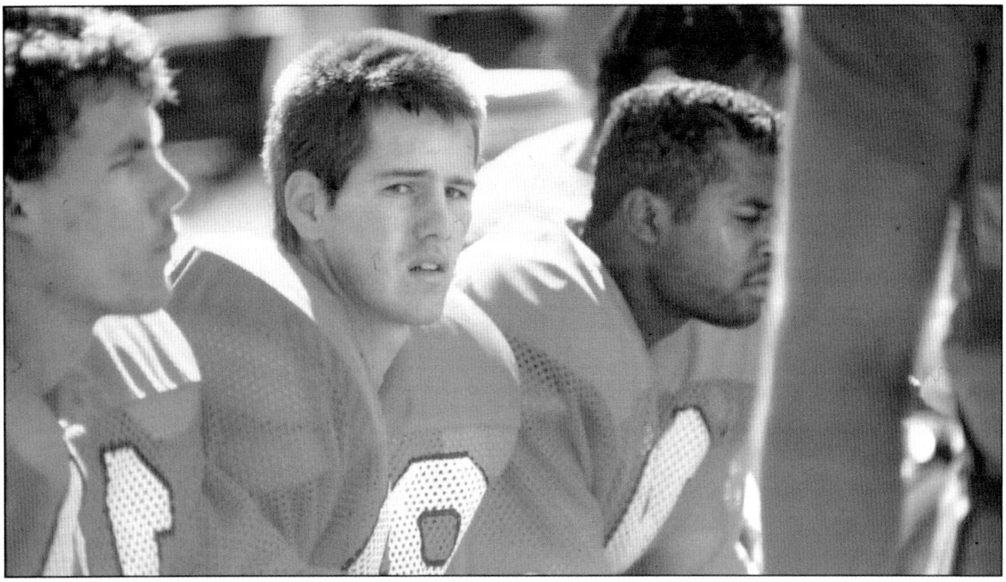

Georetown College Football. During World War II, Georgetown football was suspended for a few years due to the lack of male students. Georgetown athletic teams played under the Kentucky Athletic Intercollegiate Conference (KAIC) during that time, but after football was revived following the war, only a few schools played in the conference. In 1950, Georgetown and Centre College were the only two schools with football teams in the conference, and Georgetown was the champion, winning the title by 7 to 3.

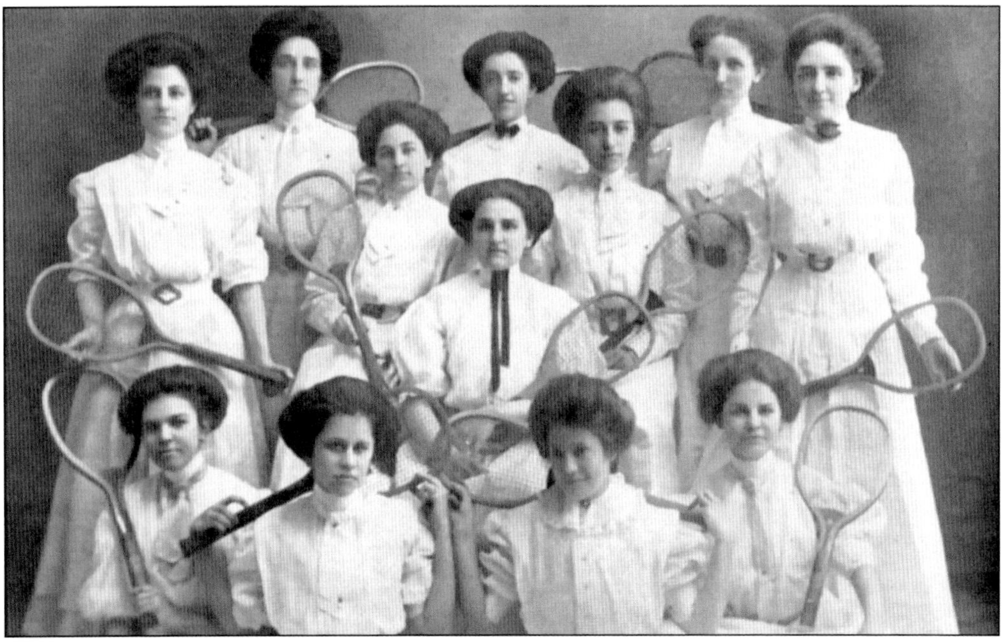

Women's Tennis Club. These young athletes are dressed for a heated game of tennis. In the early 1900s, when this photograph was presumably taken, women usually wore long dresses or skirts during athletic activity, often with bloomers underneath. This striking pose of the team with their rackets is an example of the initiative taken by female students to create clubs and new organizations for women.

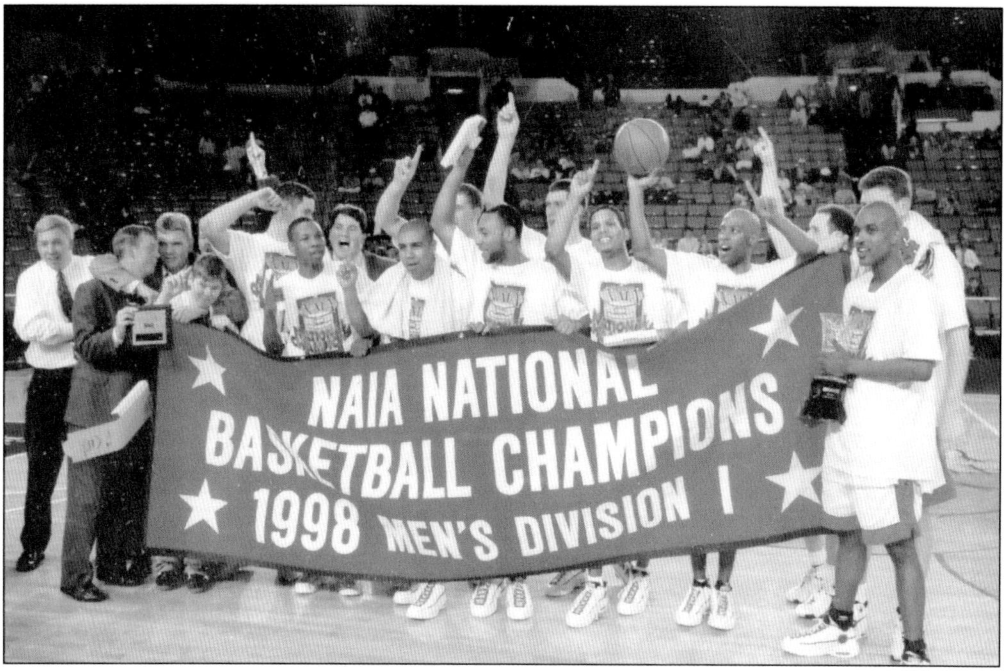

BASKETBALL CHAMPS. In 1998, the Tiger men's basketball team claimed the NAIA national championship. The team achieved their victory under the leadership of Coach Happy Osborne.

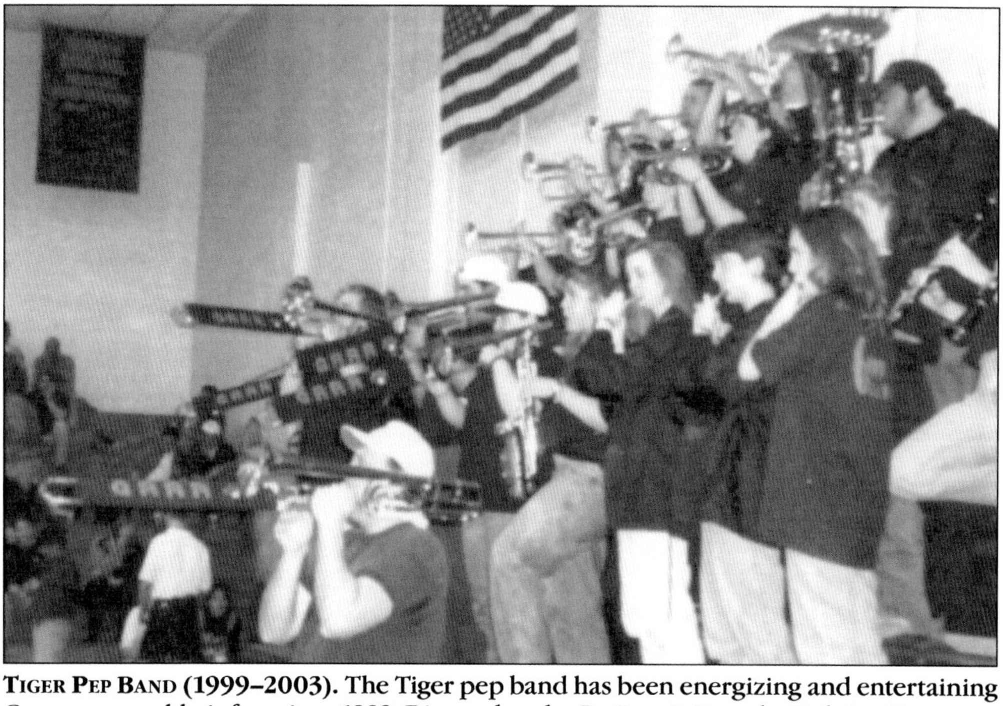

TIGER PEP BAND (1999–2003). The Tiger pep band has been energizing and entertaining Georgetown athletic fans since 1993. Directed under Dr. Pete LaRue, the Fighting Tiger Grrr . . . Pep Band upholds five band tenets including academic excellence, musical achievement, spiritual values, leadership skills, and a commitment to Georgetown College.

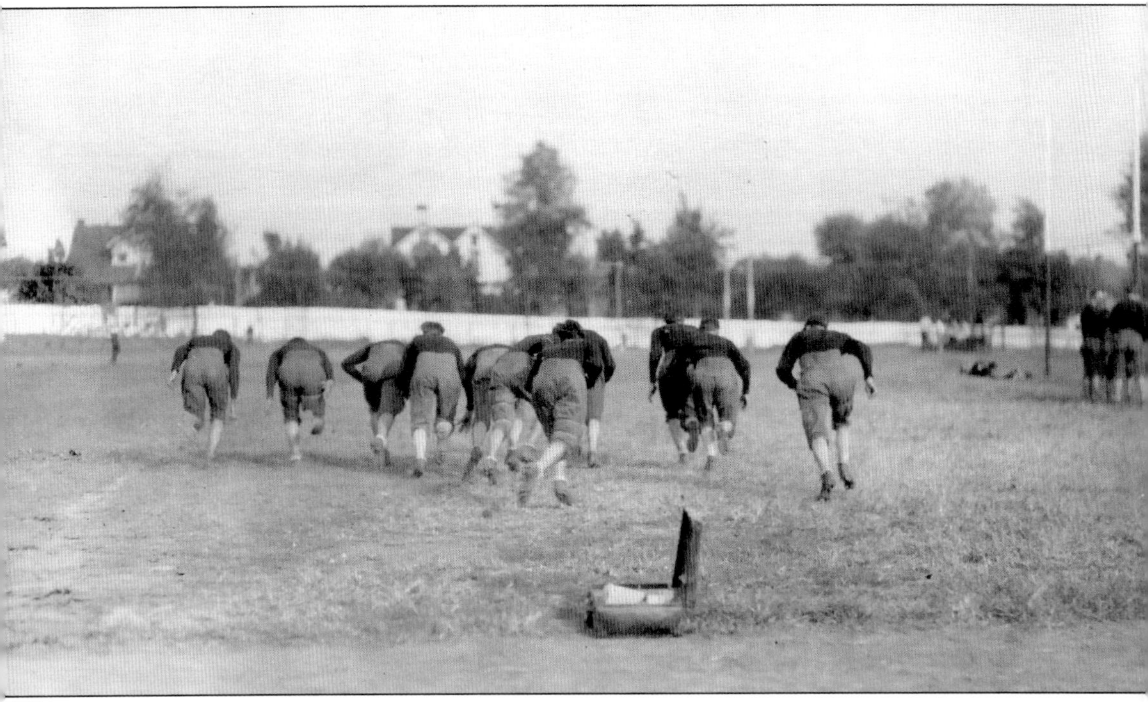

Running Football Players. Between 1908 to 1918, the athletic department provided much of the entertainment for the college under the leadership of Coach Robert Hinton. Hinton not only coached football but also basketball, baseball, and track. In 1916, the Georgetown football team defeated the University of Louisville 41-0, and from 1915 to 1917, the track team won the conference championship.

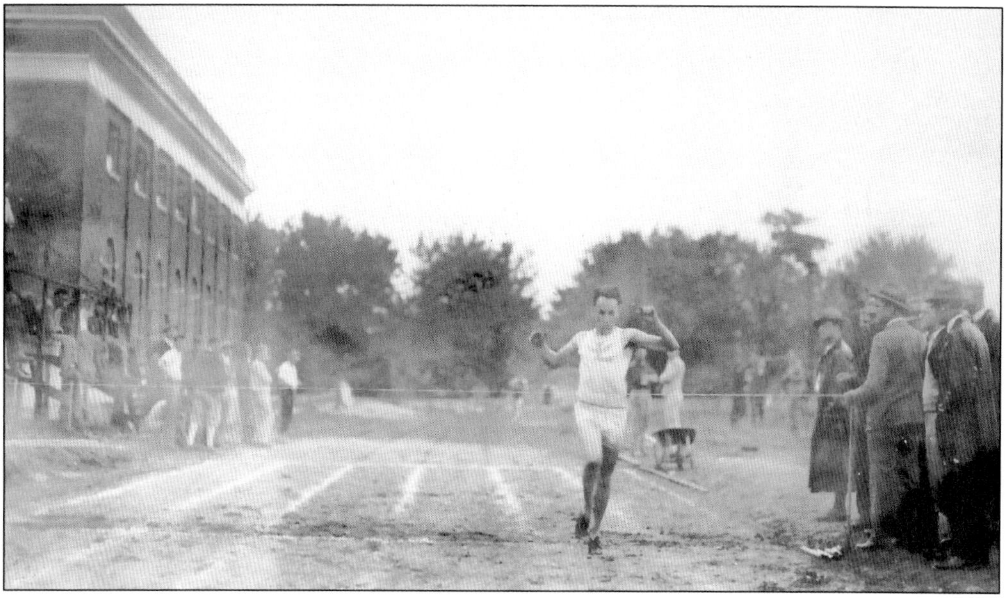

OLD TRACK MEET. This photograph features an old track meet located beside Anderson Hall. Track and field originated as a sport from field days, which were granted to students in order to encourage exercise. Soon these simple events turned into regular competitions.

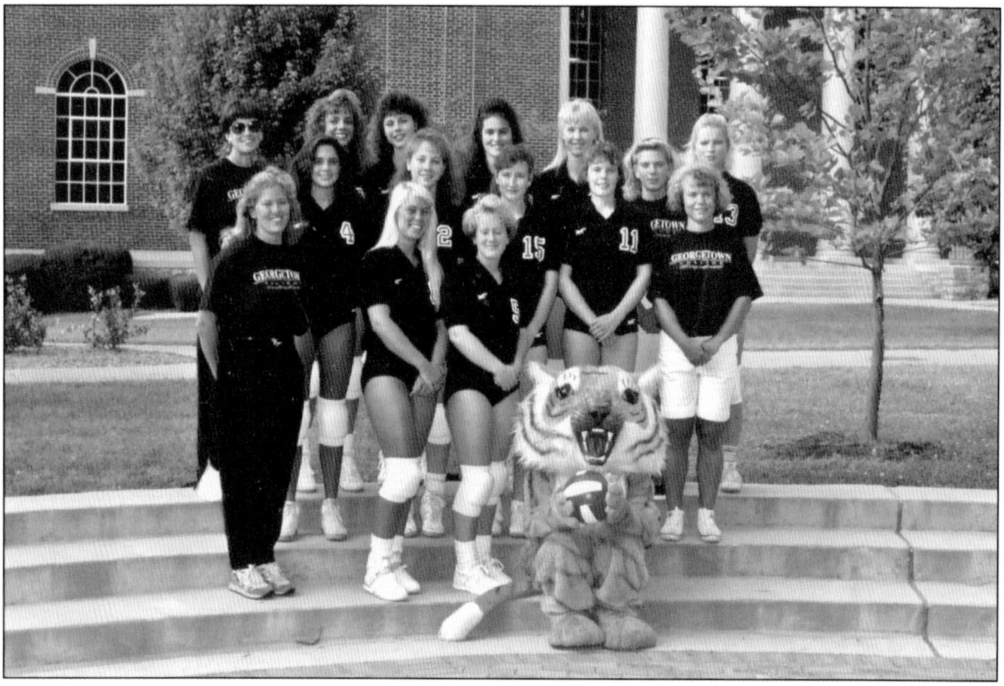

VOLLEYBALL TEAM. This photograph features the women's volleyball team from 1992, a very successful year for Tiger volleyball. The volleyball team did not emerge as a nationally recognized team at Georgetown until 1988. Under the phenomenal leadership of Coach Donna B. Hawkins, who coached for 25 seasons, Georgetown volleyball teams won the Mid-South Conference 13 years in a row and placed eighth in nationals in 1999, 2000, 2001, and 2004. This 1992 team was ranked fourth in the nation, as was the 1999 team.

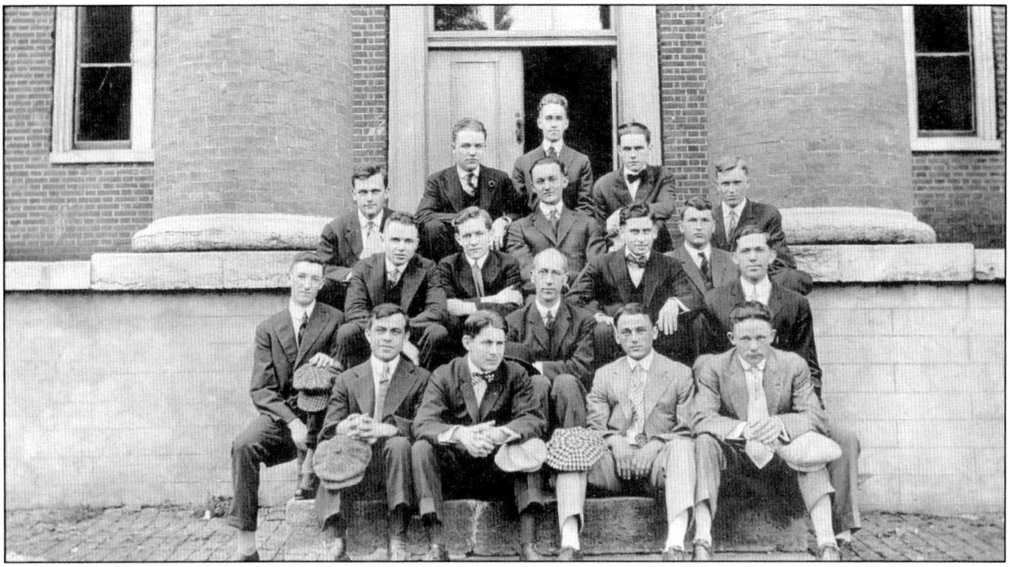

Postcard of Team. This early-1900s photograph of the college football team must have been quite popular considering that it was made into a postcard. Georgetown athletic teams participated in the KAIC for most of its athletic history, until the mid-1990s.

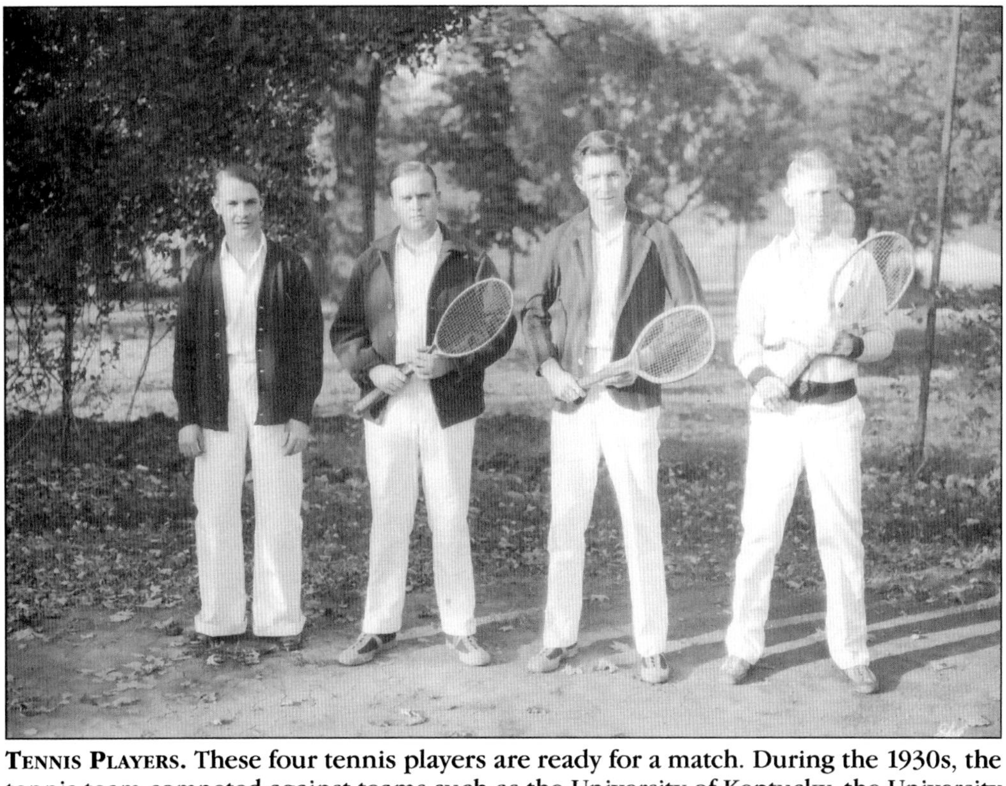

Tennis Players. These four tennis players are ready for a match. During the 1930s, the tennis team competed against teams such as the University of Kentucky, the University of Louisville, Berea College, and Centre College.

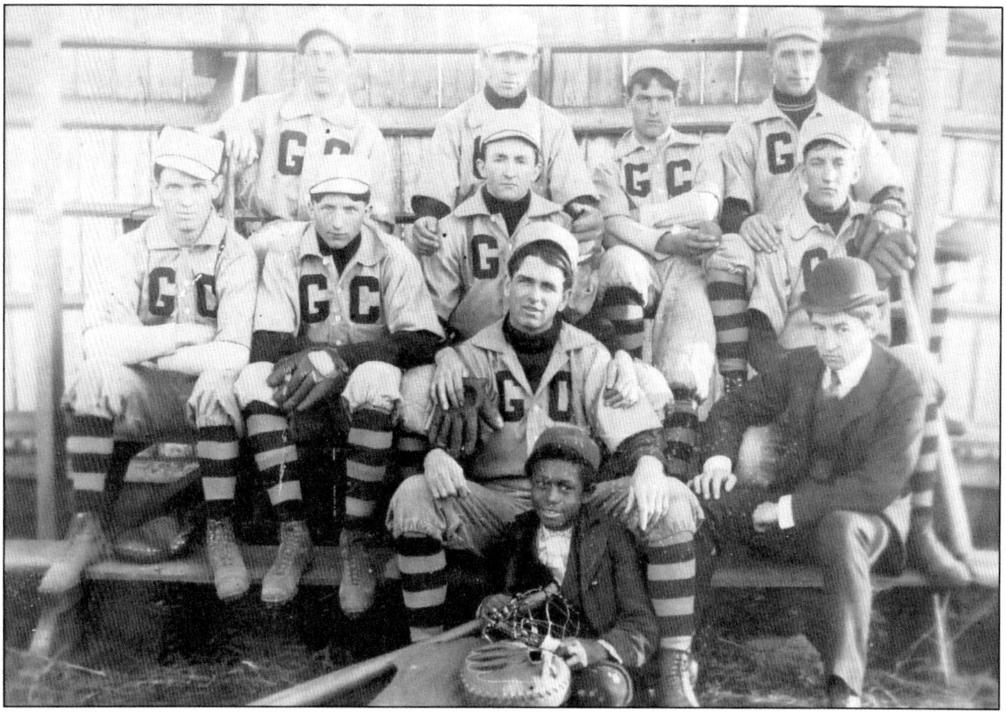

BASEBALL TEAM. The 1901 baseball team poses for a photograph with its coaches and even its ballboy in the front and center.

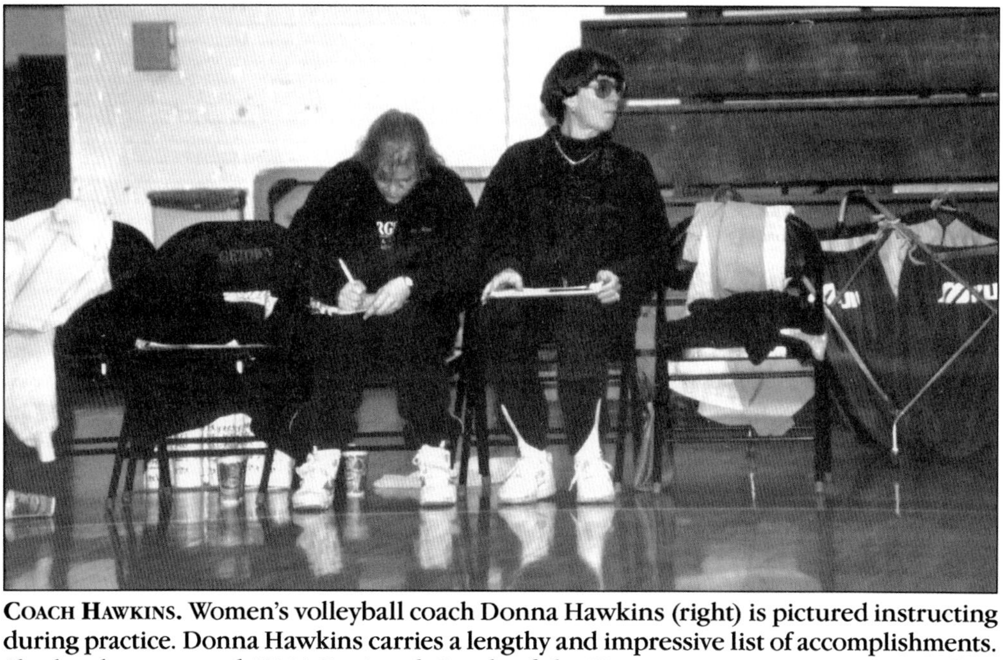

COACH HAWKINS. Women's volleyball coach Donna Hawkins (right) is pictured instructing during practice. Donna Hawkins carries a lengthy and impressive list of accomplishments. She has been named NAIA Regional Coach of the Year on seven occasions as well as NAIA National Volleyball Coach in 1999. In 2000, she was inducted into the NAIA Hall of Fame and has achieved nine team appearances at the NAIA National Championship. In her 25 seasons at Georgetown College, she has witnessed 756 victories.

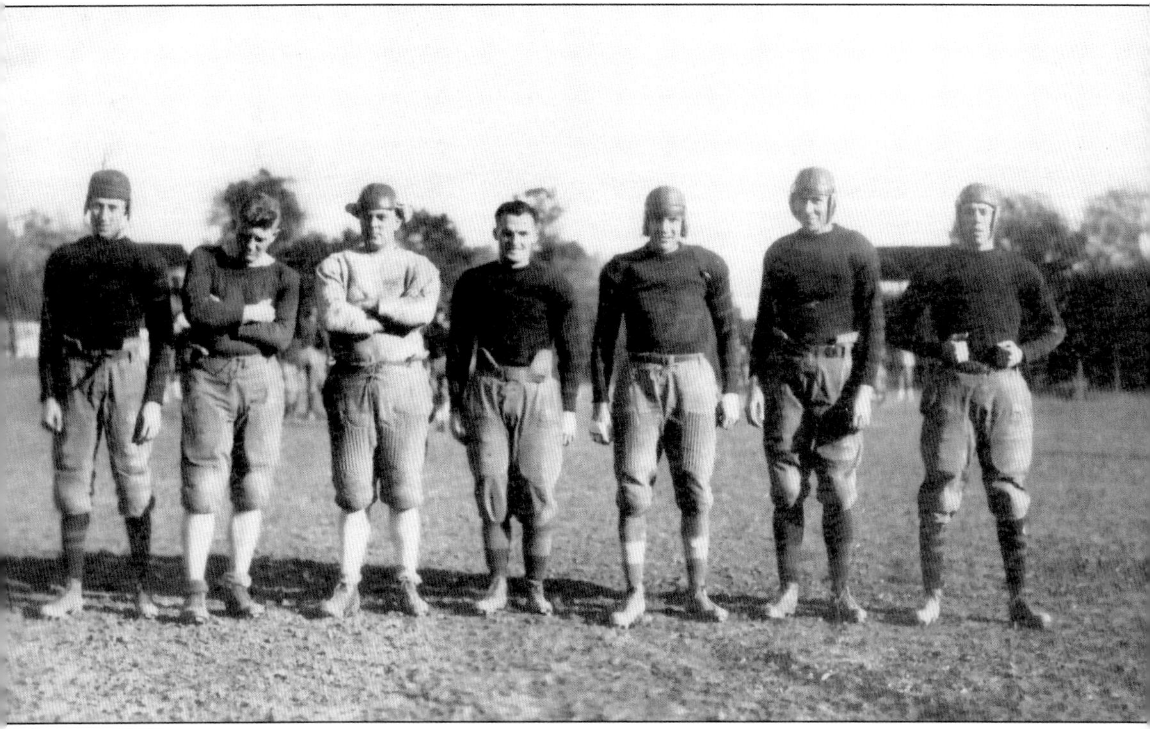

FOOTBALL LINE. The old Georgetown football team was quite popular and successful. Starting in the 1960s, it grew even more successful and continued to escalate to the high standard of today's teams. In 1965, under Coach Lester Craft, /the football team went undefeated for the first time since 1912.

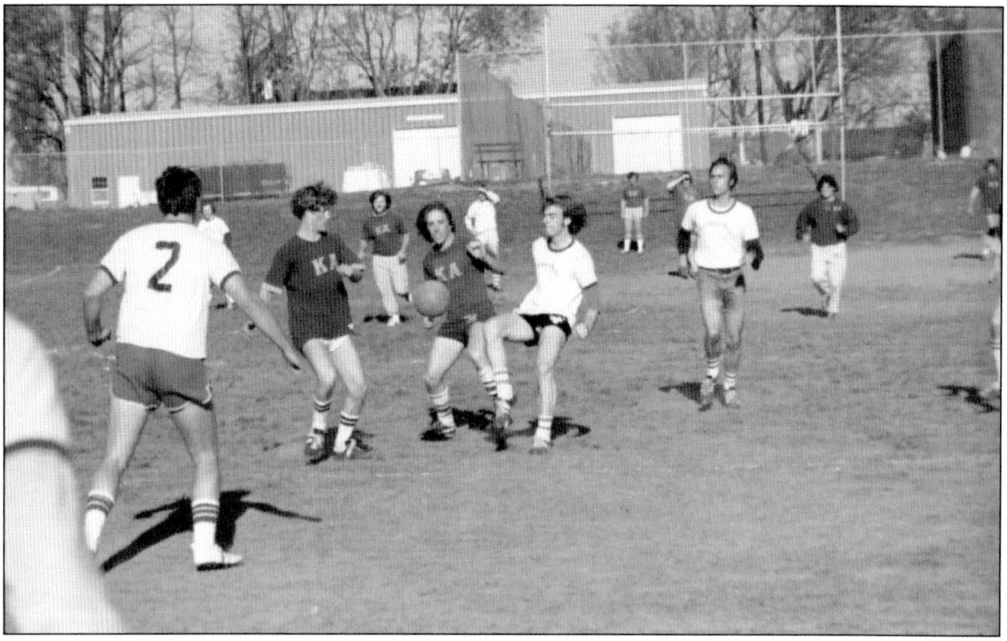

Intramurals. In the past 30 years at Georgetown, intramurals have become an enlarged aspect of the college's athletic life. Teams formed by residence halls or formed by choice are invited to participate. Today intramural sports range from water polo to dodgeball to ultimate Frisbee and include traditional sports such as football, basketball, and volleyball.

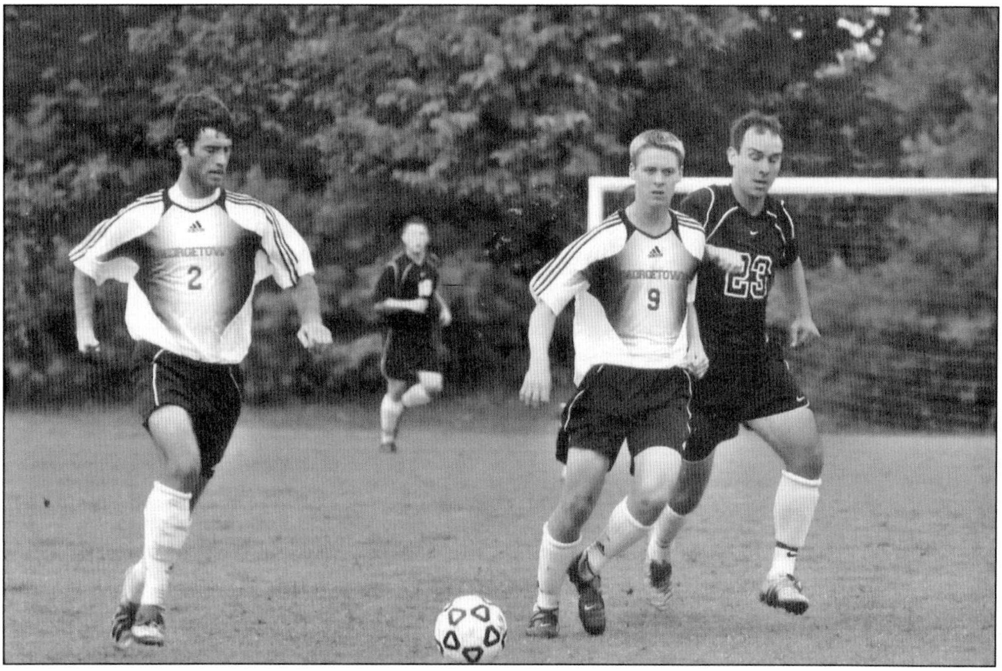

Tiger Soccer. Beginning in 1975, the Tiger men's and women's soccer teams have excelled considerably. Jim Tussey, head coach of the women's soccer team and former head coach of the men's team, has led the Lady Tigers now for 11 years. In 1996, Tussey was named the Mid-South Conference Coach of the Year.

Five

STUDENT LIFE

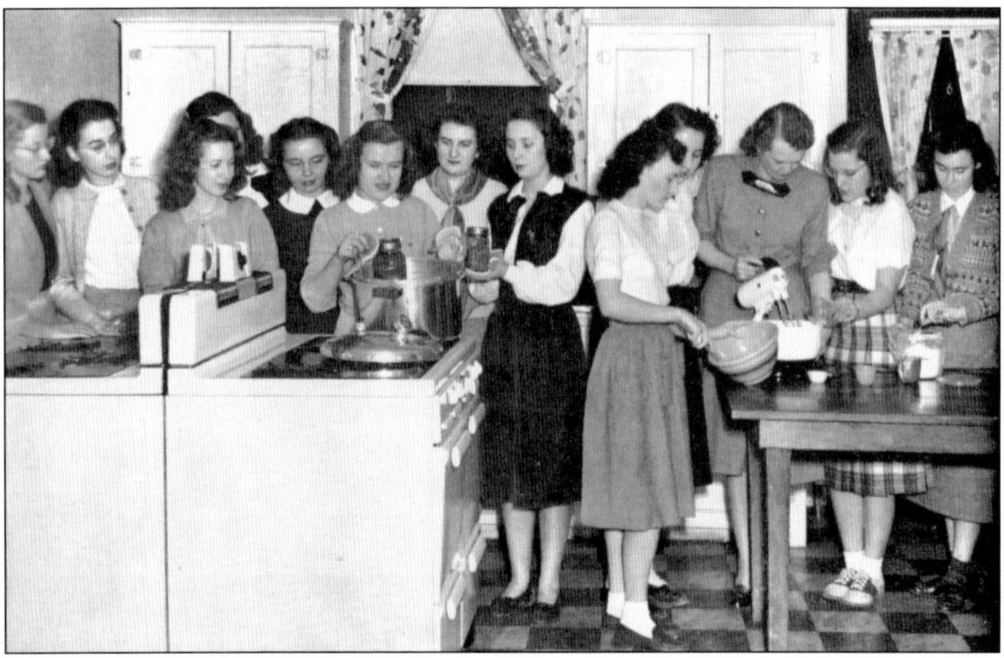

HOME EC CLUB. Students pursuing the field of home economics often joined the home ec club, pictured here. Home economics majors were required to live for a substantial amount of time at the home demonstration house, where they would perform all of the domestic duties of homemaking. Students also threw fine dinner parties for faculty members, and the home economics students were graded on their abilities and overall success of the evening.

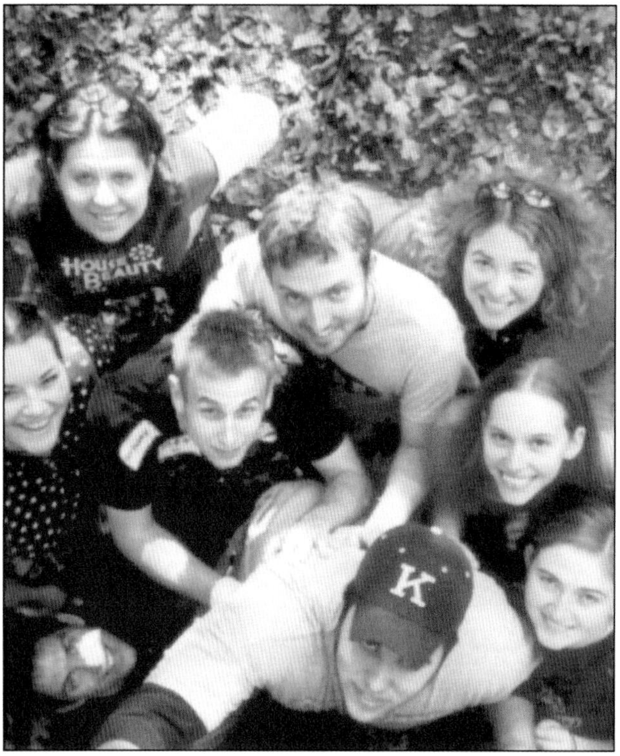

BSU Retreat. Current campus ministries at Georgetown provide a rich array of spiritual activities for students who are seeking to build more intimate relationships with Christ or who are searching for higher meaning in their lives. Fall retreats, "Common Ground" (a weekly devotional service offered to students and led by campus ministries), devotionals, freshmen family groups, creative ministries, and spring break mission trips are a few examples of activities. A council made up of Baptist Student Union leaders and representatives forms the nucleus of the student spiritual life on campus that is so unique and traditional to Georgetown College.

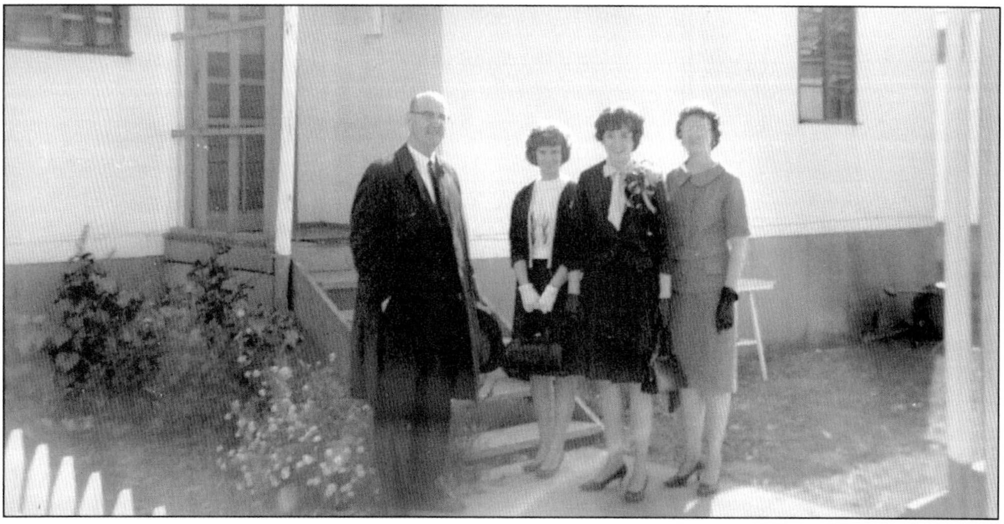

Warrandale Apartments. Located behind Military Street, the tiny shack-like structures set up after World War II to house married students were known as Warrandale Apartments, also called "the barracks." The temporary housing somewhat relieved Georgetown of the problem of inadequate housing, which many colleges encountered upon soldiers' return home. The students living at Warrandale even created their own social circles for the women living in the apartments. Shown here from left to right during the 1966–1967 school year are Carl Griesser, Peggy Griesser Roberts (Carl's daughter), Marie Dash Griesser, and Dorotha Griesser (Peggy's mother). Peggy and her parents are all Georgetown graduates. (Photograph courtesy of Carla Cook.)

May Day. May Day originated from a pagan holiday celebrating the first spring planting and featured games, feasting, and ribbon dances around a maypole. Like Georgetown's tradition of selecting a May queen and her court, villages in the early centuries even until the 1600s elected a queen from the eligible young women of the community.

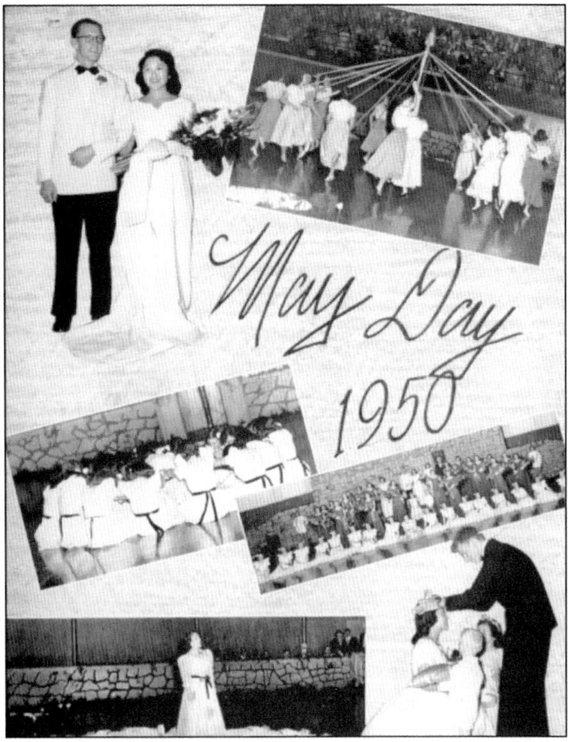

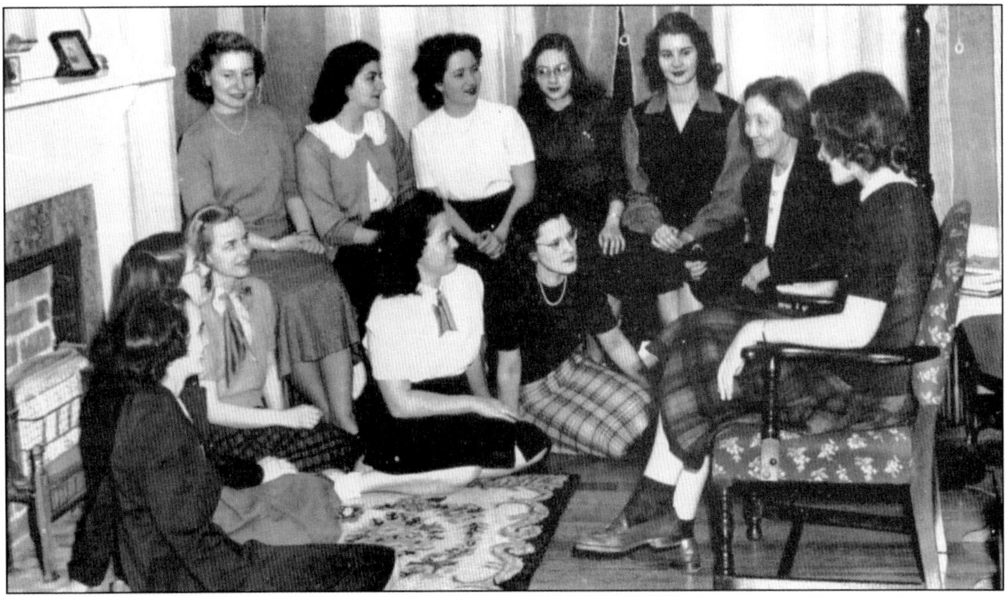

Student Government's Ladies. Student government remains an active sector of student life today, as it appeared to be in this 1948 photograph. Now known as the Association of Georgetown Students (AGS), student government today is no longer divided into two separate entities for men and women, but instead is divided into several offices, whose leaders listen and voice the concerns of students. AGS also possesses the power to make needed improvements as well as the responsibility to host special events such as Songfest, Hanging of the Green, and the annual Belle of the Blue Pageant.

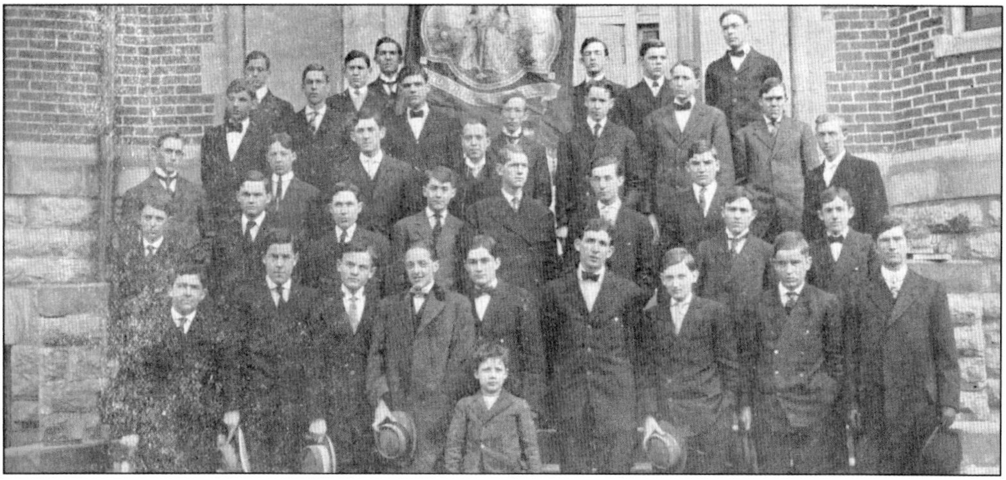

Ciceronian Society. The Ciceronian Society was established in 1837 at the old Rittenhouse Academy—the prior school on the property of what is now Georgetown College—for the purpose of promoting the development of public speaking skills. The agenda for meetings usually consisted of a reading, declamation, debate, intellectual comments, and criticism. Matching competition on campus from its rival, the Tau Theta Kappa Society, kept the fraternal-like society flourishing. An all-men's society, the Ciceronian Society was named for "Old Cicero," the orator and politician of the ancient Roman republic, and those associated with the society held its values and purposes dear to their hearts. Both literary societies on campus sported their own colors and banners, cheered their own mottoes, and participated in locally held contests. Events like these honed the wits and speaking skills of many college students.

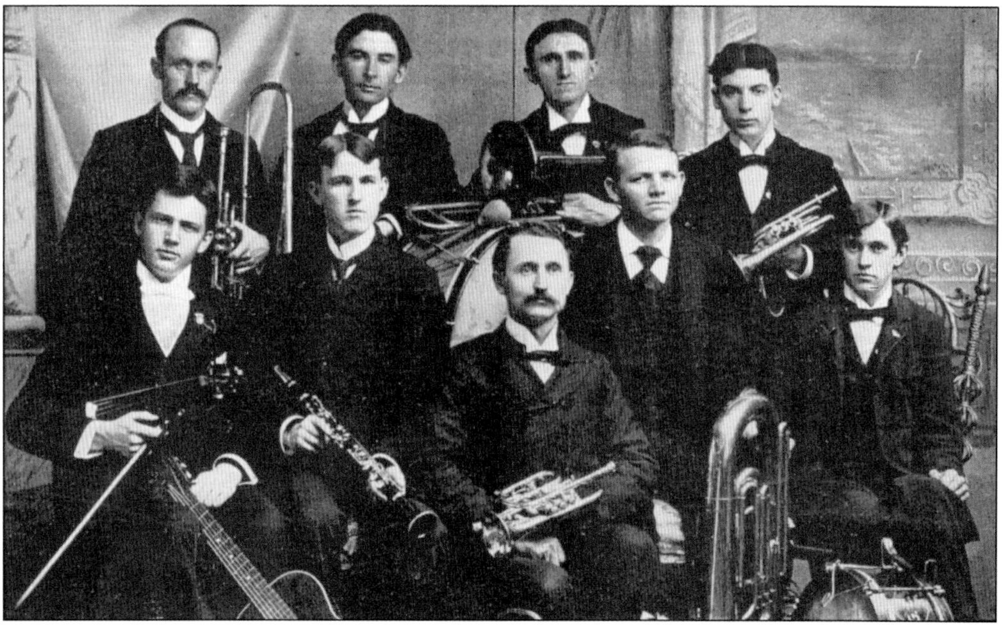

College Orchestra. The Georgetown College Orchestra provided musical entertainment before the existence of a pep band and a concert band. This 1898 group includes W. M. Smith, Lee Kirkpatrick, R. F. Gaither, W. J. Conley, Geo. P. Gibson, M. L. Orem, Hockenberry, I. N. Forward, and Wm. Marksberry.

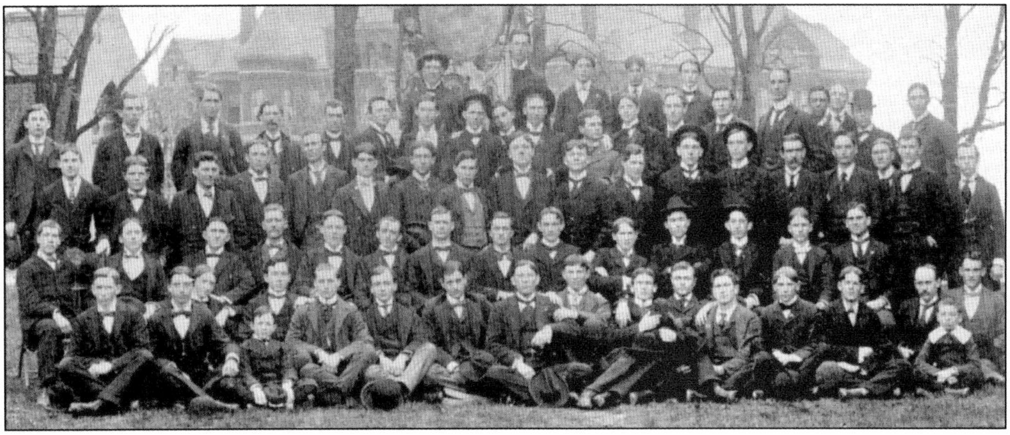

TAU THETA KAPPA SOCIETY. The rivaling partner of the Ciceronian Society, the Tau Theta Kappa Literary Society prided itself on victories in debate and oratorical skills. Most of its members proudly claimed their origins as Kentucky or the Deep South. During the sectional struggle prior to the Civil War, members debated on the topic of secession and the Southern Confederacy. In fact, this Southern sentiment proved to be so strong that Sen. Jefferson Davis accepted an invitation in 1858 to become an honorary member of the society, to which he gladly accepted. The outright support of the Confederacy from groups of students naturally increased tension on campus, and the school closed due to the strife for the autumn of 1862. Classes were dismissed after a riot broke out in response to the surrender of Fort Sumter in April 1861, and since classes were too small, the fall session of 1862 was suspended.

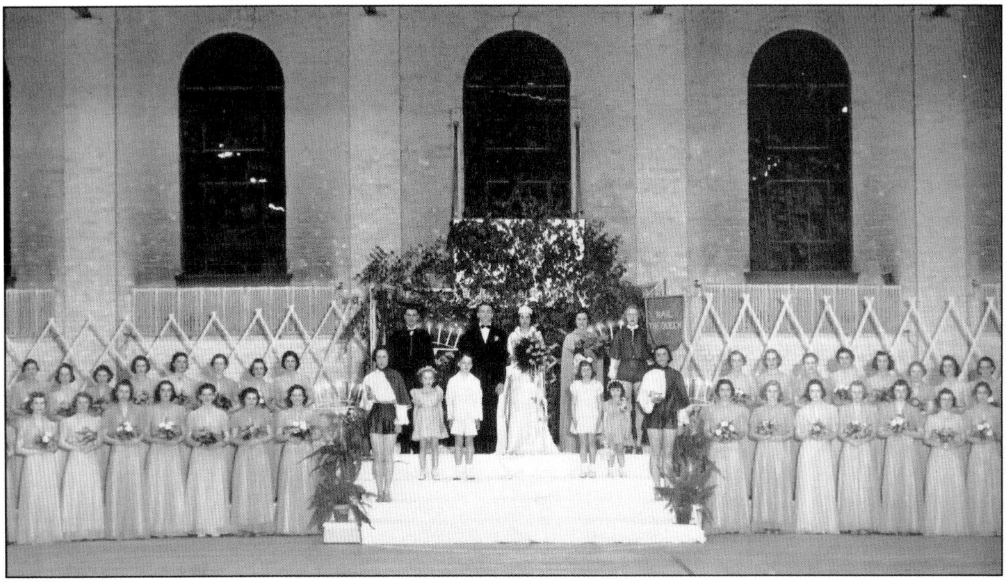

MAY DAY COURT. The procession of the queen's court during May Day festivities at Georgetown College was a serious and regal event during the 1920s and 1930s. When May Day ceased at Georgetown in 1972, the tradition of the queen's court remained in an event called Spring Fever. The event was usually held in the gymnasium after its completion in 1926, and physical education classes learned special dances for the occasion in order to perform in front of the queen's court. This photograph features the May Day court of 1938.

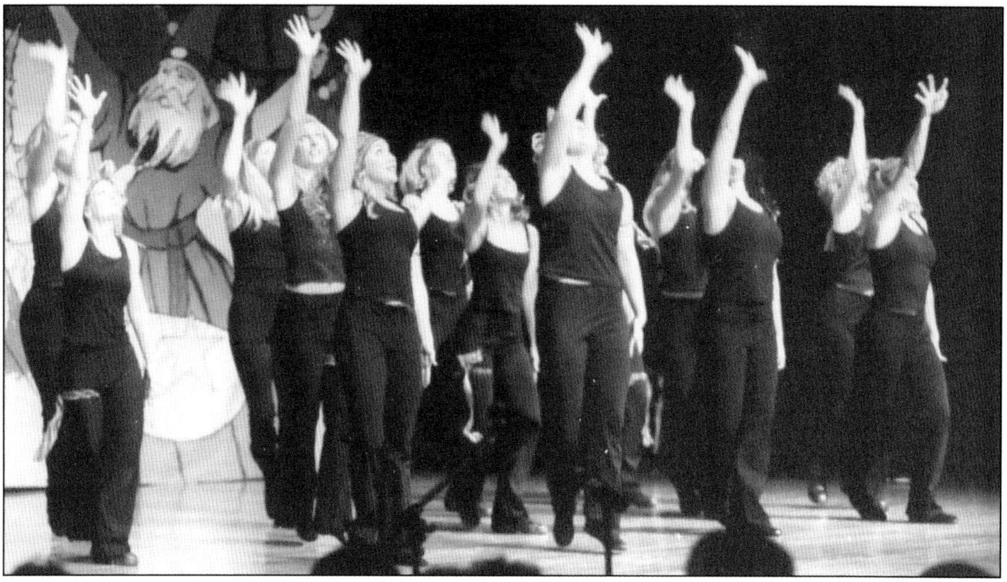

Songfest. As one of Georgetown's most popular social events of the year, Songfest showcases the college's residence halls in a competition of song and dance production, as shown in this 2001 photograph. The recent 2004 performance included mass references to movies; the theme being "Tinseltown." Groups like Lamda Chi Alpha rebelled against the movie theme by suggesting reading for sport through their rendition of *Reading Rainbow*.

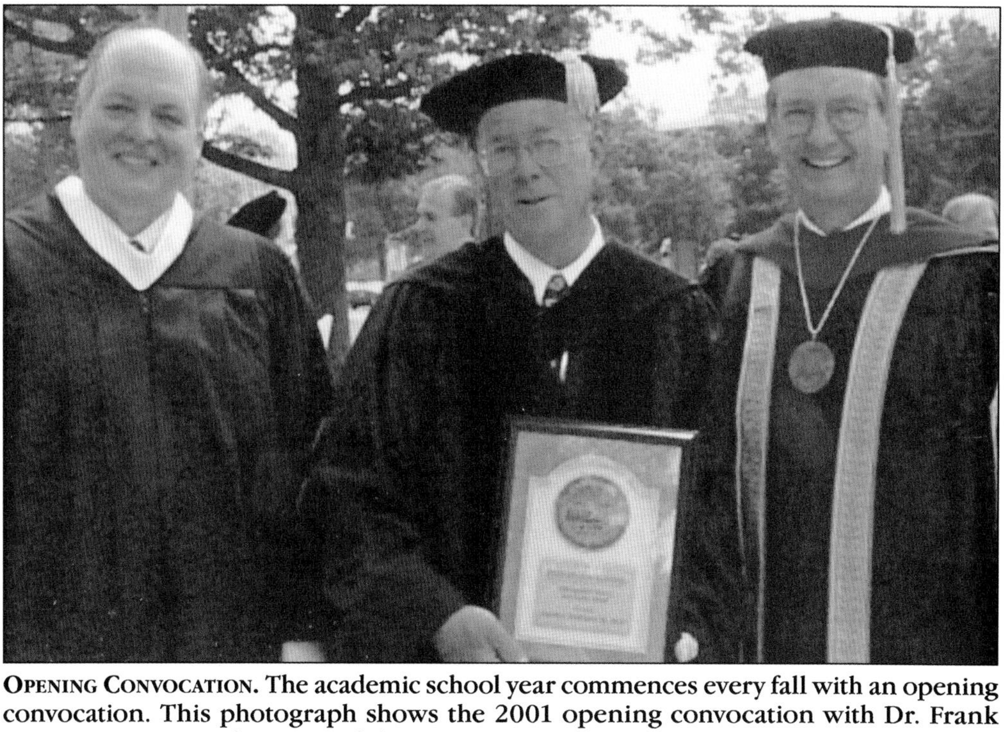

Opening Convocation. The academic school year commences every fall with an opening convocation. This photograph shows the 2001 opening convocation with Dr. Frank Wiseman (center), who received the Manning Distinguished Mentor and Teacher Award; Dr. William H. Crouch Jr. (right), president of Georgetown College; and Dr. James P. Hackett (left), president and C.E.O. of Steelcase Corporation.

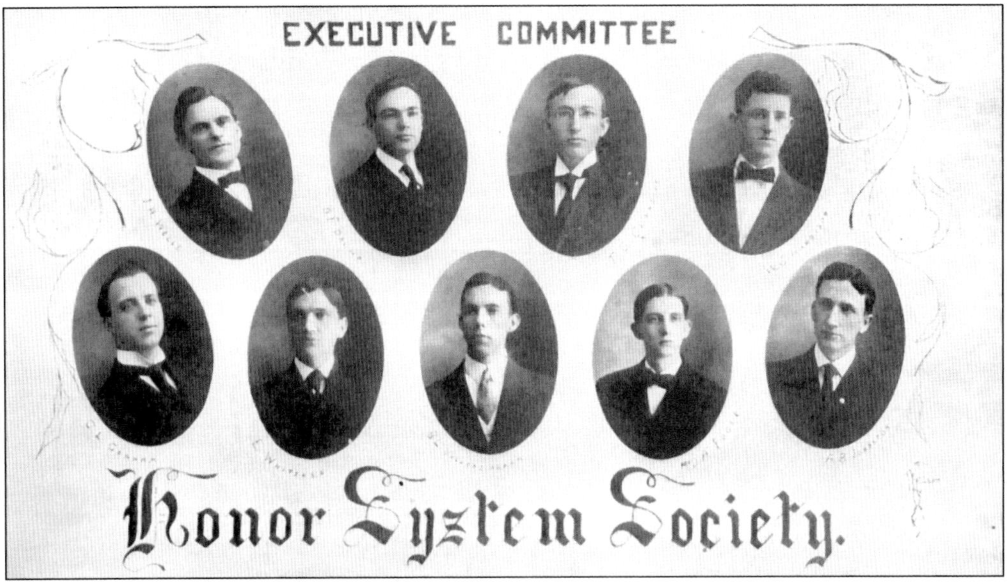

Honor System Society. Installed as a system of reform of cheating and dishonesty, the honor system societies were established in 1908 but remain today only as policy. The act of cheating, if witnessed, was curtailed through a committee that then examined the accused, finding them guilty or innocent. If the student was found guilty, he was asked to leave the college and the case was then submitted to the faculty. Two separate societies existed for both the male and female students.

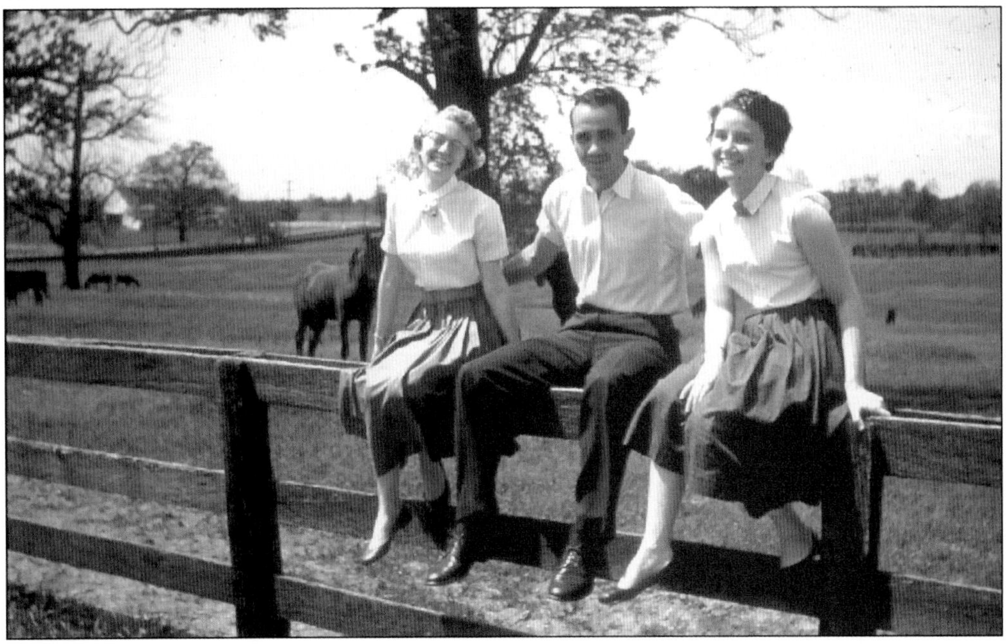

Students on a Fence. Students in this picturesque scene enjoy the outdoors at a local horse farm in Georgetown. Taken in the 1950s by photographer Ed Boden, students sitting on the fence, from left to right, are Eula Jones, Ray Rice, and Helen Poynter Boden. Today students at Georgetown College are less likely to frequent these outdoor local jewels in the surrounding community.

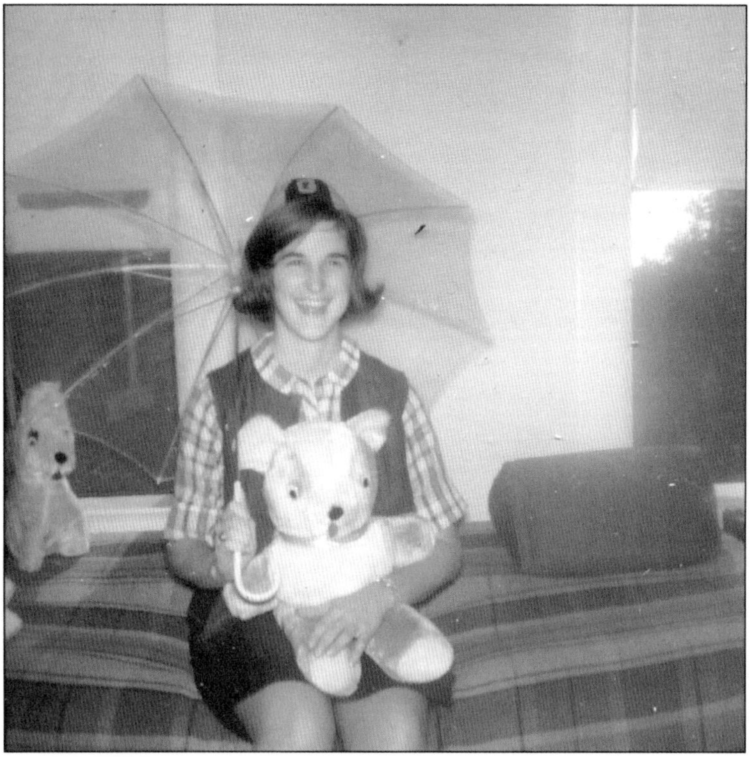

Wearing a Beanie. Becky Richards Bishop, a freshman in 1965, poses in her dorm room in Rucker Hall. Notice that she is wearing a "beanie" on her head, a freshman tradition that came to a halt in the early 1970s. (Photograph courtesy of Becky Bishop.)

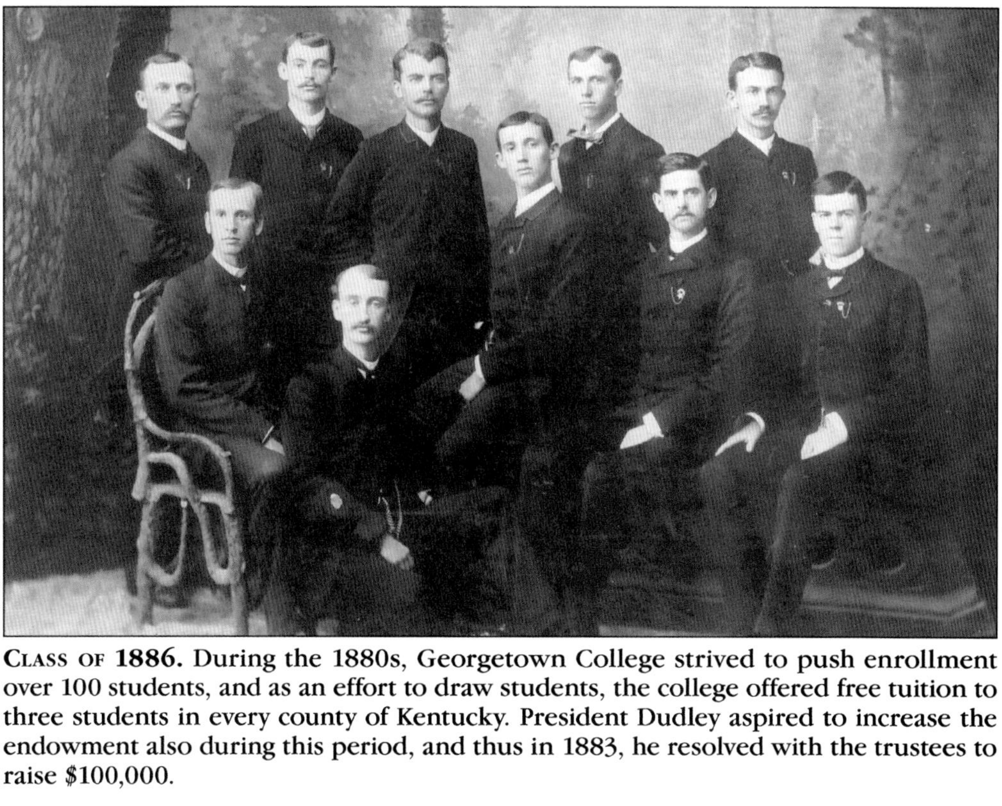

Class of 1886. During the 1880s, Georgetown College strived to push enrollment over 100 students, and as an effort to draw students, the college offered free tuition to three students in every county of Kentucky. President Dudley aspired to increase the endowment also during this period, and thus in 1883, he resolved with the trustees to raise $100,000.

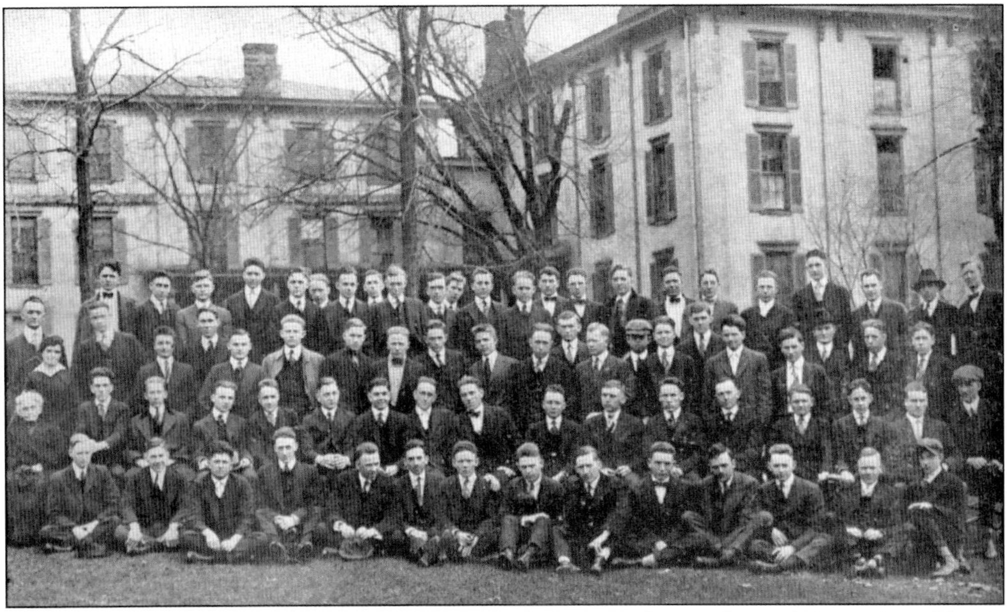

"Old Sem" Diners. Dinner required a formal dress code for students during the college's early years and also when the new cafeteria wing was added onto Rucker Hall, called the "Bristow" cafeteria. Men dined in suits while women wore dresses and skirts. However, when the Cralle Student Center opened in 1965, the new cafeteria, known today as "the caf," created a more relaxed atmosphere, as clothing trends likewise drifted to a more informal style.

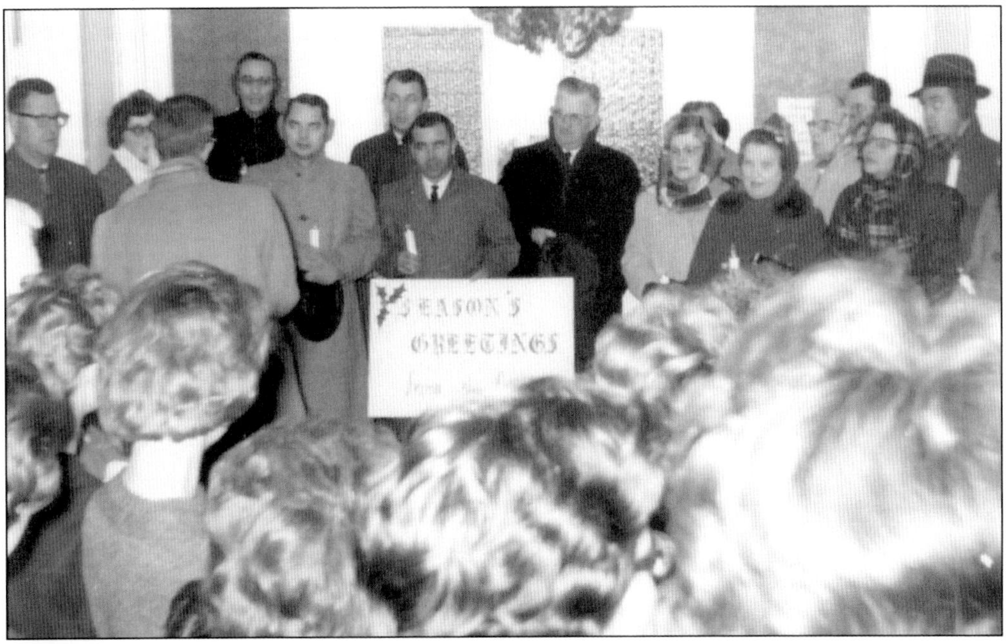

Christmas Carols/Party in Rucker Hall. Serenades were enjoyed by the women of Rucker Hall, especially during Christmastime. Women and men sang carols and enjoyed each other's company at the Rucker Hall Christmas party. The students are standing in the entryway of Rucker, which consisted of a corridor with a double staircase.

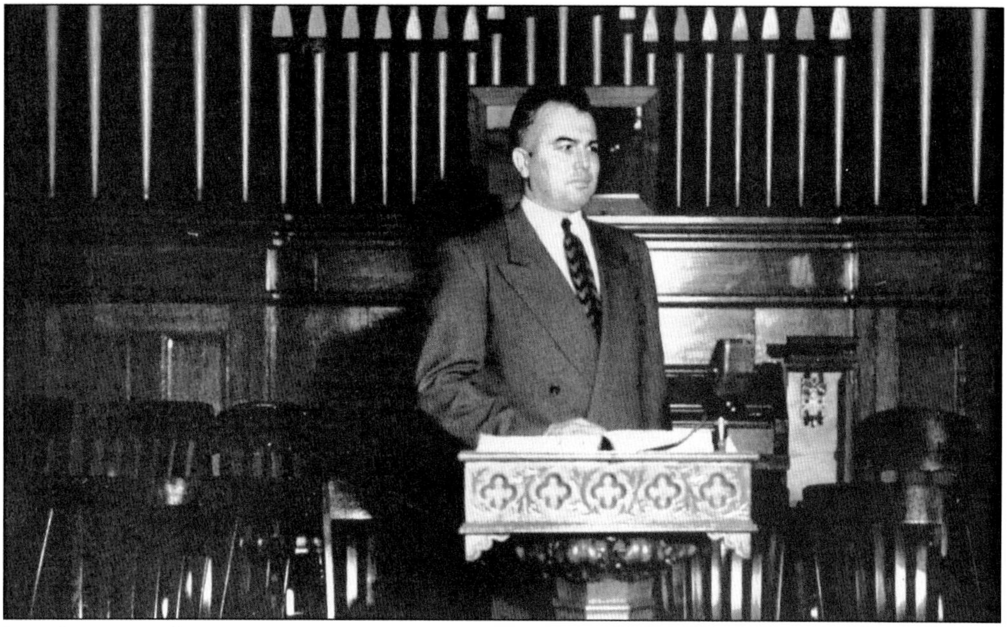

Dr. Skiles. Religious activity on campus is an ever-blossoming facet of Georgetown College. Students attended chapel services, joined local churches, and participated in the Baptist Student Union and other campus ministerial events. Revivals, chapel choirs, and vesper services were some of the popular religious activities. This photograph features Dr. Elwin Skiles, who students enjoyed hearing and who eventually served as president of Hardin Simmons University in Texas.

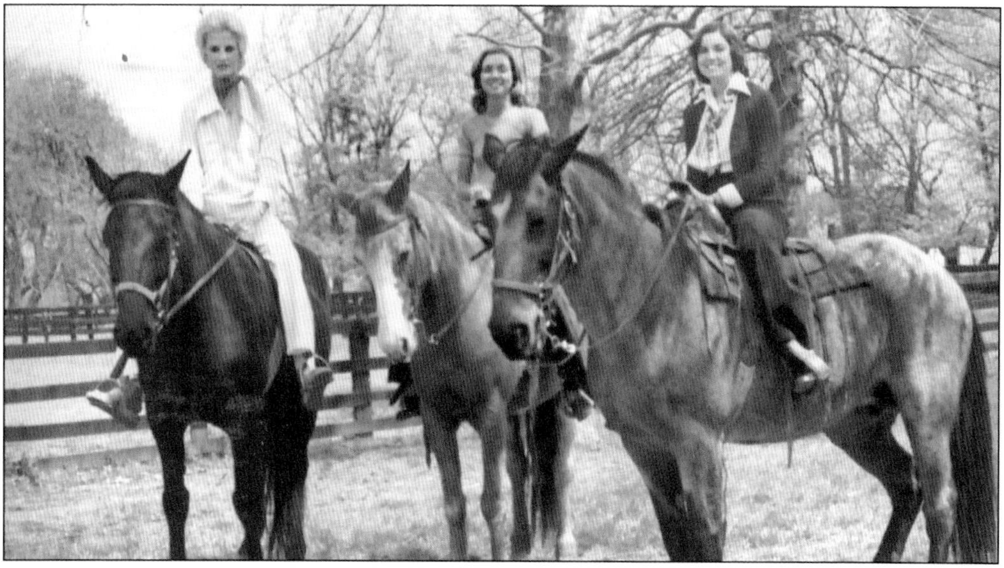

Girls on Horses. Equestrian activity, traditionally a prized sport in the state of Kentucky, was by no means void at Georgetown College. A former Georgetown student in the 1940s remembers the current maintenance building was utilized as the training facility for students enrolled in horseback riding classes. Today the tradition continues with the horsemanship class, granting physical education credit at the college. Students in the class travel to Burr Oak farm in Georgetown to learn the art of riding and caring for horses.

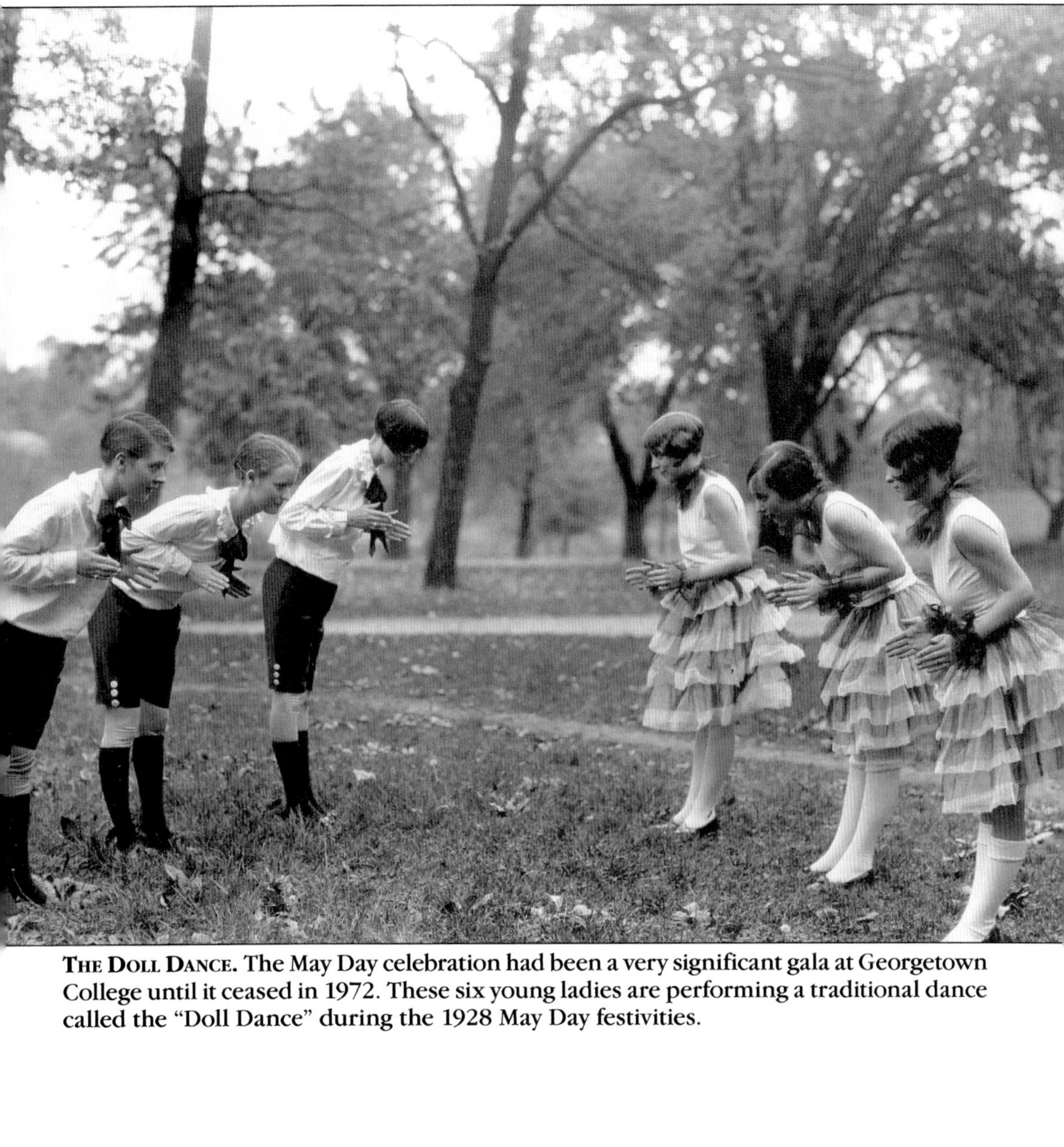

The Doll Dance. The May Day celebration had been a very significant gala at Georgetown College until it ceased in 1972. These six young ladies are performing a traditional dance called the "Doll Dance" during the 1928 May Day festivities.

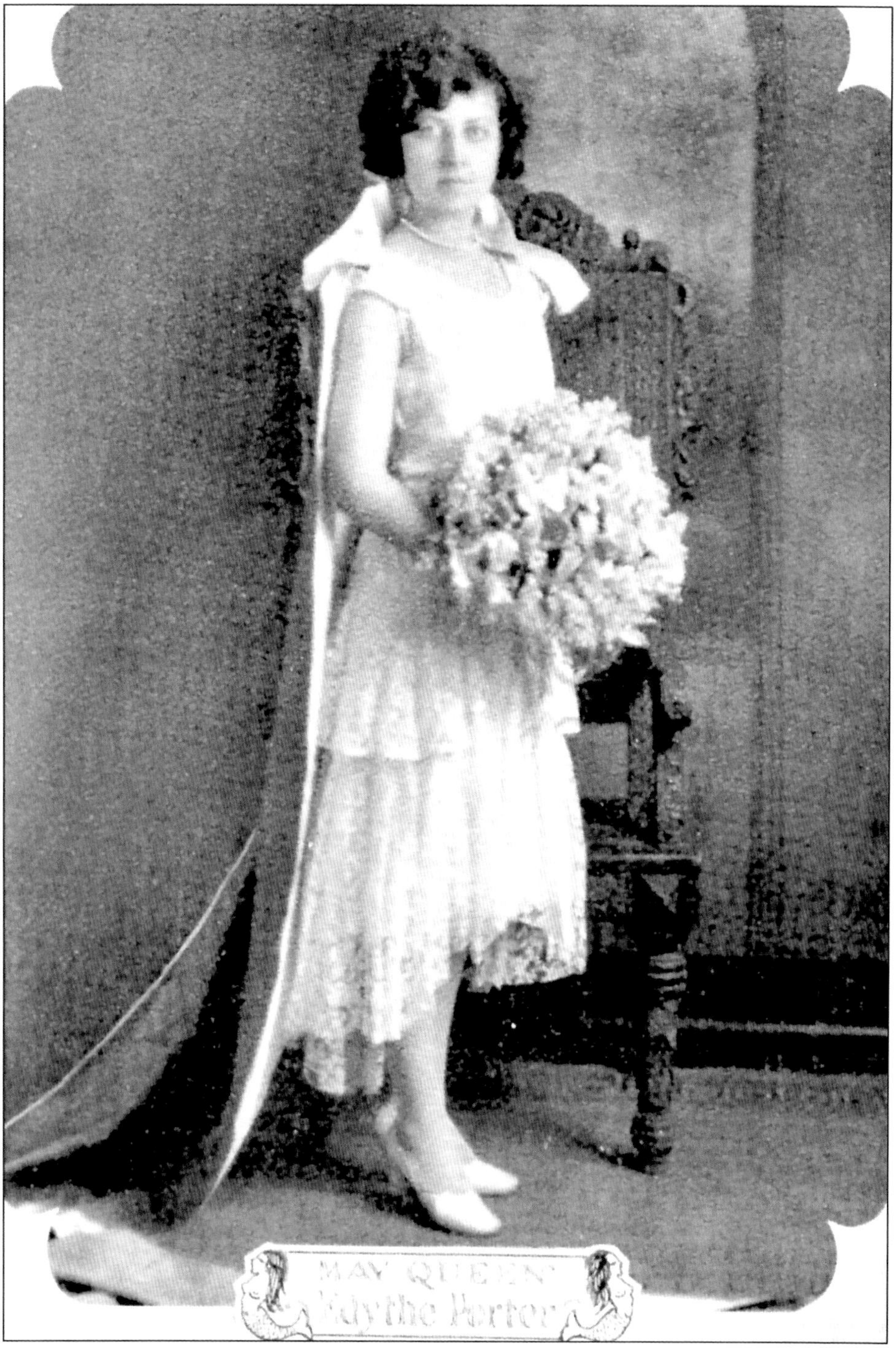

Edythe Porter. The lovely Edythe Porter poses as the 1930 May Queen. The description of May Day as a majestic celebration, including a full court proceeding down a red carpet while children bear the queen's crown, explains why Miss Porter is looking quite regal in this image. The name in the corner is Bradley, a well-known Kentucky photographer. (Photograph courtesy of Maribeth Hambrick, niece of Edythe Porter Woodall.)

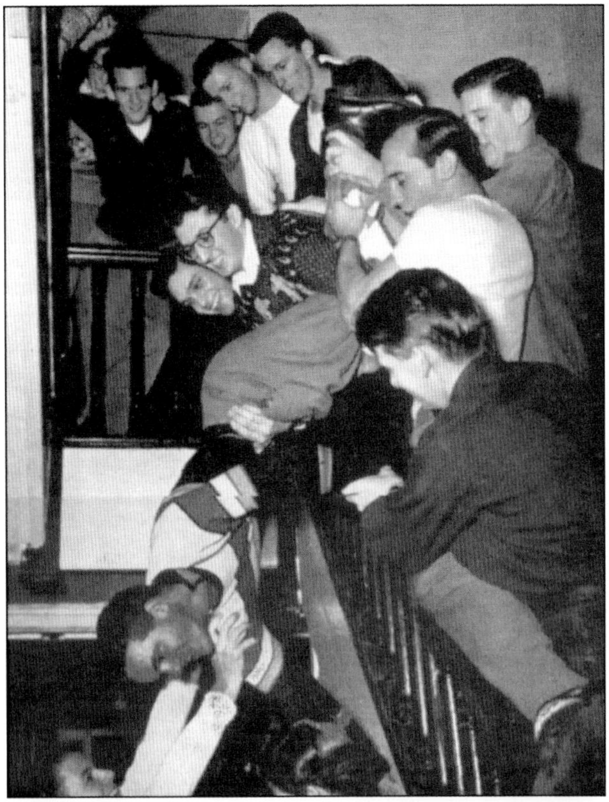

PAWLING "CATCH." Pawling Hall, constructed in 1844 and expanded in 1877, primarily served as a men's dormitory. As in most male dorms, roughhousing is inevitable, as witnessed in this photograph where students are attempting to throw a fellow comrade over the staircase. Today the renovated Pawling Hall serves as classrooms and faculty offices.

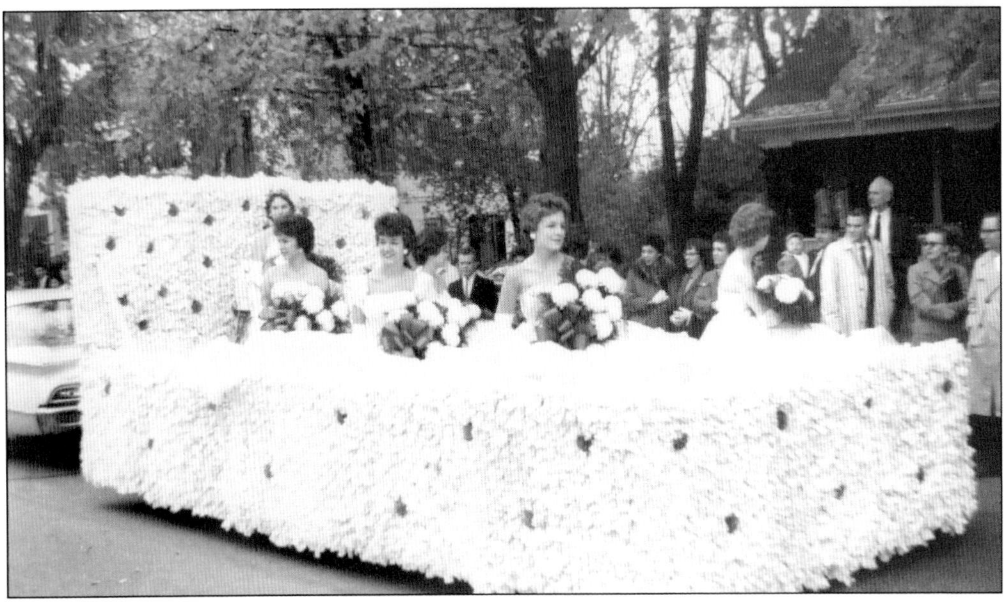

HOMECOMING COURT, 1961. The decadent homecoming parade not only featured floats traveling down Main Street in Georgetown, but also the homecoming court. The ladies in this 1961 parade resemble fluffy snowballs in their light-hued dresses made of ruffles and chiffon. Notice that most of the dresses are strapless and A-line in form, as was the style in the late 1950s and early 1960s.

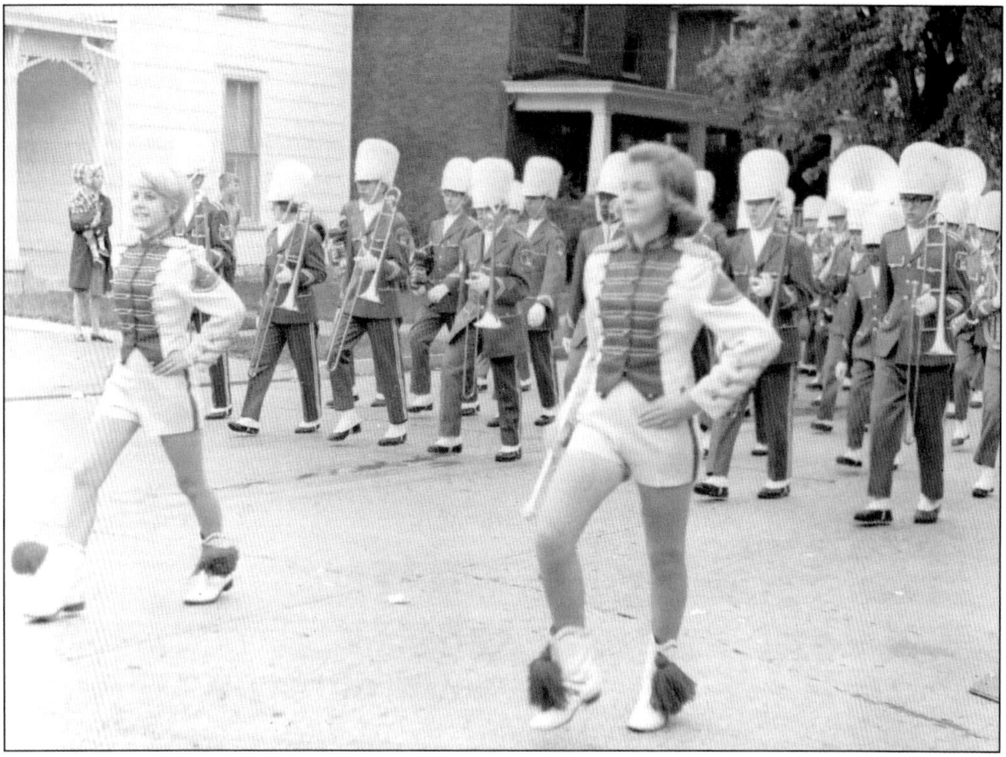

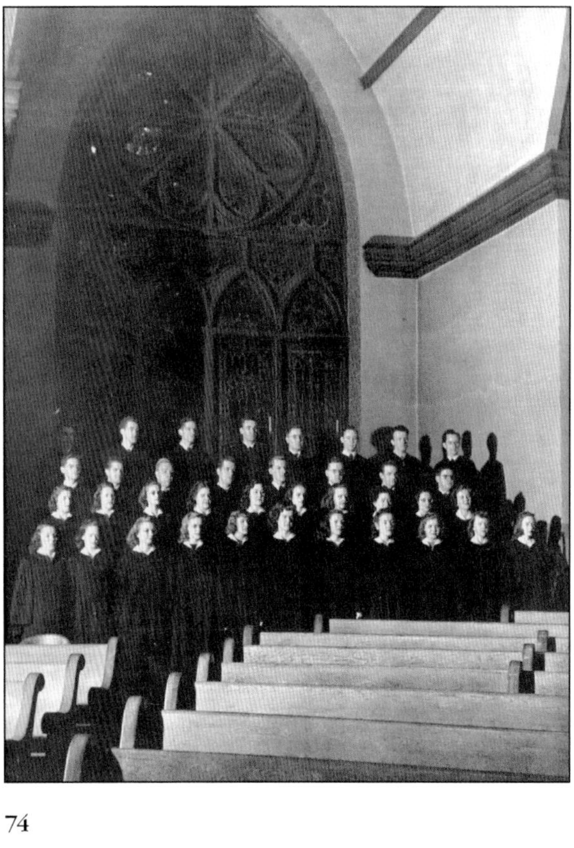

Marching Band. In 1958, a marching band was established, adding to the spirit of Georgetown College. Performing in parades and at football games, the marching band played the "Tiger Rag" for the crowds of cheering alumni and students. Today a marching band no longer exists, but the Tiger pep band leads athletic supporters at football and basketball games.

Chapel Choir. Open to all students, today's college concert choir performs in the chapel as well as in various churches. Another choral group, Chorale, formerly the a cappella choir, is determined only through auditions. All music majors not in band are required to participate in concert-choir.

Six

Greeks and Social Societies

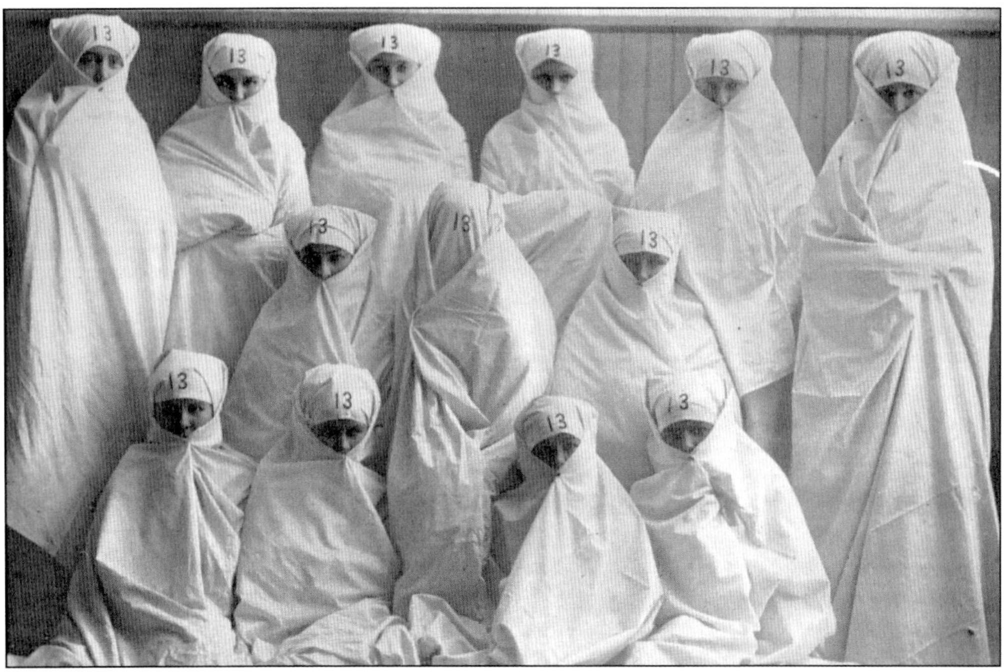

Mystic 13. The Mystic 13 is shown here mysteriously concealing their identities. Not until the 1916 annual does one find a photograph openly revealing the group members. Such "13" groups were quite common among colleges during the early 20th century, many of them performing mysterious, ritualistic acts on the 13th day of the month or gestures with the symbolic 13. For example, today at Yale University, a group called "the 13s" has provided 13 bagels to the admission office on a busy day.

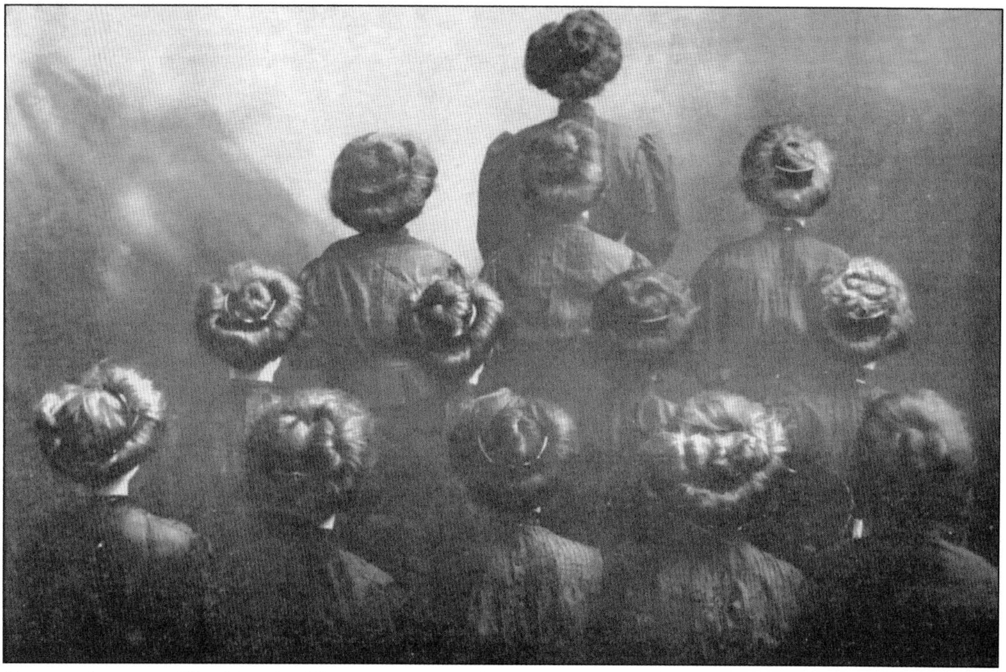

Secret Society. The Mystic 13 was a women's organization that existed from approximately 1908 to 1916. In the early years of the 20th century, social clubs increased in popularity. The Louisville Club and, in the 1920s, the Bobbed Hair Club are a few examples. Because students did not have cars to go into other towns for recreation, these clubs provided the desired social diversion. The Mystic 13 hides all its members in secrecy.

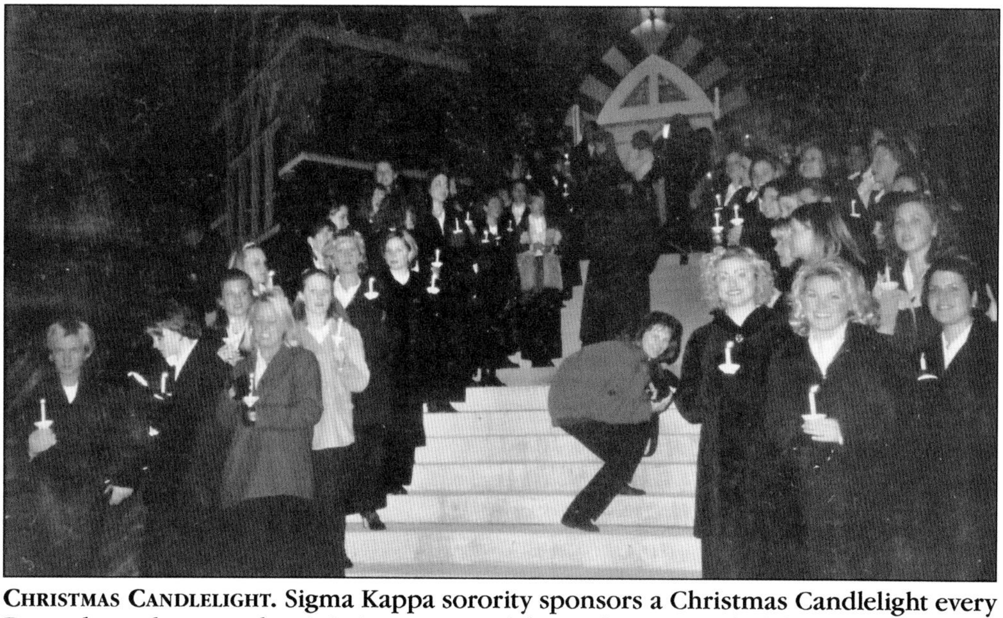

Christmas Candlelight. Sigma Kappa sorority sponsors a Christmas Candlelight every December, where carolers join in song to celebrate the coming holiday. Usually held at Georgetown Baptist Church, a host of alumni return to Georgetown to celebrate the Christmas spirit through song with the chapter. Here members pose on the steps of the church during the 1999 Christmas Candlelight.

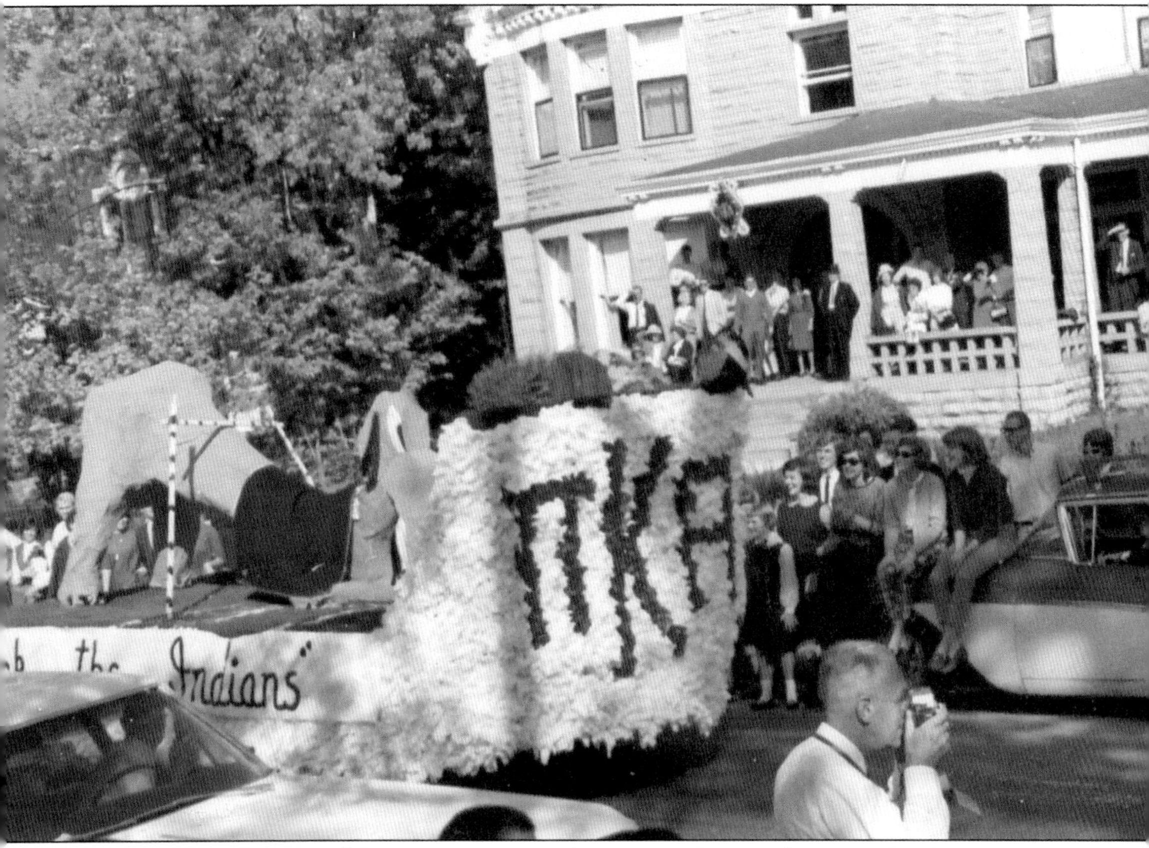

Homecoming. The annual homecoming parade gave students a chance to let their creative juices flow by designing and assembling a float for their residence hall. The float in this photograph was created by the Pi Kappa Alpha fraternity and is incidentally passing the large Pi Kappa Alpha house, built in 1897.

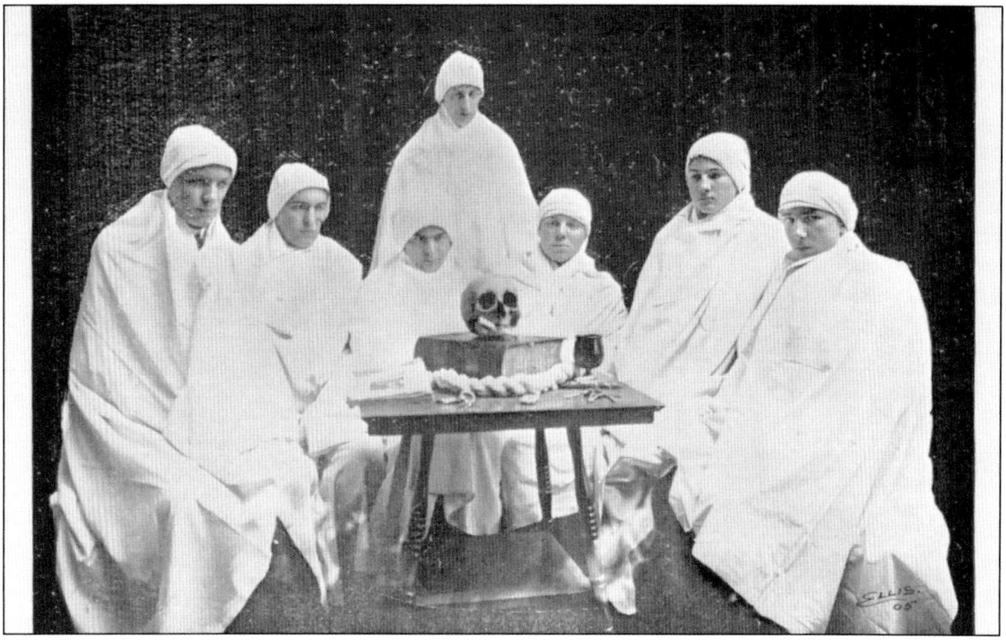

Les Enfantes Du Diable. Clubs and social societies are an extremely popular venue for students at Georgetown College. Many clubs had a ritualistic and more serious image like this one in 1901, called Les Enfantes Du Diable. Other clubs existed primarily for fun and for meeting new comrades. Among others were the PHADs, the Seven Devils, and the Nicotine Club for men, and the Canines and Whitecaps for women.

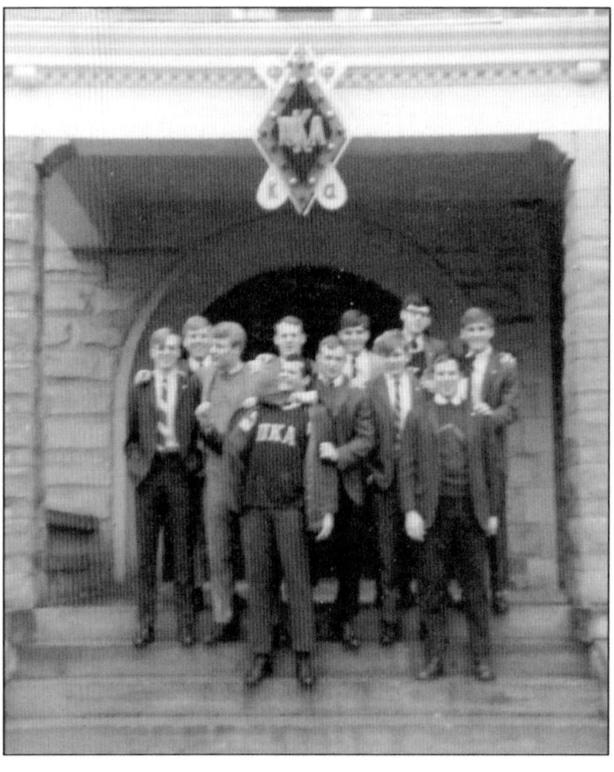

PIKES on the Porch. These Pi Kappa Alpha brothers pose on the porch of their Main Street home, built in 1897 and purchased in 1926 by the college. The basement of the house was likely used for ritualistic pledging activities. Travis Burton, class of 2006, reports his experience with Pi Kappa Alpha in an interview: "I feel a great base of support; no matter what challenges arise, I have many people to turn to." Today the "PIKES" stress leadership in their fraternity, exemplified through their involvement in Association of Georgetown Students (AGS). In 2003, they held four of the nine seats on AGS, and in 2004, the PIKES accounted for three of the seats.

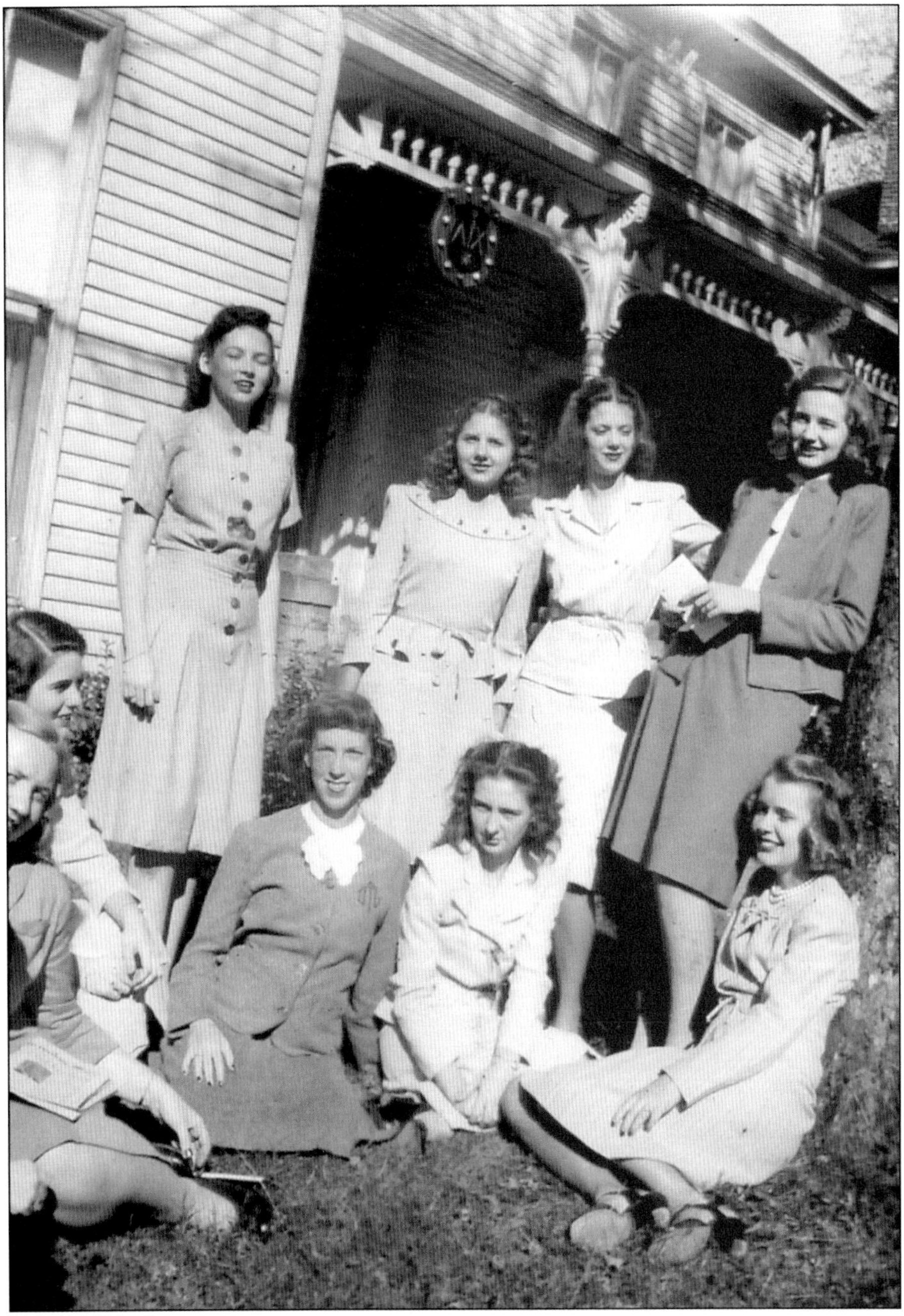

KDs in Front of Old House. The Kappa Delta sorority, chartered at Georgetown in 1946, originally formed their home in President Yager's old house on Main Street. It was formerly named Yager Hall. The "KDs," like most Greek fraternities and sororities on campus, retained about 20 members during the 1940s. Greeks during this period remained in the minority compared to independents; the largest social group was the Rucker Hall girls followed by the men of Pawling Hall. Because fraternities and sororities were smaller than today, they could often fit all their members into the large older homes on Main Street, like this former Kappa Delta House.

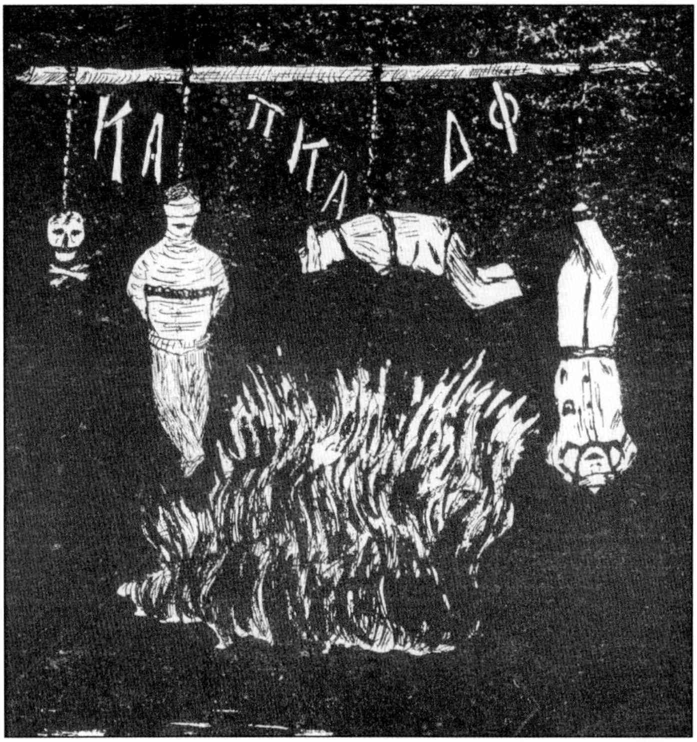

Land of the Fratdogs. Horror images of skulls, crossbones, and blindfolded men often accompanied Greek propaganda. Other popular cartoons frequently associated with Georgetown College fraternities were images of goats, coffins, and individuals completely draped with sheets. This particular image, taken from the 1908 *Belle of the Blue*, represented the three fraternities in existence during that year: Kappa Alpha, Pi Kappa Alpha, and Delta Phi.

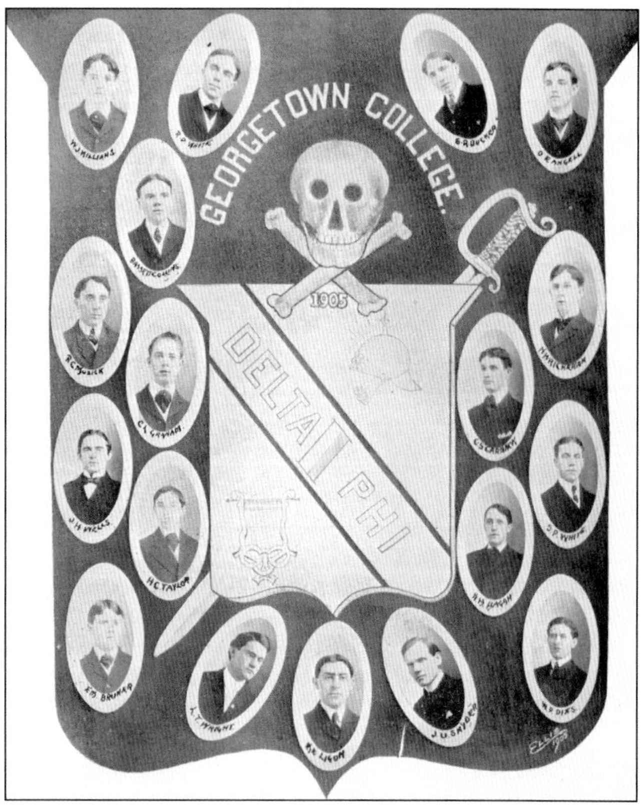

Delta Phi. Delta Phi, a local fraternity, was established on Georgetown's campus in 1904. The fraternity's motto, "Princes inter pares," motivated its members to lend help to the weaker brother. The group strove to live by ideals that lifted the fraternity to a higher intellectual and moral plane.

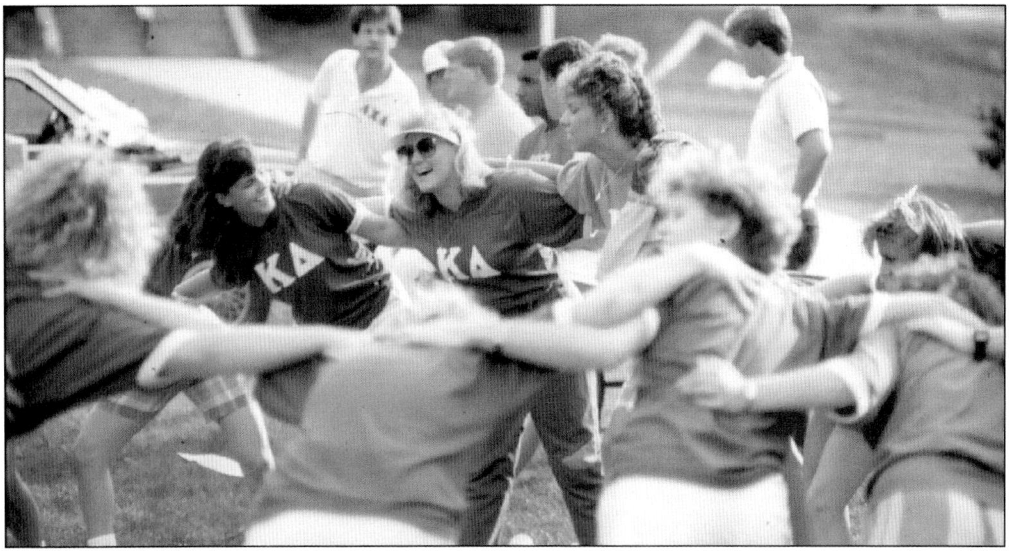

KD Circle Up. One tradition at Georgetown College, especially during special events such as homecoming, Songfest, and especially Chapel Day, is for each Greek organization to "circle up." This includes shouting a chorus of songs, chants, and cheers of the organization by members in a circle. This display of Greek spirit is today performed after weekly meetings of the sorority or fraternity.

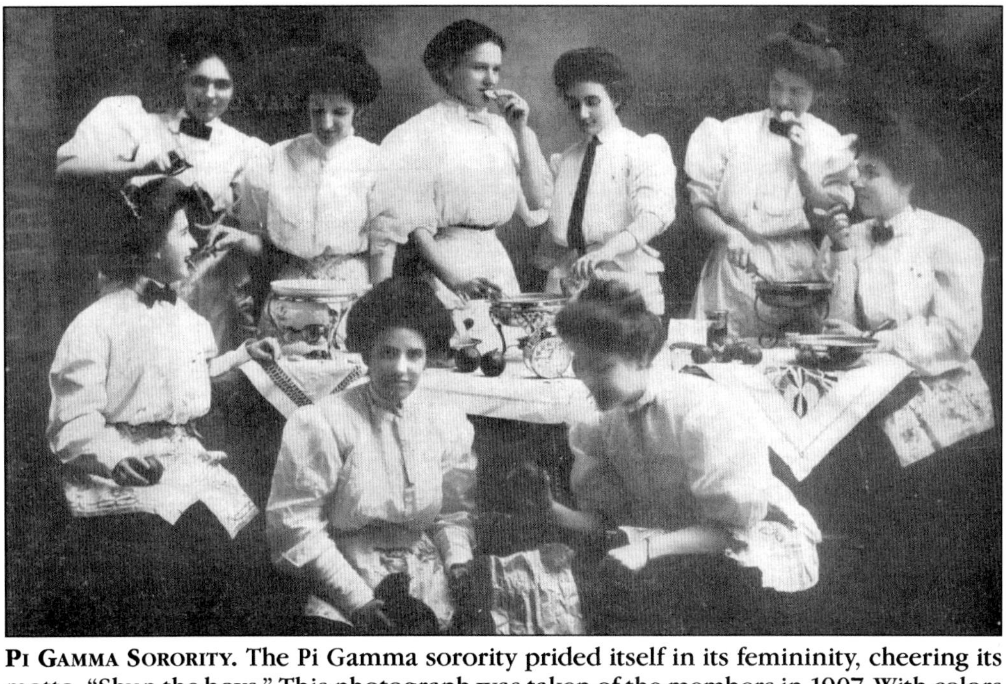

Pi Gamma Sorority. The Pi Gamma sorority prided itself in its femininity, cheering its motto, "Shun the boys." This photograph was taken of the members in 1907. With colors of turquoise and gold and the forget-me-not as its flower, Pi Gamma Sorority failed to remain on campus, lasting only a few short years. Many Greek organizations on campus likewise were unstable. Pictured from left to right are (first row) Miss Miller, Miss Tolin, Miss Burgess, and Miss Thompson; (second row) Miss Creason, Miss Revill, Miss Sayers, Miss Duiguid, and Miss Revill.

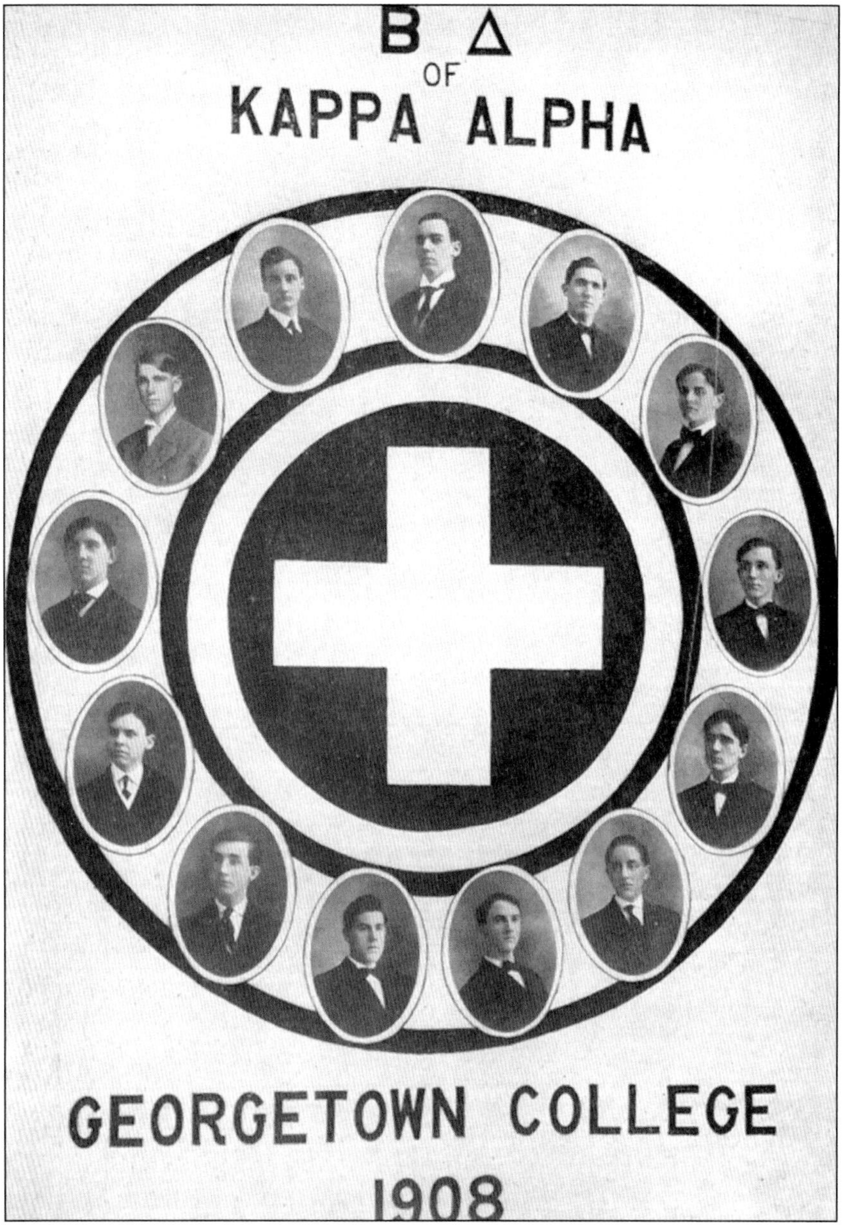

Kappa Alpha Order. The Kappa Alpha Order, founded in 1865 at Washington and Lee University, was the first fraternity to establish a home at Georgetown College in 1904. Rooted in the old principles of chivalry, students bound themselves together in a brotherhood in order to preserve ideals represented in this quote: "When man for war was born, with God and ladies as their battle song." The colors of Kappa Alpha are crimson and gold, and their badge of membership is shaped in the form of a shield, symbolic of the fraternity's association with heraldry and knighthood. The Beta Delta chapter at Georgetown remains active and celebrated its centennial in the spring of 2004. The last name of students pictured in this 1908 roster of Kappa Alpha are (clockwise from top center) Allen, Weakley, Stites, Branham, Ardery, Bristow, Covington, Barnett, Larimore, Gaines, Rossell, Carpenter, and Herring.

GRUBFEST: PHI MU. The annual event of Grubfest has always been a time to get down and dirty in the mud. Fun games enhanced by spaghetti sauce, chocolate syrup, flour, and water balloons leave students' skin barely visible. The muck dripping from their bodies leaves footprints in every dorm that lead straight to the showers. During Grubfest, residence halls form teams which then compete against each other with one objective: to get dirty. This photograph shows the Phi Mu Grubfest team of 2001 as they participate in the messiest but perhaps most enjoyable campus games of the year.

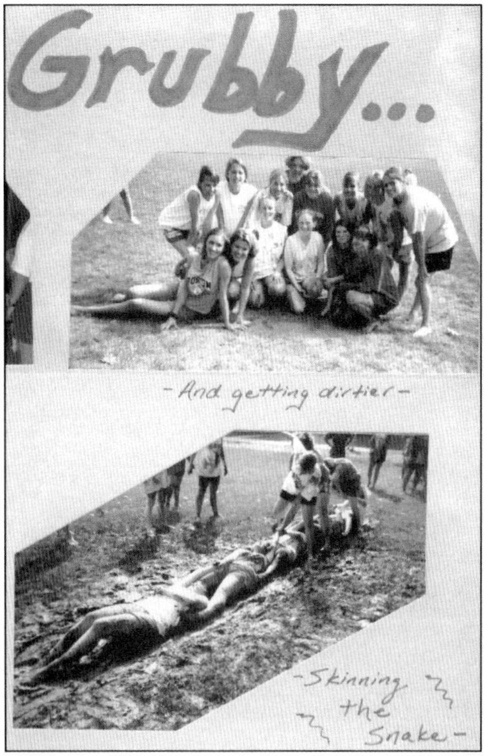

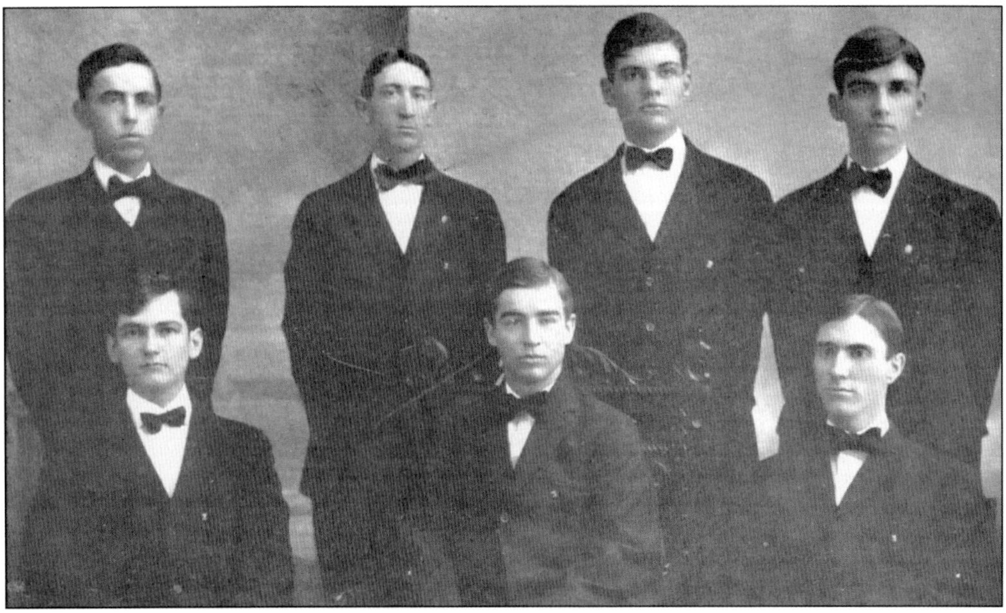

PI KAPPA ALPHA. The Alpha Lambda chapter of Pi Kappa Alpha was chartered in 1906 at Georgetown College. The national fraternity celebrated its centennial in 1968 and the Georgetown chapter held a local celebration for the event. Pi Kappa Alpha originally hails from the South; the North lacked a chapter until 1909. The "PIKES" or "PiKaps" dress in colors of garnet and old gold to display their spirit on men's bid day, and their official symbols are "Shield and Diamonds" and "Dagger and Key."

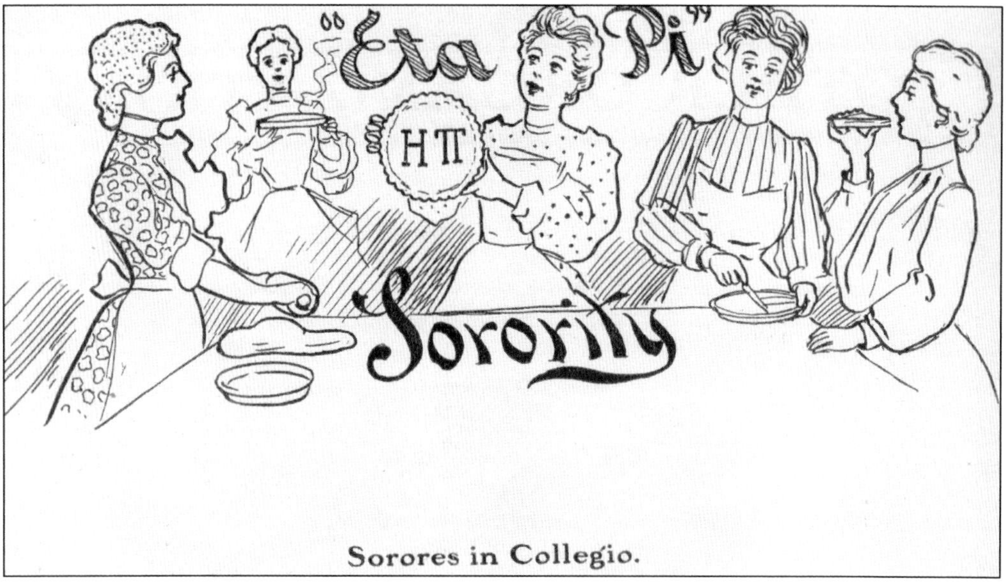

Eta Pi. This mock sorority, called "Eta Pi," was a club for women in the early 1900s. Clubs on campus during this era were in abundance at Georgetown, sometimes becoming very specific in nature. For example, a Nicotine Club once existed at Georgetown as well as a Bobbed Hair Club. Notice in this photograph the women are baking and eating pies to play on the words of "Eta Pi."

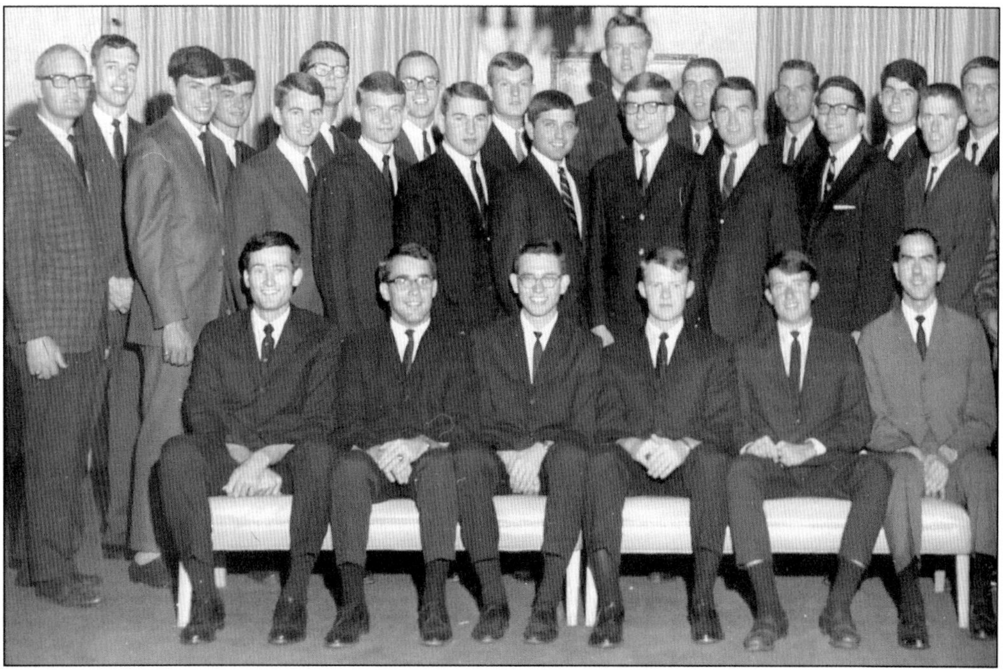

PHA. The President's House Association (PHA) was formed in 1964 with the purpose of creating a local group of Christianity, scholarship, and brotherhood. This photograph of the handsome new group was taken in 1967. During PHA's early years as a brotherhood, ministerial students tended to dominate the non-Greek fraternity and as a result the group was called the "monastery." (Photograph courtesy of Becky Bishop.)

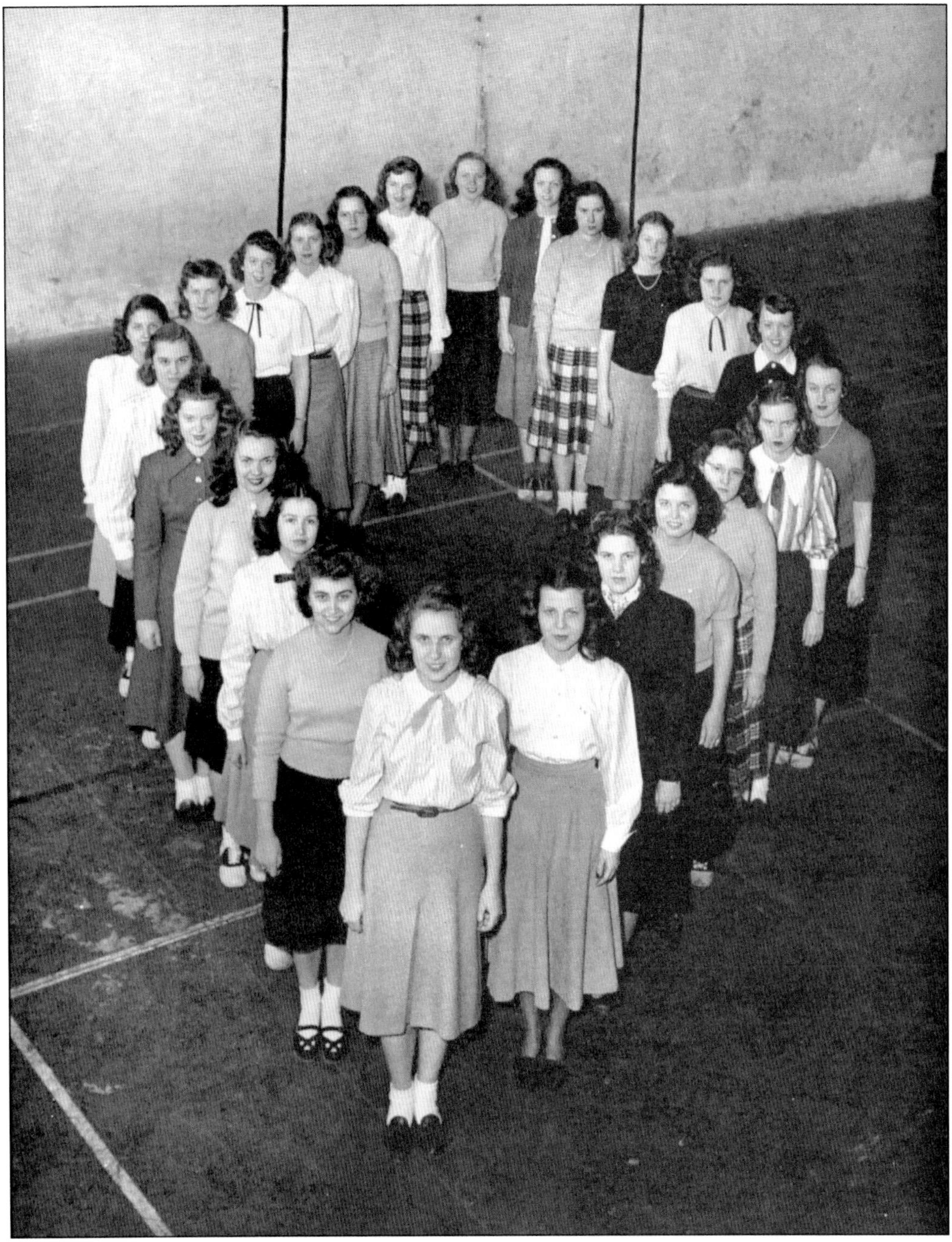

Kappa Delta. With the colors of olive green and pearl white, the Beta Lambda chapter at Georgetown College chartered its founding in 1942. Philanthropic events of Kappa Delta benefit the Girl Scouts and Prevent Child Abuse America. This photograph, taken in 1948, shows 25 members positioned in the outline of the "KD" badge.

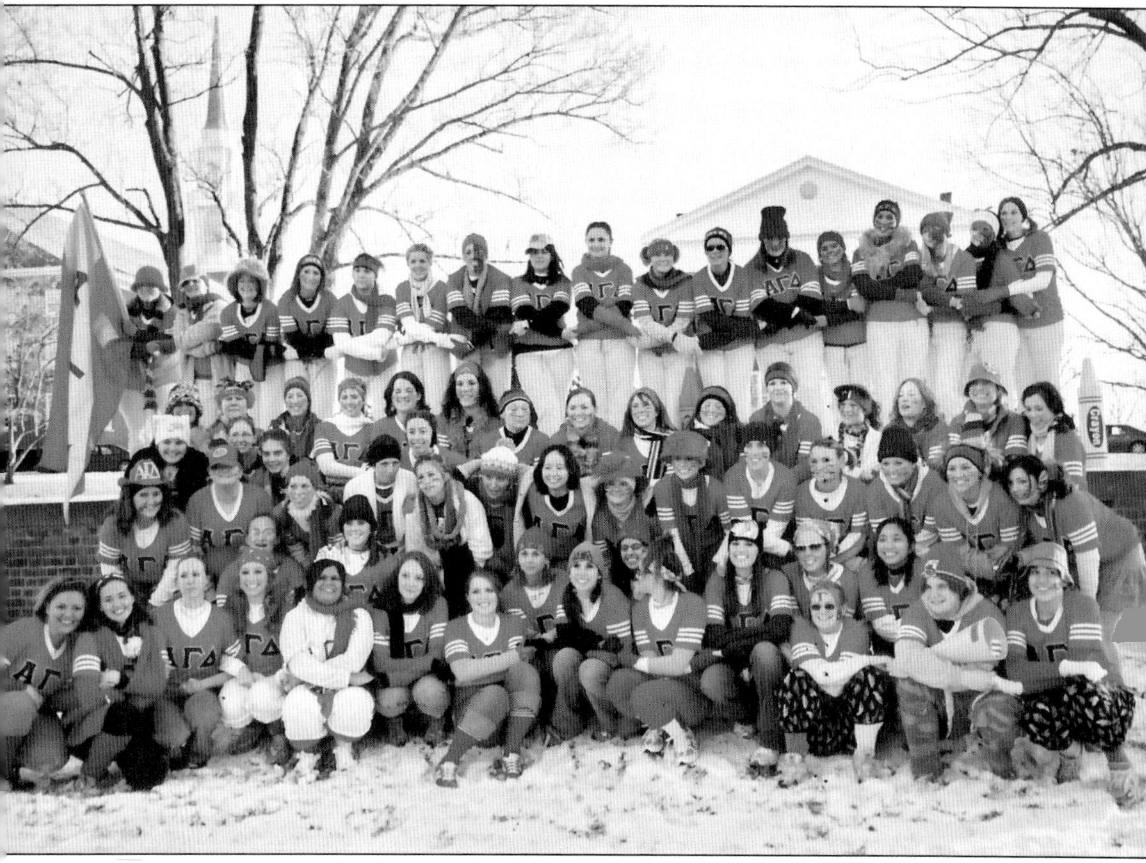

AGD Chapel Day 2005. The Theta Upsilon chapter of Alpha Gamma Delta was chartered in 1999 and became the fourth Greek female organization on campus still in existence. Wearing the colors of red, buff, and green, the "Alpha Gams" promote their squirrel mascot and currently occupy what was formerly known as Dudley Apartments. Much like their national motto, "Inspire the woman, impact the world," the Theta Upsilon chapter has been inspiring to the Panhellenic community, exemplified in their growth and achievement since 1999. In 2004, Alpha Gamma Delta celebrated its centennial and the Theta Upsilon chapter was honored at the national convention with the prestigious New Chapter Achievement Award.

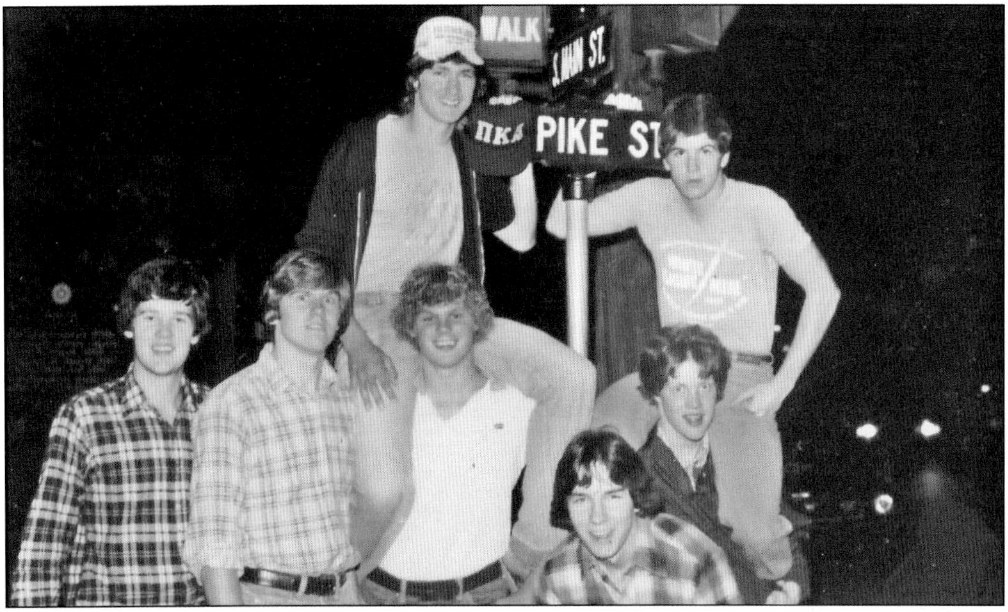

PKA Spring Pledge Class. A Pi Kappa Alpha pledge class poses on the corner of Pike Street. Tyler Bostic, class of 2008, sums up his PIKE fraternity experience by stating that "Pi Kappa Alpha is a family outside my own family." Bostic's predecessors in his "fraternity family line" include three former AGS presidents, a telling example of Pi Kappa Alpha's level of campus involvement.

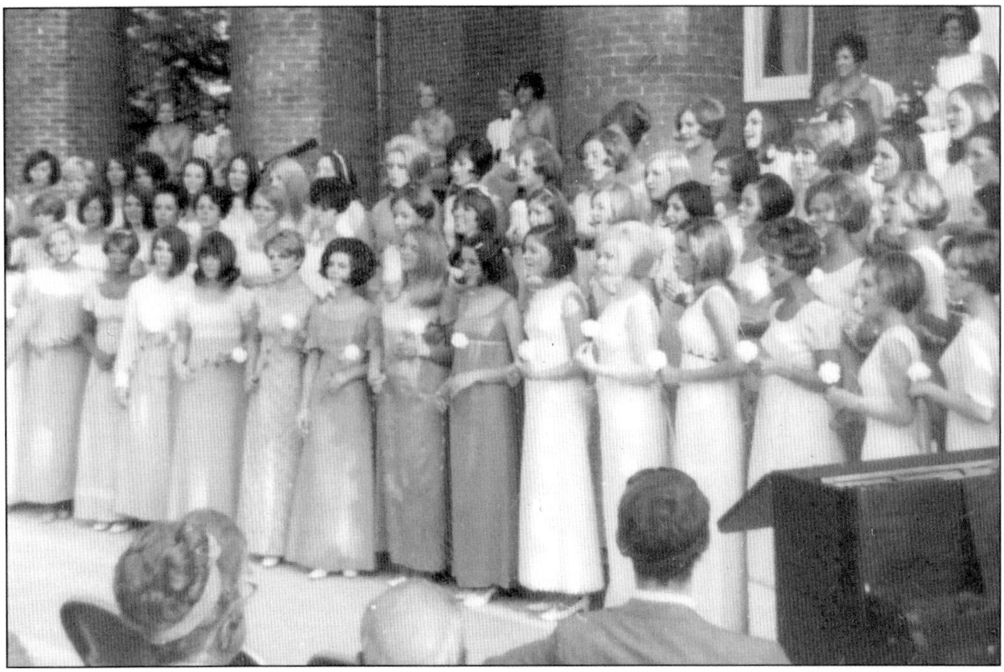

KDs in May Sing. A choral tradition at Georgetown, May Sing (also called Campus Sing) invited Greek organizations to compete in song. This tradition ceased in 1976 and was replaced in 1986 by Songfest. This photograph features the ladies of Kappa Delta dressed in their spring attire at the May Sing competition.

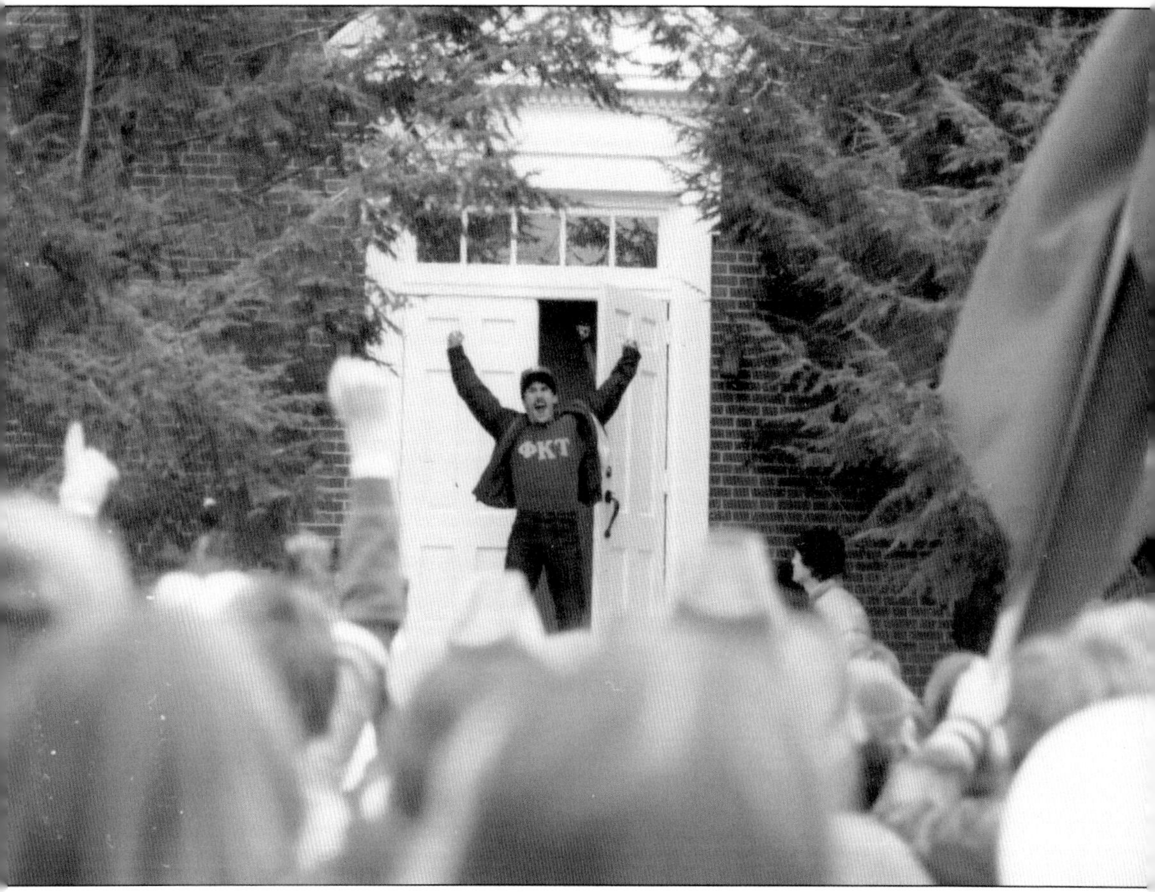

Phi Tau Chapel Day. New Phi Tau pledges run out the side entrance down to their proud and spirited fraternity brothers. Chartered in 1968 on Georgetown's campus, Phi Kappa Tau fraternity today shows elaborate creativity in dress on men's bid day. Ranging from superhero costumes to "Clifford the Red Dog" suits, the recent Phi Tau costumes are a unique contrast to the traditional letter shirts of their earlier brothers.

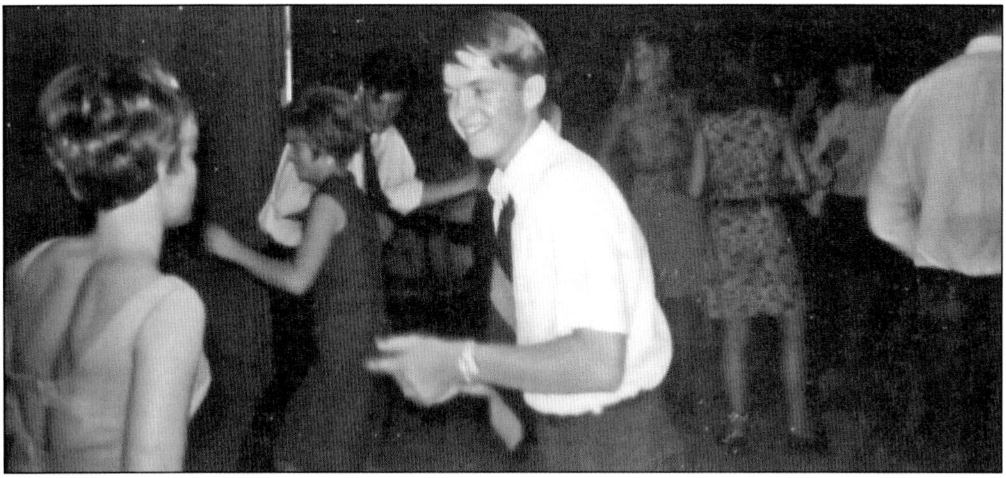

PKA Pledge Party. Fraternity pledge parties have been a popular pastime since the 1960s. Today female supporters attend fraternity parties on the night of men's bid day to celebrate the organization's new members. This particular party of Pi Kappa Alpha includes many of its female affiliates, called "diamonds," in attendance. Before 1968, dancing was banned on Georgetown's campus. But students argued that dancing was too minor of an issue for the school to battle in comparison to dilemmas such as the Vietnam War and racism.

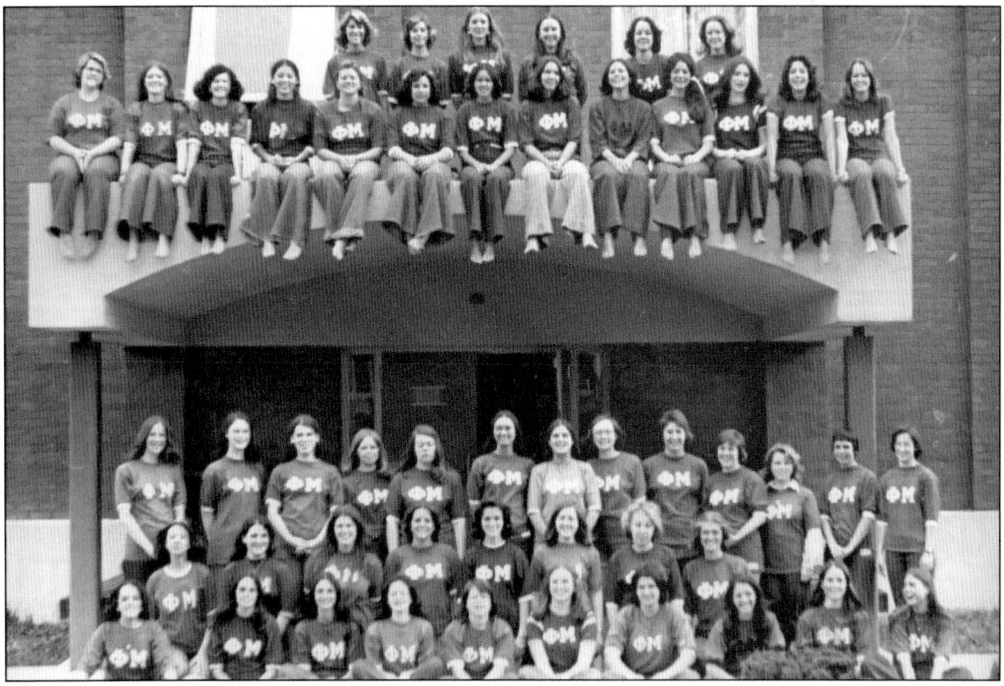

Phi Mu. The ladies of Phi Mu adorn their house nicely in a traditional group photograph. Founded in 1852 at Wesleyan College in Macon, Georgia, Phi Mu is the second-oldest women's fraternity in the nation. Formed in 1969 on Georgetown's campus, Phi Mu's symbols consist of the lion, the color pink, and the Confederate flag. A fraternity rich in Southern heritage, the Phi Mu crest was designed by Robert E. Lee. Today Phi Mu remains extremely active on campus, winning the Presidents' Cup, a Panhellenic honor, in 2003, 2004, and 2005.

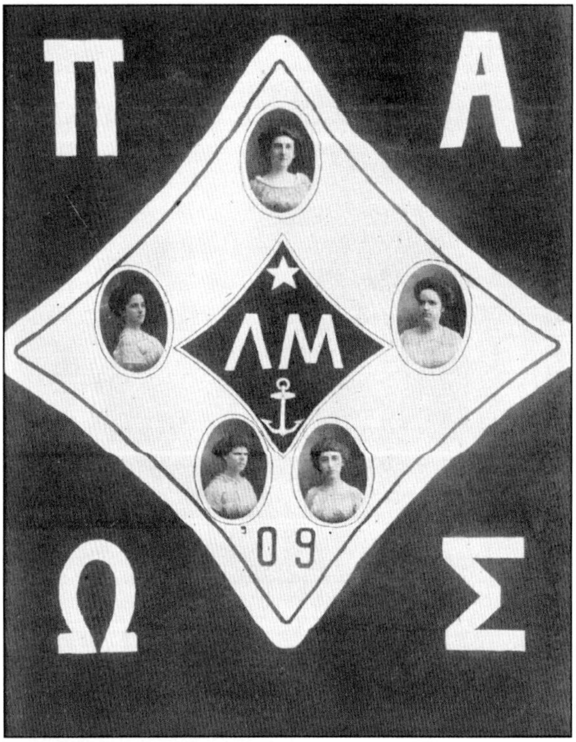

Lambda Mu. One of the earliest sororities founded at Georgetown College, Lambda Mu formed through a band of girls in 1905 whose ambition it was to promote social and intellectual intercourse and to develop mutual helpfulness. In 1916, the group contained 13 active members. Pictured clockwise from the top are Miss Ward, Miss Shockency, Miss Garrett, Miss Radford, and Miss Garrott.

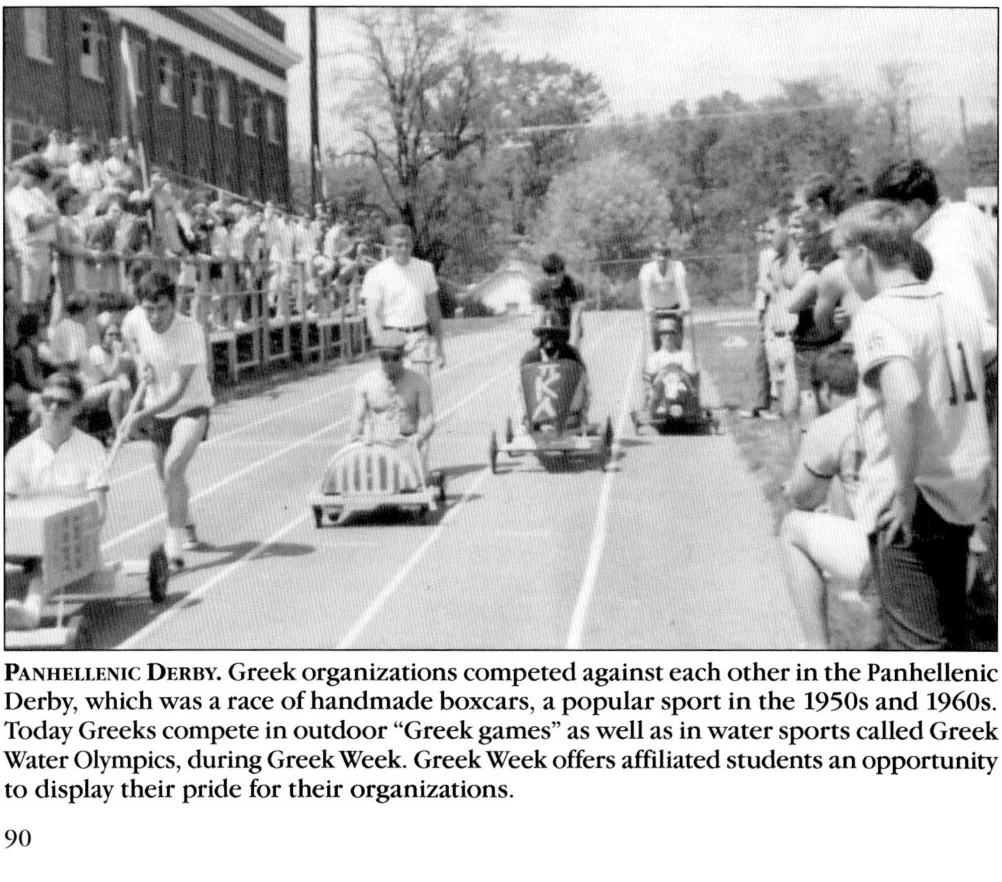

Panhellenic Derby. Greek organizations competed against each other in the Panhellenic Derby, which was a race of handmade boxcars, a popular sport in the 1950s and 1960s. Today Greeks compete in outdoor "Greek games" as well as in water sports called Greek Water Olympics, during Greek Week. Greek Week offers affiliated students an opportunity to display their pride for their organizations.

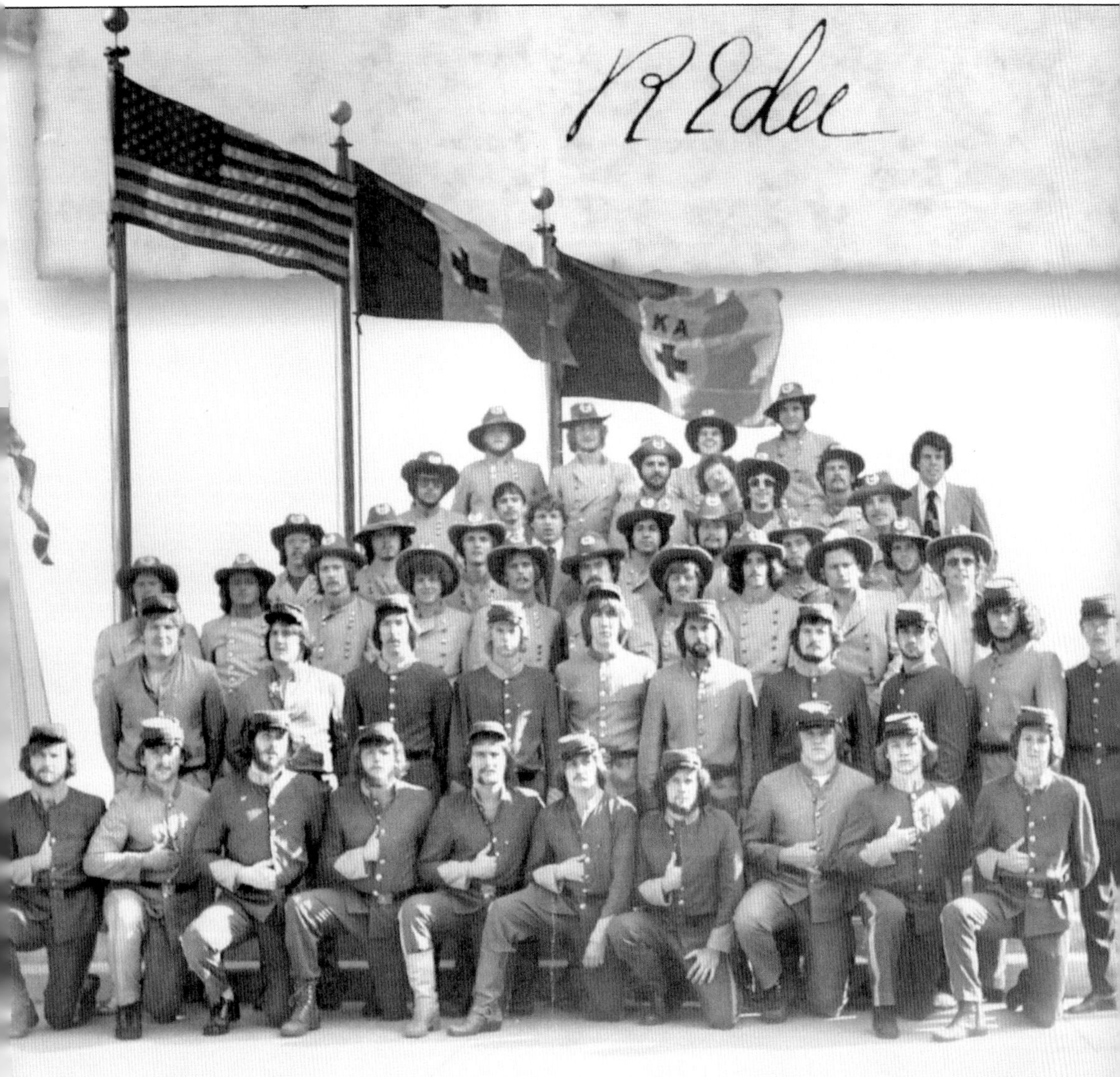

KA Class Dressed in Uniform. The KA class of 1976 poses for a photograph dressed in Confederate uniforms, ready for their "Old South" weekend. Georgetown graduate Dana Snyder Dale remembers the KA's beards and their serenades of the ladies' dorms at 7:00 every morning during "Old South" week. (Photograph courtesy of Clifford Dale.)

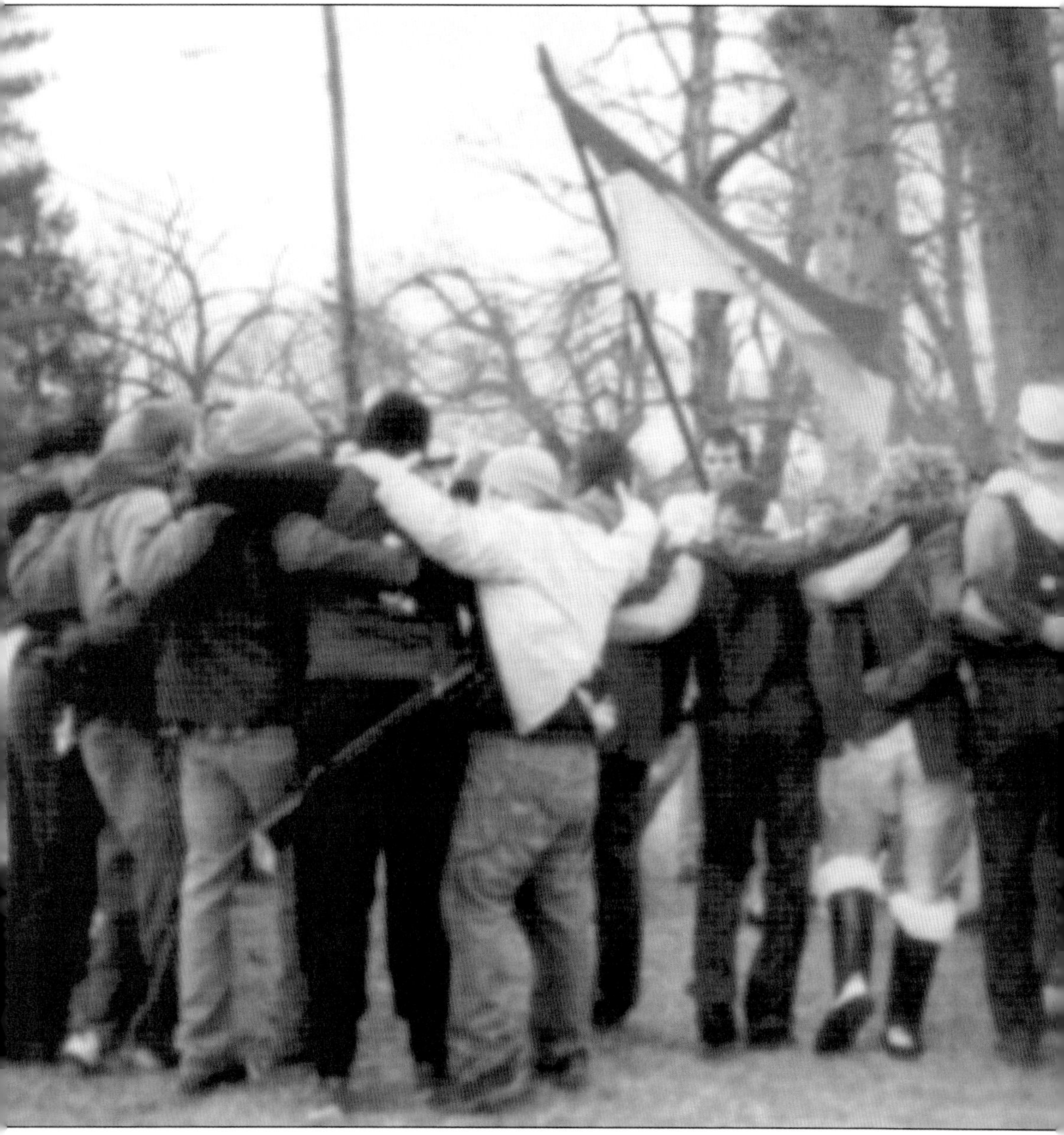

MEN'S BID DAY. This photograph of men's bid day depicts the annual tradition of men departing the chapel and running to the waiting fraternity brothers of their choice. However, this tradition has changed a bit since then. Today men dressed in spirited attire run out of the Cooke Memorial Library rather than the chapel to the fraternity brothers of their choice, who are also dressed in crazy garb. Zack Wolfe, Phi Tau president of 2005, states, "We've [Phi Tau] dressed as randomly as possible for bid day the past four years just for fun."

Seven

Georgetown During Conflict

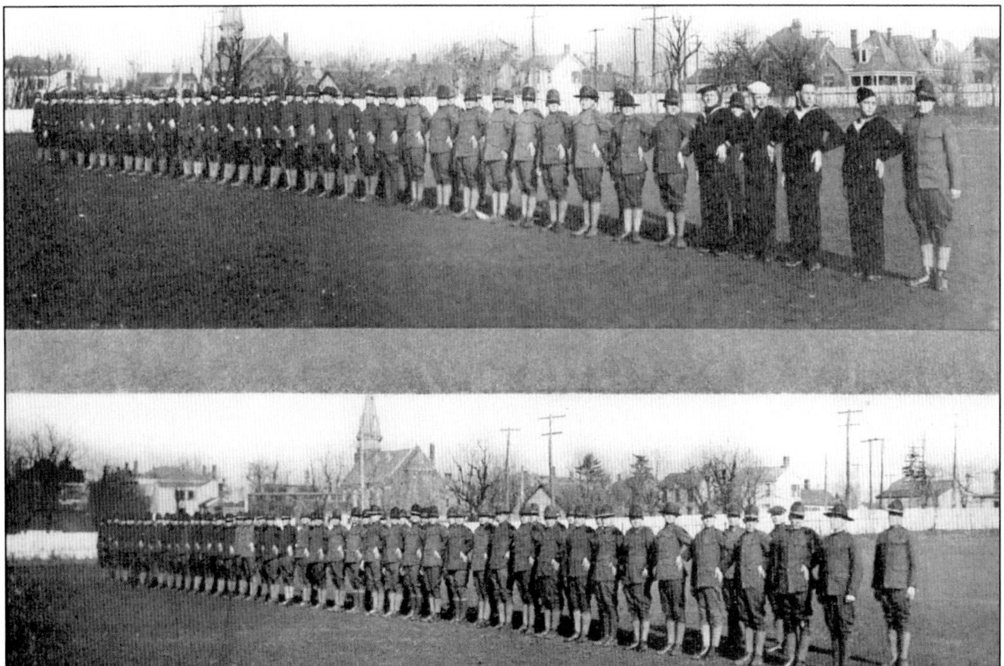

SATC Companies. In 1918, during World War I, the Students Army Training Corps (SATC) at Georgetown College accepted 140 students. However, the ill-fated SATC companies at Georgetown were affected by the merciless influenza epidemic that year, when hundreds died across the country. The Georgetown College girls morphed into nurses as Rucker and Pawling Halls converted into hospitals and the college closed for a week.

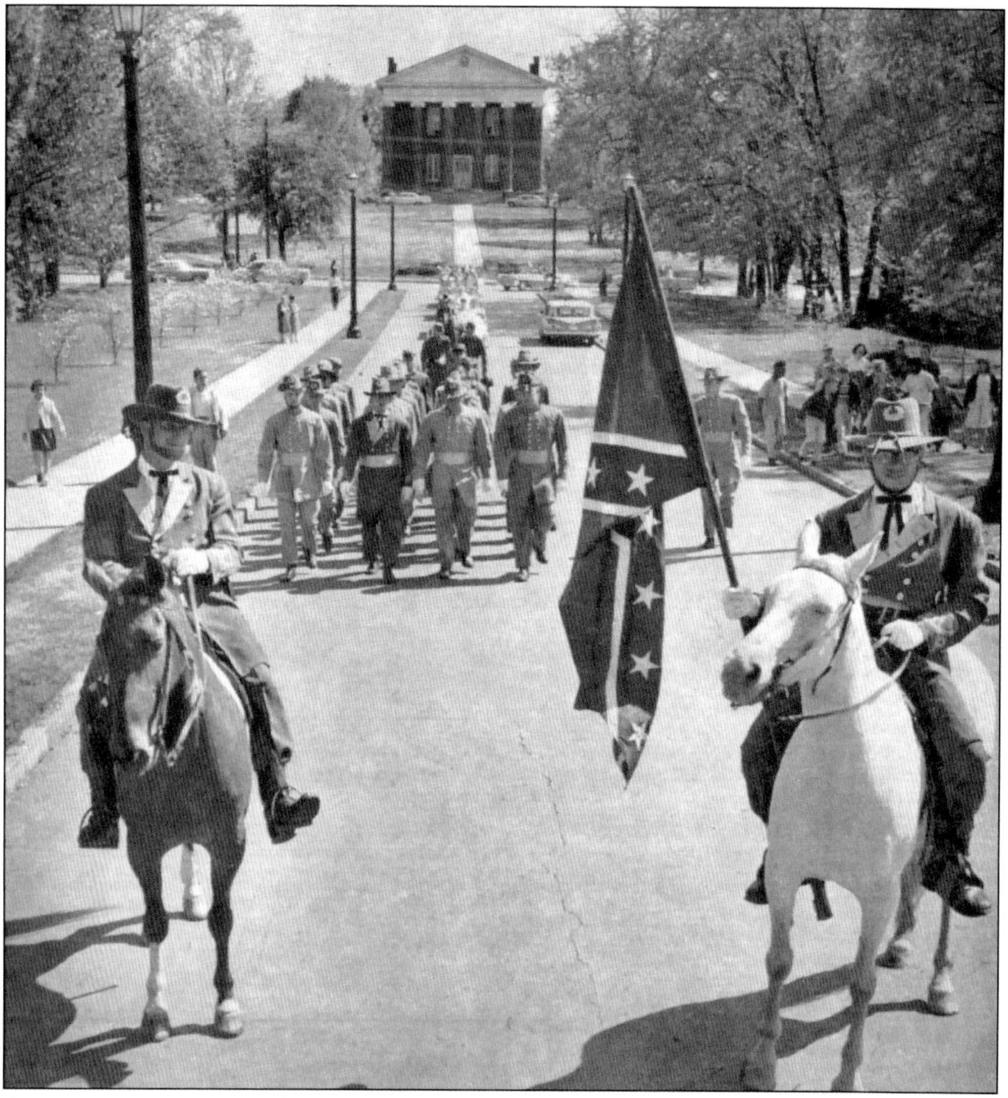

Old South Procession. The Kappa Alpha fraternity, pictured here marching from Giddings Hall in 1960, tried to "capture" the city during their re-enactment of the city's role in the Civil War as part of the group's traditional "Old South" weekend. Dressed in Confederate uniforms, the Kappa Alpha's and their female counterparts held a brief ceremony at the nearby cemetery in which 18 Confederate soldiers are buried in a memorial plot. Attending the ceremony and the procession were two daughters of former Civil War soldiers, Miss Jane Lewis and Miss Elnora Allen. In 1860, tension was aroused when the Southern sympathizers within the Tau Theta Kappa Literary Society hoisted a Confederate flag from the northeast corner of Giddings Hall. It was pulled down by Dr. Stephen F. Gano, a college trustee, after the sympathizers refused to cut it down. Fortunately Gano was not killed by disapproving townspeople that had gathered to watch.

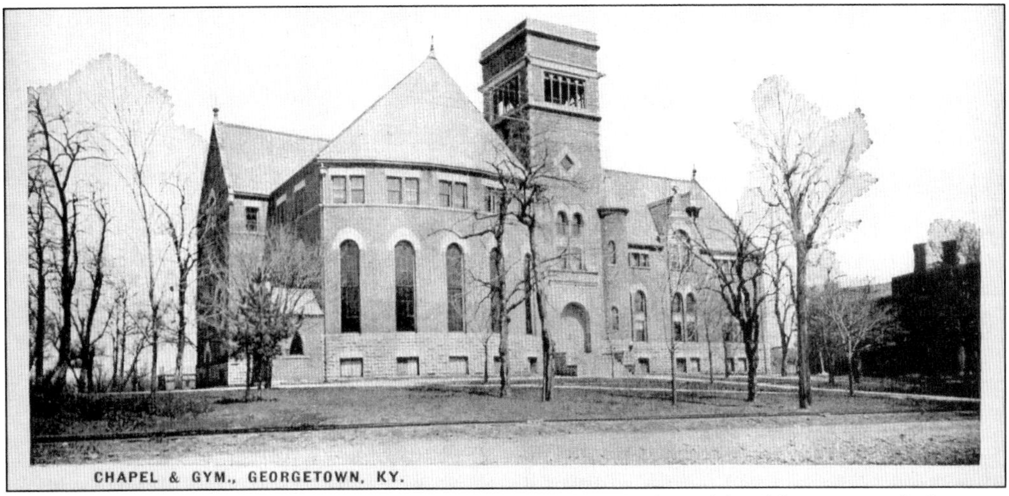

OUTSIDE OF OLD CHAPEL BUILDING. The multi-purpose chapel building provided space for religious activity, which has permeated so much of the life of Georgetown College. At times, controversial subjects have caused conflict because of the Kentucky Baptists' devout religious views, such as the 1924 debate over the teaching of evolution. Faculty members were asked questions on various theories of evolution and other principles of the Bible by the Kentucky Baptist Mission Board, and due to the controversy, two professors resigned. Not long after the questionnaires, Georgetown trustees signed a resolution, created by the Southern Baptist Convention, condemning evolution theories.

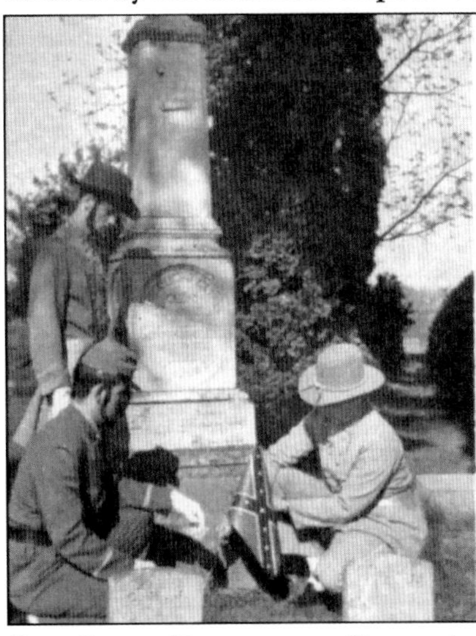

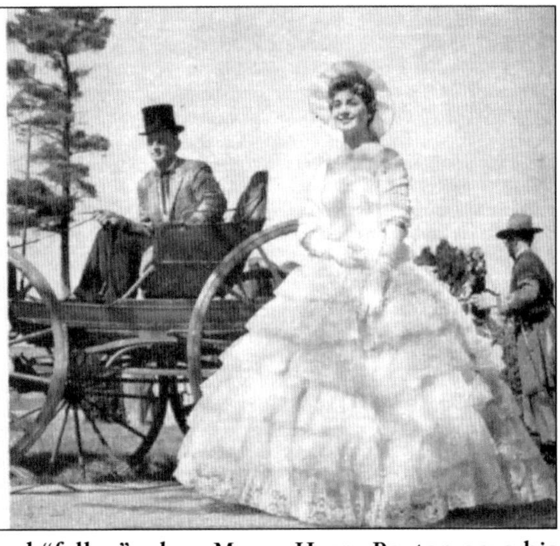

OLD SOUTH PROCESSION. Georgetown had "fallen" when Mayor Harry Paxton gave his sword to a student leader as his "surrender" during a 1960 Civil War re-enactment of the capture of the city of Georgetown. This was only one of the events held for Kappa Alpha fraternity's "Old South" weekend. In the fraternity's earlier years, they had formally seceded from the college for the whole week, abstaining from chapel and classes. Today "Old South" consists of a public and oral invitation given by the members to "accept this rose" to the fraternity's formal dance. The lucky girls who are asked to "Old South" await their formal invitations and roses while dressed in ruffled hoop skirts. With ringlets decorating their hair, the girls are quickly swept away by the young KAs, who are dressed in Confederate uniforms with artillery as they approach every residence hall.

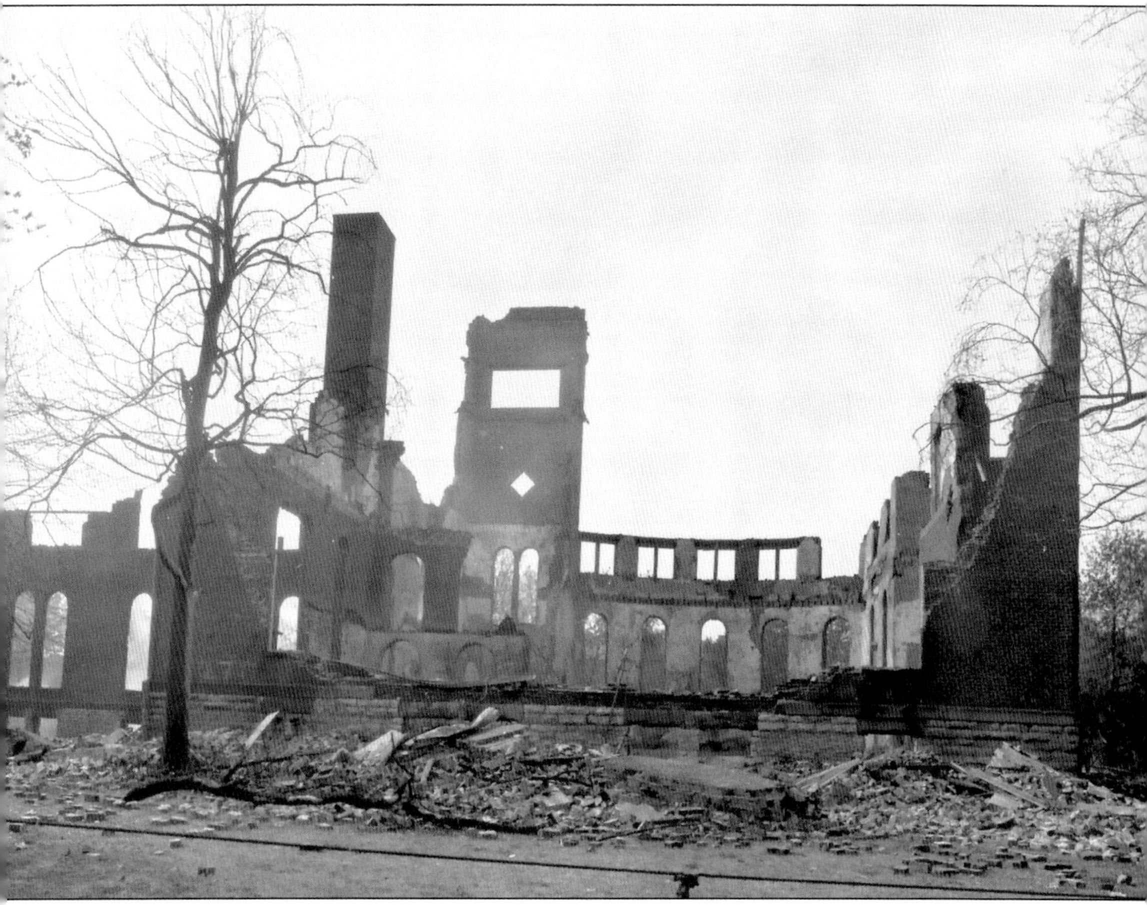

Chapel Fire Ruins. The Chapel/Library Building blaze was not only destructive to the college community, but also to the Scott County residents living nearby. Dr. Horace Hambrick, a former Georgetown student and faculty member, remembers as a child his mother not allowing the family to watch the fire on campus because the flames were so massive that cinders fell all over downtown Georgetown, potentially endangering his own house.

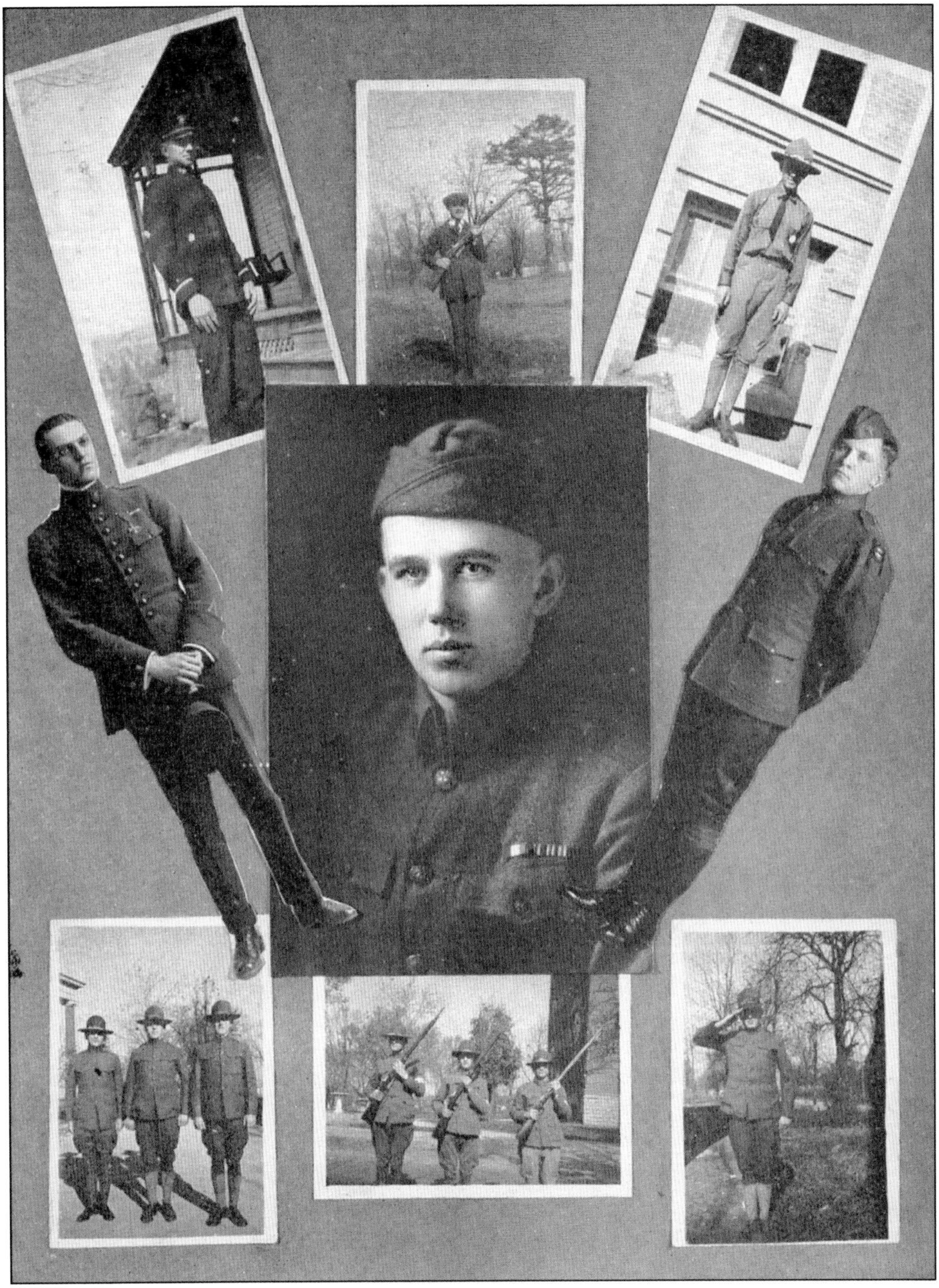

MILITARY SNAPSHOTS. A day before the Pearl Harbor attack, Dr. Henry Sherwood, president of Georgetown College, was forced to resign. The Sherwood Affair, as it is termed, was due to the fact that Dr. Sherwood had not been re-baptized in the Baptist church after coming from the Christian church. It was exaggerated to the point that the Kentucky Baptist Convention withdrew their financial support from the college. In truth, he was noted by students, trustees, and community members to be a well-loved and successful president. But because enrollment had plummeted so much from the war, Georgetown College could not afford to keep Dr. Sherwood around without support from Kentucky Baptists.

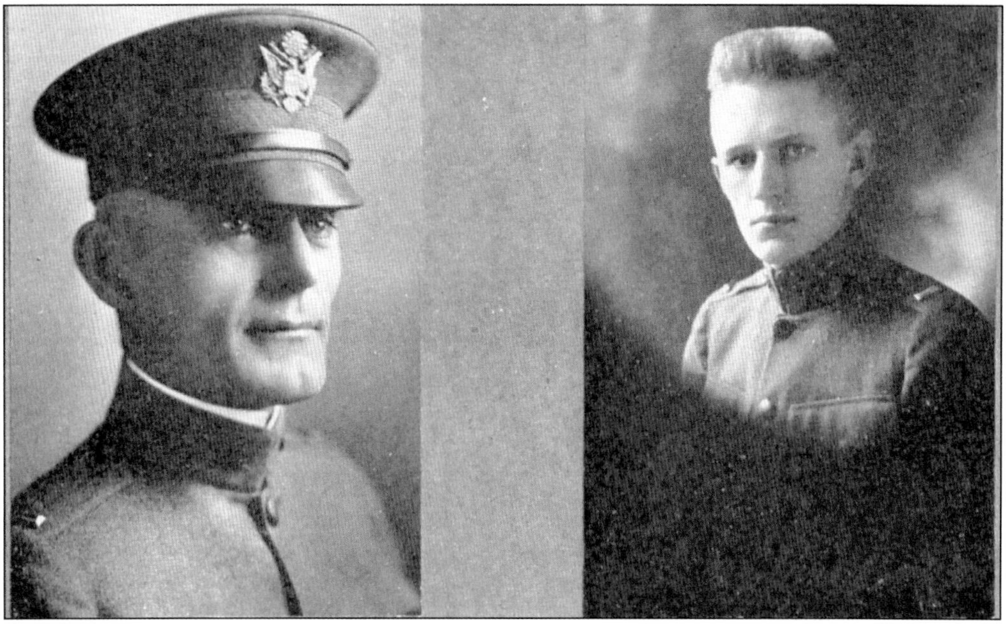

War Record. Though the college took hits through the years from all conflicts involving a draft of young men (such as these unidentified soldiers), nothing compared to the deep dent impressed on the college from World War II. The *Georgetonian*, the college newspaper, estimated there were about 300 Georgetown students serving in the military during World War II.

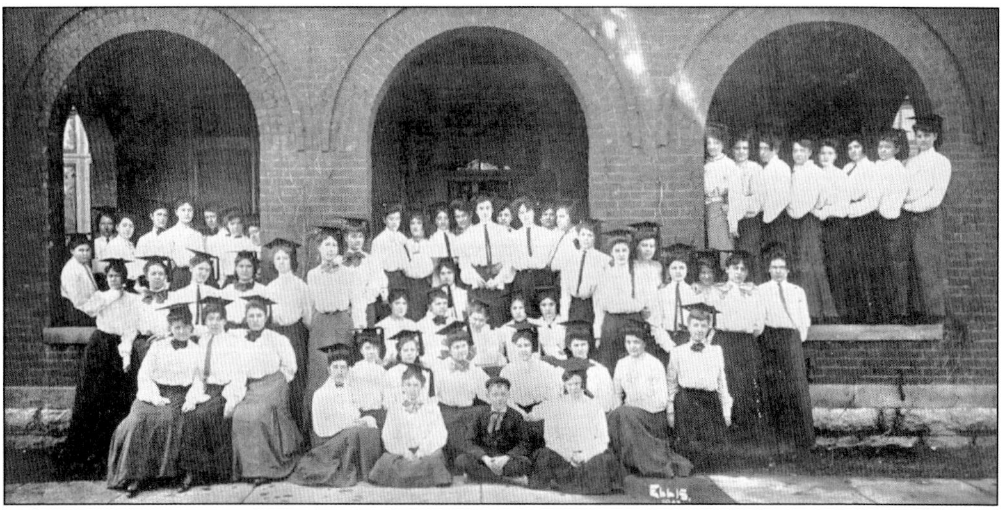

Rucker Hall Girls. Because the college joined what was later named the War Service Exchange College, an organization that provided wartime employment to students, Rucker Hall women were able to raise over $400 in 1917 through the Student Friendship War Fund, contributing to the war effort. The girls labored by knitting socks and bandages as well as by rolling bandages for the hospitals. This photograph of the girls was taken in 1917.

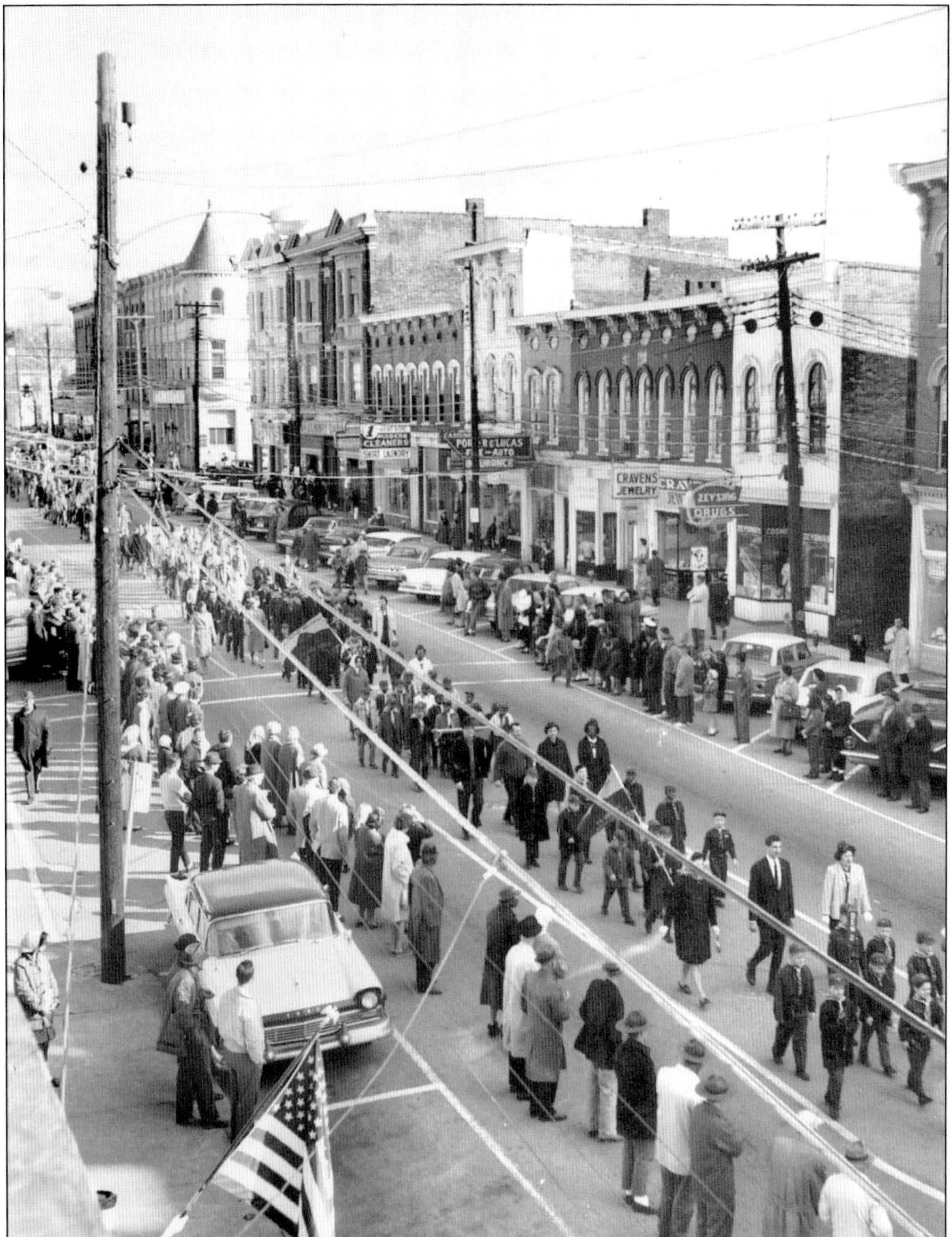

World War II Parade. With so many men and women enlisted in the service during World War II, it was a difficult period for Georgetown College. In 1942, Dr. Samuel S. Hill became president and helped to spark college development. However, in 1944, still only 13 students graduated. Today veterans who attended Georgetown College and died for America during World War II are honored with brass plaques flanking both sides of Memorial Drive. When the war was over and victory announced, the city of Georgetown celebrated with a parade down Main Street.

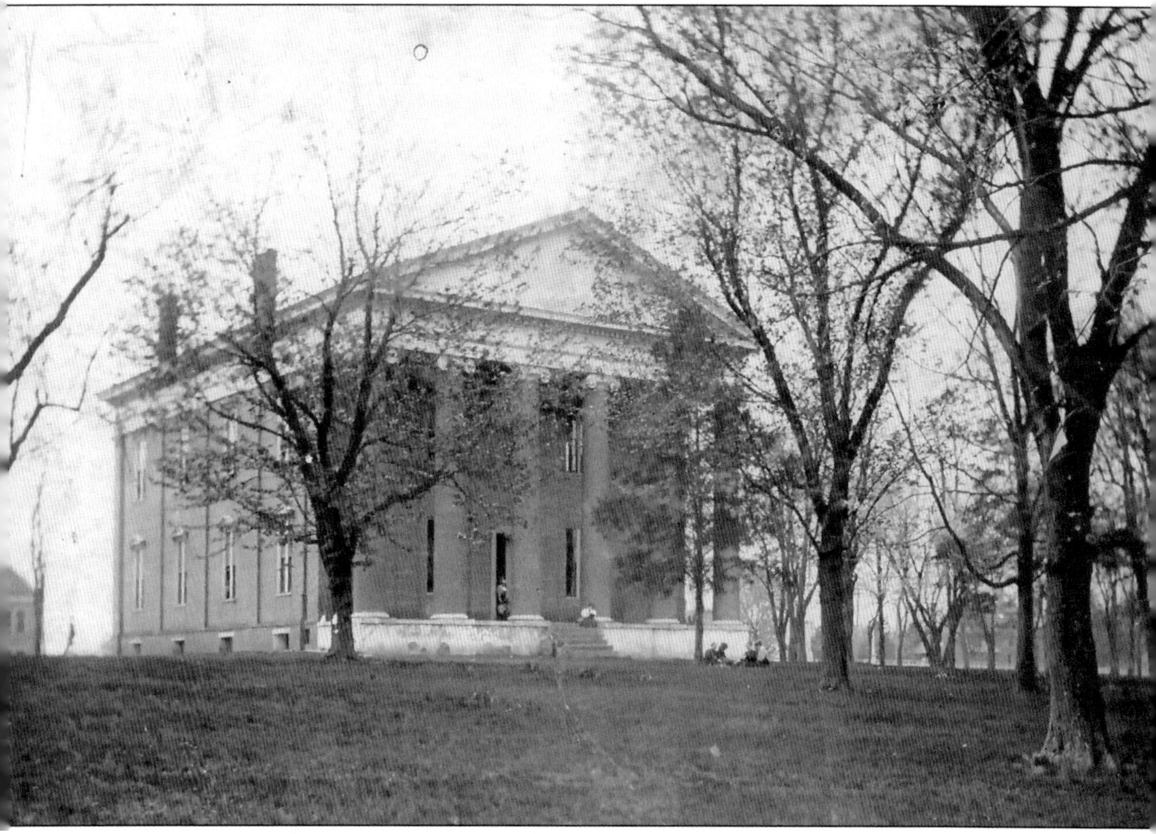

Old Giddings. Before the plans for Giddings Hall, formerly known as Recitation Hall, were even created, the old Rittenhouse Academy building was the only building standing on campus. During this period, before Rockwood Giddings served as president, Georgetown College was plagued with instability, as well as a controversy called "Campbellism." The conflict could have destroyed the college as a group of former Baptists, known as the "Campbellites," split from traditional Baptist dogma and eventually evolved into the Disciples of Christ. Much of this reform movement, led by Alexander Campbell, occurred during the term of Pres. Joel S. Bacon and that of de facto president Thornton Johnson, when the college lacked a president for four years from 1832 to 1836. However, in 1838, newly elected Pres. Rockwood Giddings provided sound leadership as he reconnected traditional Baptist views to the college.

Eight

ACADEMICS

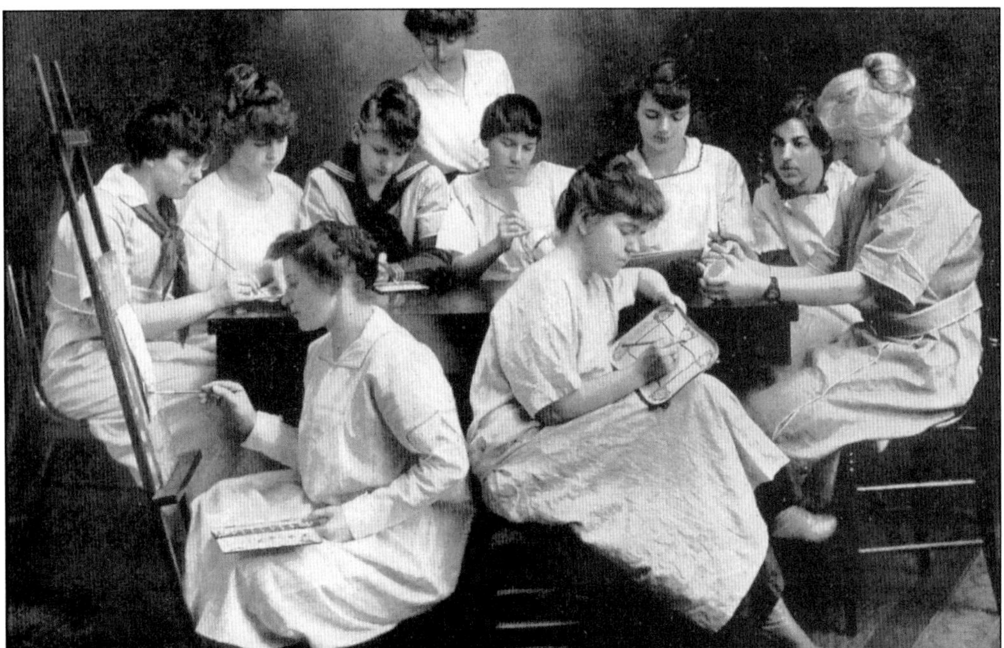

ART STUDENTS AT WORK. These students practice painting during art class in 1916. Before the establishment of co-education at Georgetown College in 1892, art classes for women were offered at the Female Seminary, taught by Mrs. Esteria Butler Farnham, in the 1840s.

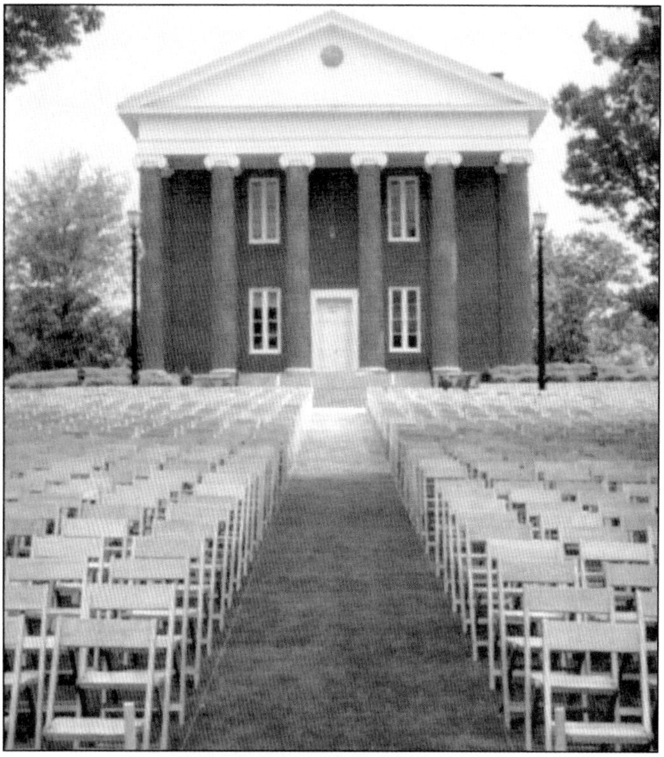

Graduation on Giddings Lawn. Early May usually produces nice weather and hopefully ensures a traditional outdoor graduation. Today the commencement ceremony is located on the lawn of Giddings. Beginning in 1842, commencement once was a week-long ordeal, perhaps the biggest event of the year. During the 1870s, women from the Female Seminary were permitted to attend graduation, one of the few occasions boys could meet the young ladies and talk in the softly lit seminary yard, which was peppered with Japanese lanterns.

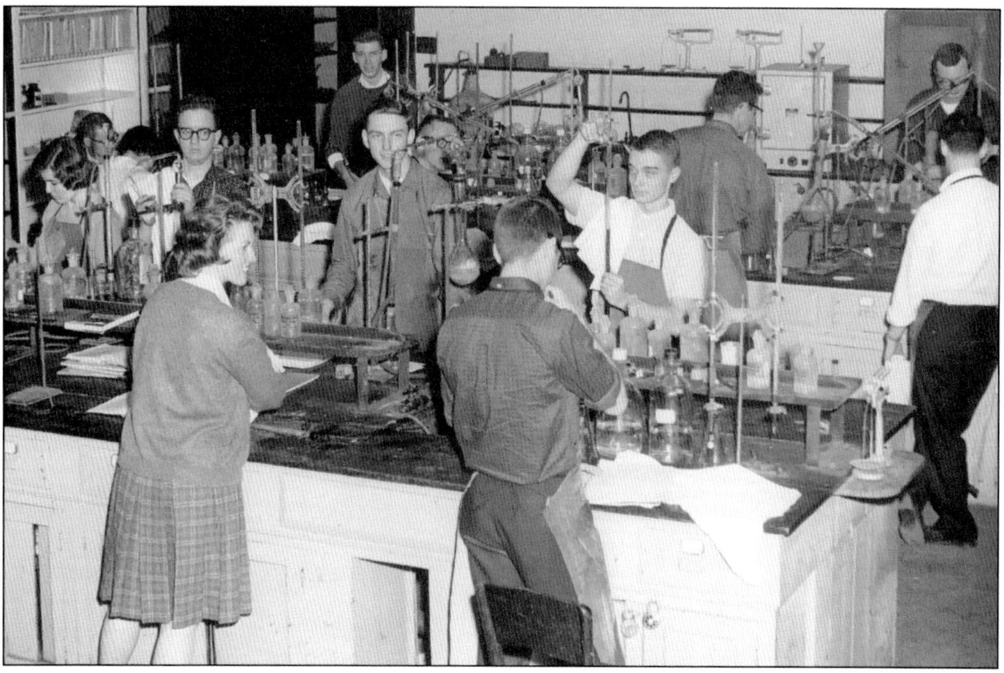

Old Chemistry Lab. The science laboratories, as seen in this photograph, were located in the old Academy Building, now Highbaugh Hall, before the science center was built. These students were most likely performing a titration in either a general lab or an analytical chemistry lab.

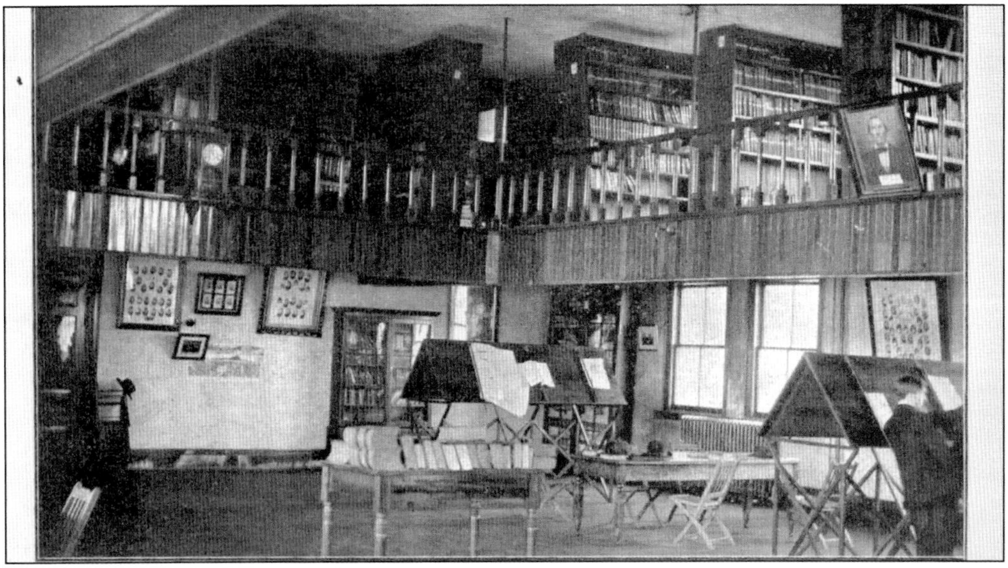

Library. This photograph, taken from the 1908 *Belle of the Blue*, presents almost a full view of the library chapel building. The library boasted an impressive collection of some 25,000 books, 5,000 of which were saved in the 1930 fire. During the burning of the building, Dean Hinton made sure that chaos did not erupt and had students file out in an orderly manner. Dr. Thomas Clark, Kentucky's historian laureate for life, performed his doctorate in this library prior to its burning.

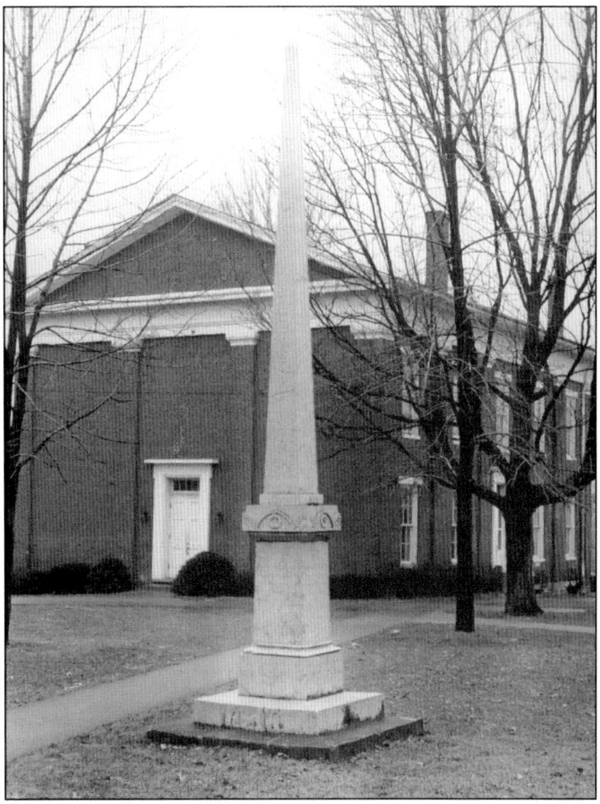

Highbaugh Hall/Academy Building. Once known as the old Academy Building, Highbaugh Hall was the third building built on campus, replacing the small Rittenhouse Academy structure in 1861. The building has been utilized for many purposes and is renamed for its benefactor, LeRoy Highbaugh. Housing the science classes, Highbaugh Hall also became known as the physics building around the time of World War I. Today it serves as the location of the registrar, business office, and human resources. Engraved on either side of Highbaugh Hall are the names of the Tau Theta Kappa members and the Ciceronian literary societies, who originally met in the building. From 1861 to the early 1900s, it held the college's preparatory school, which prepared students for college-level education.

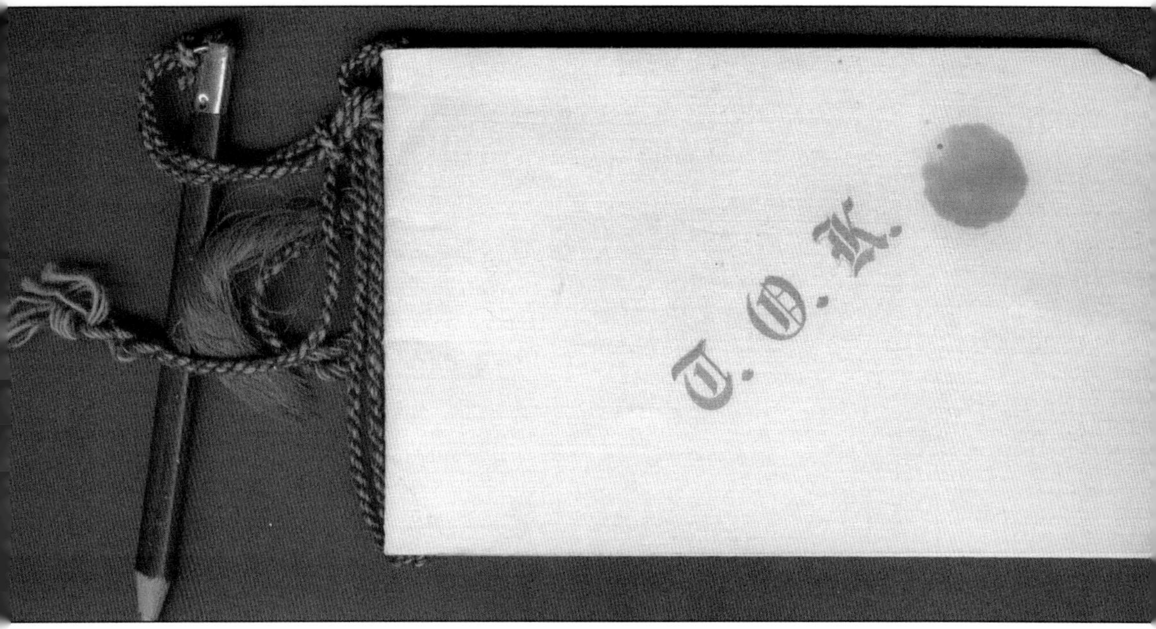

TAU THETA KAPPA PROGRAM. The Tau Theta Kappa Society, a literary society founded in 1839, debated academic, philosophical, and political issues and was housed in the Academy Building, now Highbaugh Hall. The literary societies at Georgetown debated in their respective halls complete with a stage and programs. This miniscule program is from the November 10, 1916, meeting of the Tau Theta Kappa Society. The schedule consisted of a devotional, roll call, welcome, oration, and declamation, and finally proceeded to the debate with music and criticisms afterwards. This particular meeting's topic of debate "resolved that the faculty of Georgetown College should be abolished." A miniature-sized pencil is attached to the program by a cord for autographs and notes. In addition to obtaining a degree from Georgetown, students were also awarded a degree from the literary society of which they were a member. (Program courtesy of Maribeth Hambrick.)

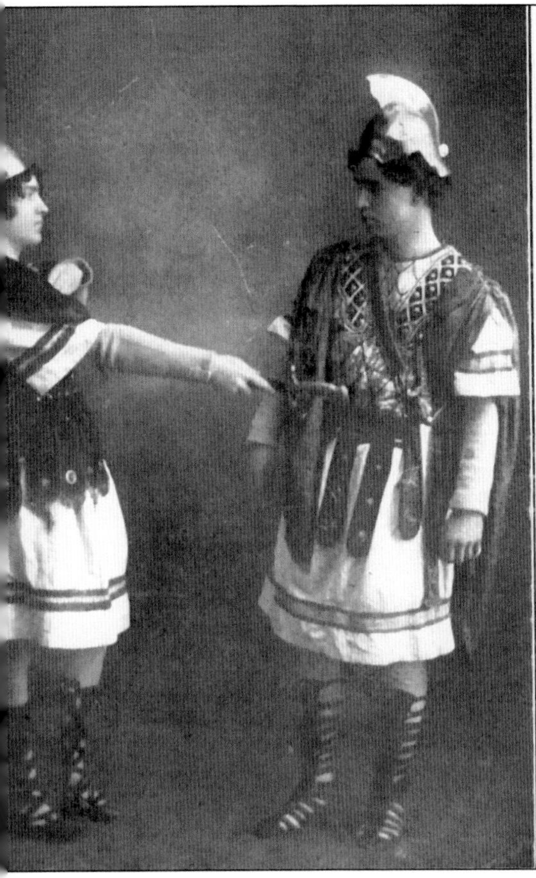 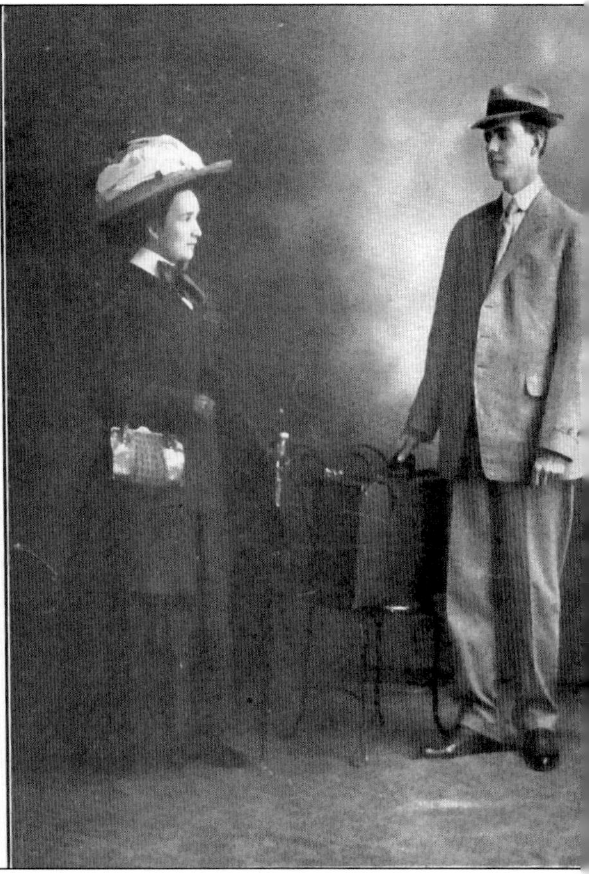

Elocution Department. Established in 1899, the elocution department was headed by Miss Elizabeth Broderick Armstrong, a graduate of the New York School of Expression. The department enriched the skills of many and honed oratorical expression. The college now possesses a theater department rather than an "elocution" department. Theater students comprise the club called Maskrafters, which is the oldest theater club/group in Kentucky.

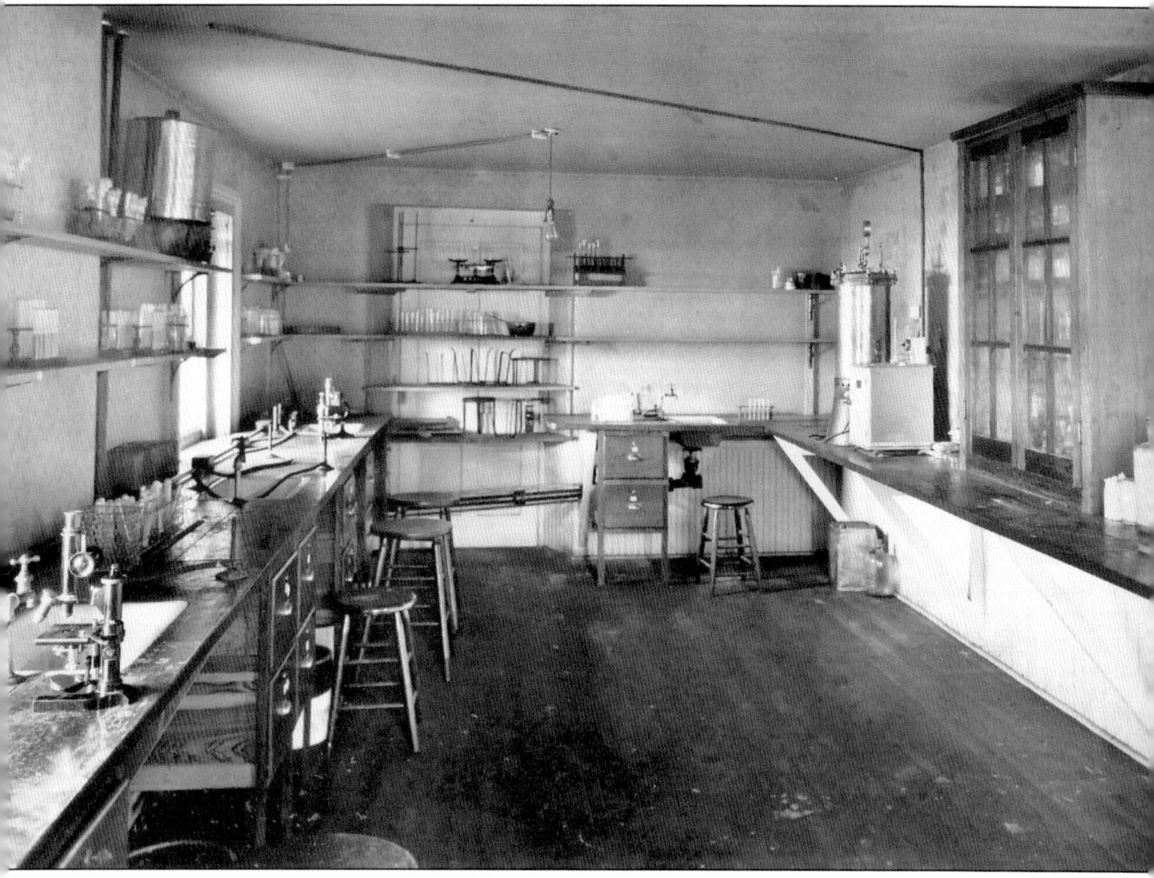

Old Science Laboratory. The old chemistry and physics laboratories were formerly located in the Academy Building, now renamed Highbaugh Hall. Today the science labs and classes are held in the George Matt Asher Science Center, which houses a greenhouse and small planetarium as well.

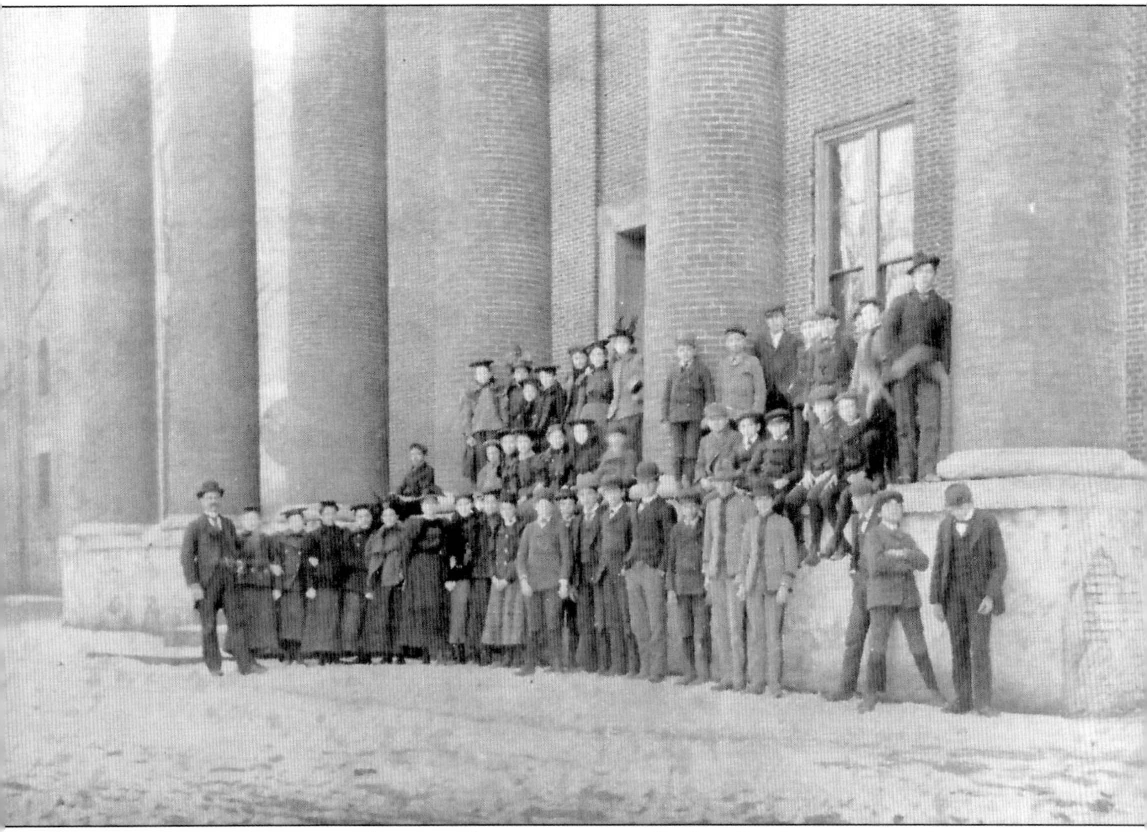

The Academy Group. Academy students were enrolled in the Preparatory Department, which was organized in the late 1830s. With the absence of high schools, the academy prepared students to do college-level work. The Preparatory Department was discontinued around 1916.

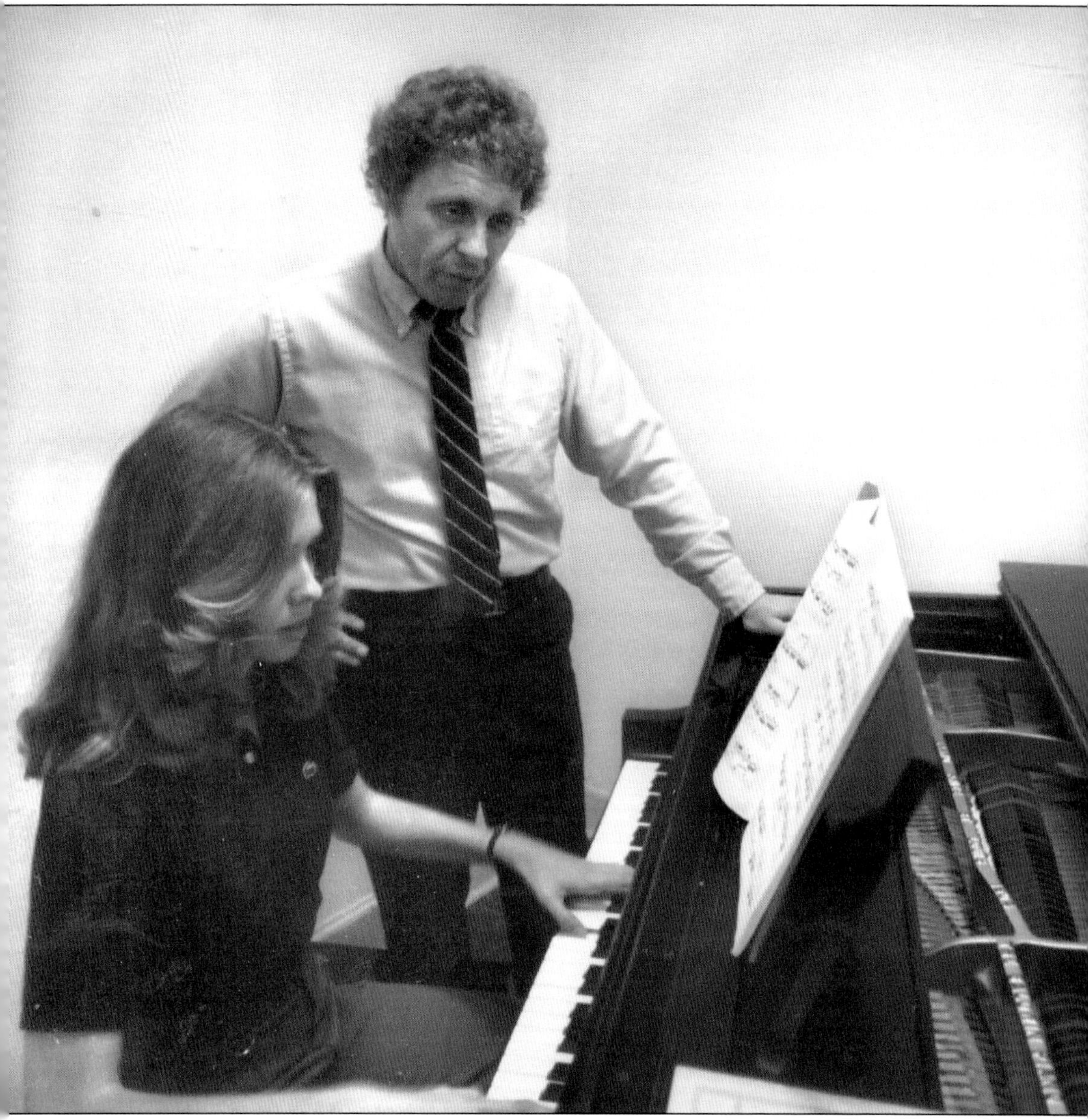

Prof. Danny Tilford. In this photograph, music professor Danny Tilford instructs a student in piano. Danny Tilford served as chair of the music department, and today his son, Stephen Tilford, also teaches piano at Georgetown College. Music has been an integral and enjoyable part of campus life throughout Georgetown's history.

Nine

STUDENT PUBLICATIONS

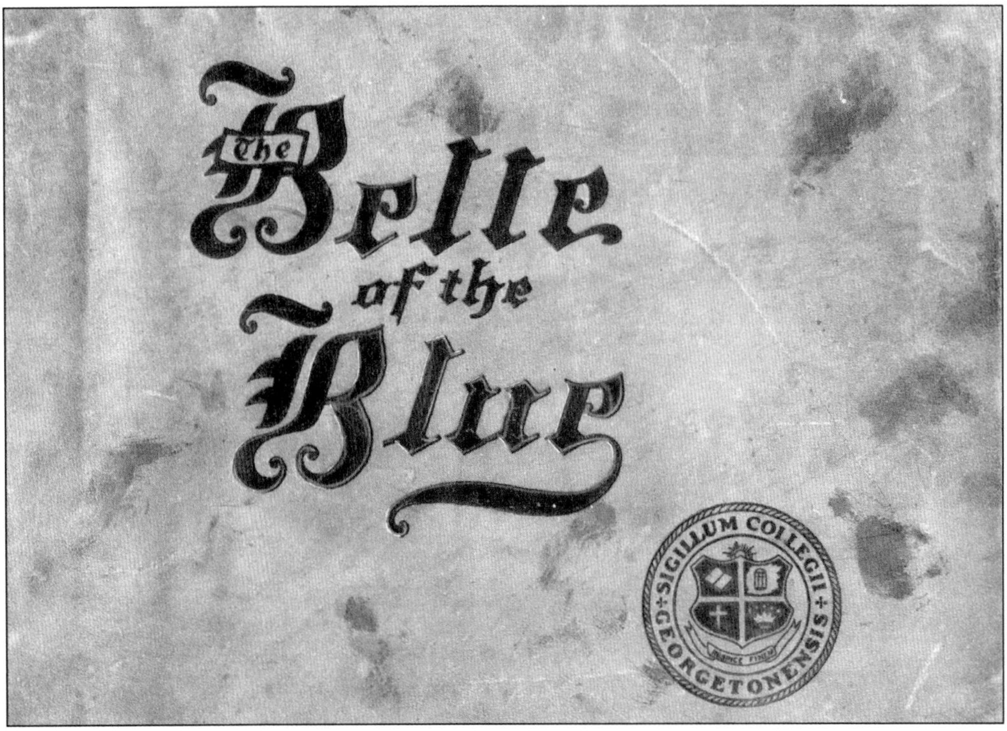

COVER OF *OLD BELLE OF THE BLUE*. The name of the Georgetown College 1909 annual, *The Belle of the Blue*, is based on a classic description of Georgetown: the heart or "belle" of bluegrass. *The Belle of the Blue* yearbooks not only included student and faculty photographs, but also were colorful pictorial histories of athletics, clubs, organizations, campus buildings, and student literary works. The first edition of *The Belle of the Blue* was published in 1898.

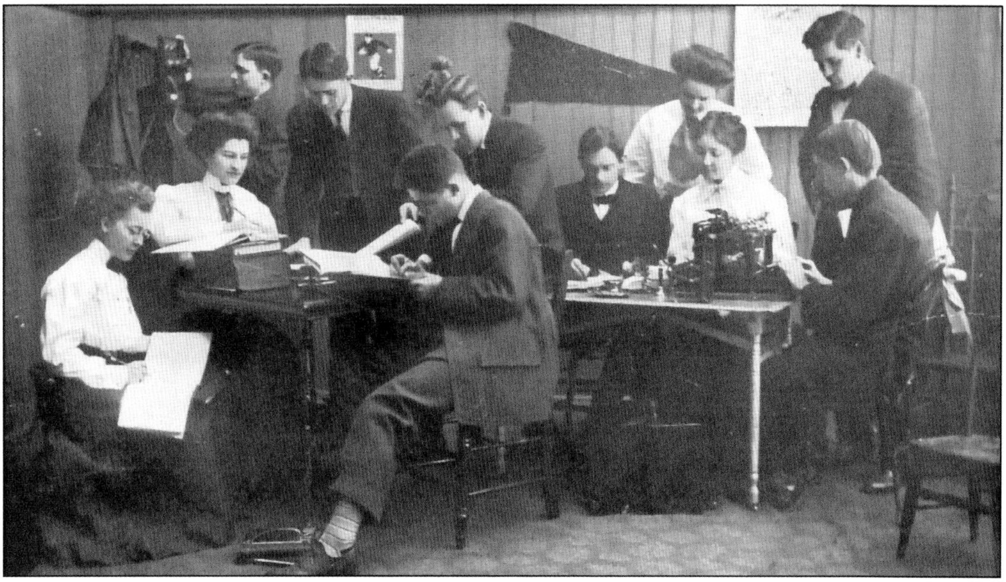

"BEFORE." *The Belle of the Blue* editorial staff diligently begins their work on the creation of the 1909 *Belle of the Blue* yearbook. The staff pictured here includes Jesse H. Wells, Rena Calhoun, McDowell A. Fogle, Myra L. Davis, Lester L. McHargue, Arthur W. Allen, Mary A. Shockeney, Patty F. Revill, W. Emerson Gwynne, Fay Ardery, and Virgil L. Christian. Yearbook staff positions ranged from editor-in-chief to business manager to art and literary editors.

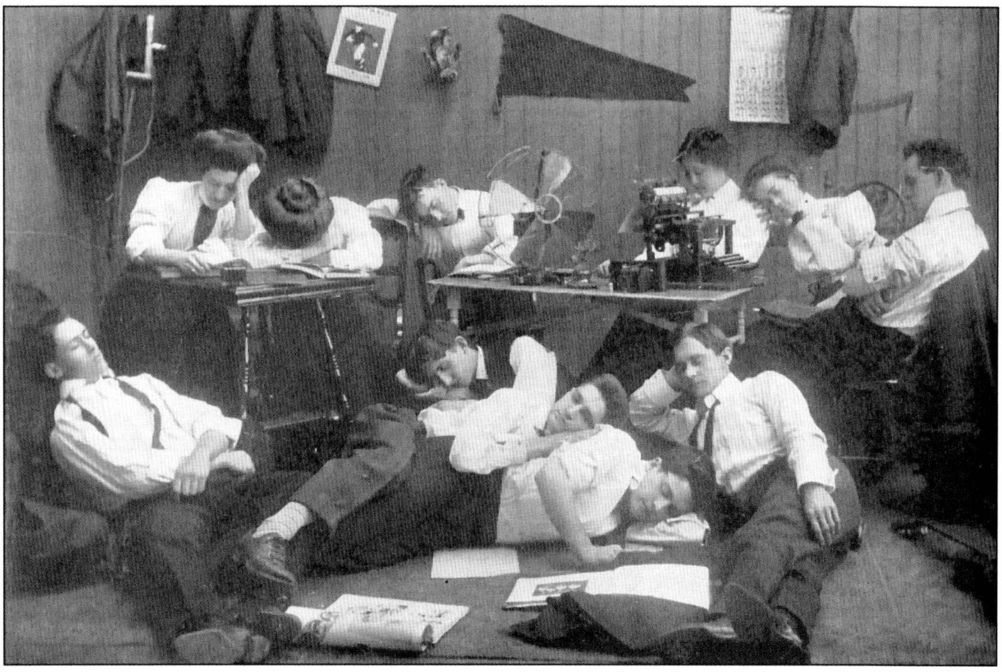

"AFTER." *The Belle of the Blue* editorial staff poses utterly exhausted after their laborious effort to produce the 1909 yearbook. The early yearbooks of Georgetown College not only contained photographs, but also an abundant number of literary pieces including short stories, songs, and even detailed student artwork.

THE BEST SCANDAL SHEET
Of
The Bluegrass
Circulation Unlimited

The Gawgetownian

READ OUR ADS
There's a
KICK
in Every Line

"May our 'Bull,' Like the Elkhorn, Flow on Forever"

ANY OLE BULL SESSION | GEORGETOWN, KY., ON THE BANKS OF THE ELKHORN, MIDNIGHT | PRICE—ONE HINTON PENNY

COLLEGE BOOK STORE OPENS; GIRL FAINTS

INTELLIGENCE TEST FLOORS DOC TOLMAN

REPORTER BEATS PROF AT OWN GAME

Pedagogue Unable to Cope With Witty Cub From Gawgetownian Staff.

In an effort to learn the exact identity of some of the intelligence tests which have been given in the Education Department of Georgetown College, the star reporter of the "Gawgetownian" sought to interview Dr. Judson A. Tolman, head of the Department of Education.

Dr. Tolman, however, would not listen to the young man's entreaties. The reporter begged and begged. Dr. Tolman kept his tenacity intact, however, and would not allow the young man to question him.

Finally, in a fit of desperation, the reporter had an idea.

"Say, 'Doc,' if I let you give me one of these intelligence tests, will you let me have the interview?"

Dr. Tolman, quick to grasp his opportunity, replied:

"Yes, I will I Q. you. But I give you my warning, if your I. Q. is not what it is supposed to be, you cannot have the interview."

"All right, 'Doc.' Shoot."

The questions came thick and fast.

"Sir, do you play any musical instruments?"

"Yes, sir," came the answer from the reporter.

"Sir, what instruments can you play?"

"I can play the victrola and blow my nose," said the reporter.

"Sir, are your eyes good?"

"Yes," said the reporter, for his I. Q. was at stake.

"Sir, how far can you see?"

"I can see 90 million miles."

"Sir, how is that?"

"Well, I can see the sun and it is that distance from me."

"Sir, have you any appreciation of love?"

"Yes. Once I carried my girl to the top of a mountain and I fed her wild honey and nectar."

"Sir, can you swim?"

"Yes, I used to be a street cleaner in Venice."

"Sir, have you a sense of humor?"

"Yes. I once saw a girl so fat she had to wear balloon tires for garters and it struck me as a bit odd," came the ready reply, for his I. Q. was at stake.

"Sir, do you like reporting?"

"Yes, like a hog likes garbage."

(Continued on Page 3.)

SEE WILLIAM BOSWELL

For coaching in physics. Office in parlors of Rucker Hall. Will accept only a limited number, as method calls for personal attention.

Announcing 1925 Summer Session

Announcement has been made regarding the 1925 Summer Session and the courses to be given. Under the leadership of Doc Tolman, backed up by Bobbie Hinton and Bobbie Richardson, a new course is to be given that will interest all of Kentucky's pride. At the chapel period when the session and its plans were announced Professor Hinton stated that the principal recreation and pastime of the coming term would be "necking" and "petting." At a show of hands of all who anticipated attending the summer session there were seen to be more than for either of the former summer terms and also that the girls outnumbered the boys four to one. The outlook is great, but to the boys—pax vobiscum.

CAMPUS SHEIK IN DIRE STRAIGHTS

Milam Tandy Confronted by Four Furious Females—Action Expected Soon by Stewdents.

The peace of one of G. C.'s most tranquil, most Chesterfield-like gentlemen is ruined. And the cause of it all is one little red-headed girl from Hoptown, down where they shoot the county judges, prohibit fair hops, and peddle IT in thermos bottles. This little lass of the brick top arrived on the campus suddenly the other morning, expecting to monopolize the day of her hero, the Sheik of the Pennyrile, but as usual Mr. Tandy had his morning walk scheduled with Lena Rogers, his afternoon stroll toward the Millionaire Hill of Georgetown with Jeanette Johnston, and his after-dinner walk from Rucker to Rhoton with Doris Campbell. Such a schedule had worked to perfection for months until Miss Winfrey, of Hoptown, attempted to throw over schedule, plans, and girls.

Needless to say the G. C. co-eds pulled together, just as the evening when Miss Rogers entertained Miss Johnston in Rucker Hall, and the fair visitor found herself confronted with three furious misses warning her of the penalty of intruding. At last reports little hair had been pulled and all faces were still recognizable, but the atmosphere was tense in its very presence.

A coalition of the forces of G. C., in which lots will be drawn for the privilege of taking the scalp of Milam, promises defeat for West Kentucky. The old campus, always noted for its turning of young men's fancies, has played havoc with the feelings and aims of this young swain and his advice to those who would follow in his footsteps is "There may be strength in numbers, but let 'em come one at a time."

Further reports from the scene of the conflict may be had by appearing at Rucker Hall dining room any evening at 6 p.m.

STEGAR LOSES HIS PAJAMAS

Well-Known English Shark Spends Several Nites Unpleasantly.

James Stegar, the lad who received twelve votes for May Queen last December, has lost one of his most prized articles of clothing—a pair of pink pajamas with ruffles around the bottom of the legs.

It seems that these pajamas were the pride of Mr. Stegar's life. Every night, as the town clock struck nine, Mr. Stegar would solemnly don his pink ruffled pajamas and ease off to bed. Every morning, as the town clock struck nine, he would dutifully crawl from his cot, go to his room, take off his pink ruffled pajamas, fold them carefully and lay them away in a rose-scented place.

And now they are gone and the master is in desperate straits. He avows that he is sure he wore them the last night they were in his possession. He is dead sure that he donned them at nine o'clock on that eventful last night and he is sure that he took them off at nine o'clock the next morning. Mr. Stegar says that he is dead sure on those two points.

At first Mr. Stegar was in a quandâry. Torn between love for his club brothers and attachment for his pink ruffled pajamas, he could not decide whether he should question any of his brothers as to the whereabouts of his lost article of clothing.

Finally, one night as he was sitting before the grate in his room, he overheard a conversation in the adjoining room between John York and "Pinkie" Neal.

"Neal, that garment fits you to a T. Where did you get it?"

"I picked it up in—."

Stegar did not wait for further eavesdropping. Dropping his copy of Browning abruptly, he rushed into the next room, fully expecting to find "Pinkie" Neal attired in his pair of pink ruffled pajamas!

Mr. Stegar burst into the room, buoyed by a will-o-the-wisp. He

Continued on Page 4.)

SIGHT TOO MUCH FOR MISS NEAL

Opening Saves Lives of Rodent Boarders of College Shop.

Fainting upon seeing the book store open in the morning, Miss Floy Neal, a popular member of the graduating class of Georgetown College, created a frenzied excitement on the campus Wednesday morning, April 1.

Miss Neal was going to a class in Giddings Hall, as had been her usual custom for the whole term. According to eye-witnesses, she was seen to look toward the door which leads to the book store, put her hand to her head and groan: "My Gawd! the book store is open."

In a few moments several students had gathered around Miss Neal. J. Blanford Taylor rushed pell-mell into the basketball dressing room and returned with the first-aid kit.

By the time Mr. Taylor arrived the crowd had grown so thick that Dr. Pierce ran to the chemistry laboratory and returned with a hydrogen sulphide generator, which he set in operation at once.

When the crowd had dispersed Mr. Taylor and Dr. Pierce began to apply every known means for resuscitating Miss Neal. Their labors were interrupted, however, by some shouts from the interior of the book store:

"Hey, what is that stinks so around here," Harry Mitchell cried out.

"Maybe it is those starved rats we found in the corner," B. A. Dawes answered.

"No, it can't be those rats. I have just chucked them into the candy case and shut the door," replied Harry.

"Well, there is just one other thing it can be—your feet," sneered B. A. Dawes.

"Take that crack back, you Freshman, or I will fight you," cried Harry in anger.

"Come on then, for I don't take back nothing," said B. A., getting madder.

In an instant the interior of the book store resounded with the sound of what appeared to be a mighty struggle. Glass was heard to crack, bookcases were heard to crash over, pennants were heard to drop to the floor with dull thuds and finally the Palm Olive soap machine was heard to fall to the floor.

By this time the odor of the hydrogen sulphide had dispersed far enough in the distance that the crowd of students were able

(Continued on Page 2.)

WEATHER FORECAST

A brainstorm with thunder and lightning directed toward
YE IDIOTOR

"*GAWGETONIAN*." This spread is from a 1925 *Georgetonian*, which highlights college news. Notice the headline regarding a fainting incident. The *Georgetonian* staff printed its papers at the *News and Times* office in downtown Georgetown, and every organization on campus ran an ongoing column. Greeks, literary societies, and religious organizations all reported their weekly happenings. The amusing alteration of the spelling of the *Georgetonian* in this issue refers to students' Southern drawl.

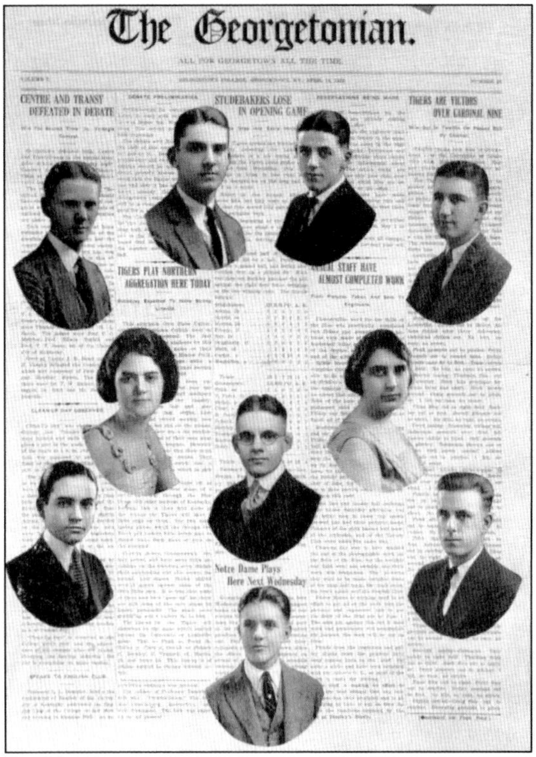

The Georgetonian.

CENTRE AND TRANSY DEFEATED IN DEBATE

STUDEBAKERS LOSE IN OPENING GAME

TIGERS ARE VICTORS OVER CARDINAL NINE

TIGERS PLAY NORTHERN AGGREGATION HERE TODAY

STAFF HAVE ALMOST COMPLETED WORK

Notre Dame Plays Here Next Wednesday

GEORGETONIAN. The *Georgetonian* magazine originated in 1896 and evolved into a weekly newspaper reporting college highlights. The 1940s versions of the *Georgetonian* newspaper included space for every campus organization's report and even enough room for a gossip column, which was indeed the most anticipated section.

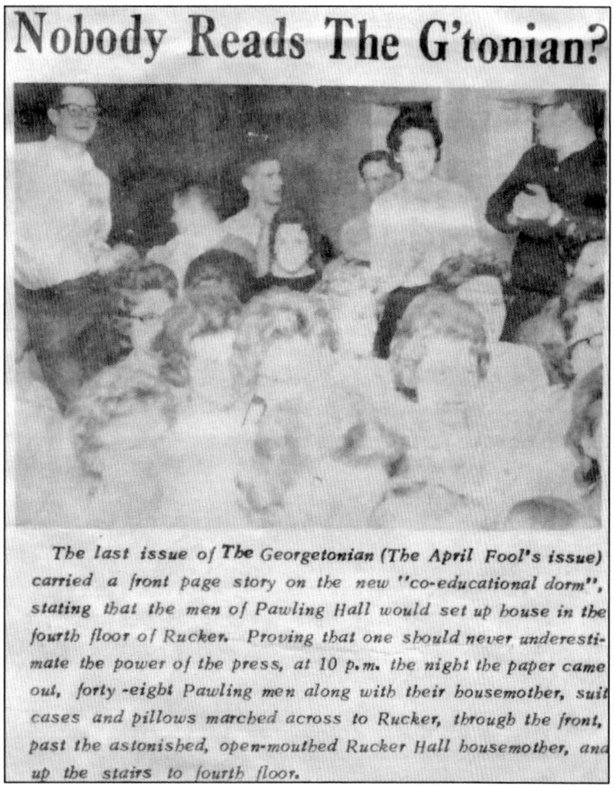

Nobody Reads The G'tonian?

The last issue of **The** Georgetonian *(The April Fool's issue) carried a front page story on the new "co-educational dorm", stating that the men of Pawling Hall would set up house in the fourth floor of Rucker. Proving that one should never underestimate the power of the press, at 10 p.m. the night the paper came out, forty -eight Pawling men along with their housemother, suit cases and pillows marched across to Rucker, through the front, past the astonished, open-mouthed Rucker Hall housemother, and up the stairs to fourth floor.*

"NOBODY READS THE G'TONIAN?" Stunned by a lack of student knowledge of what the *Georgetonian* had printed in its last issue, the staff printed a reprimanding article titled, "Nobody Reads the G'tonian?" Today the college newspaper is quite popular, providing satirical entertainment on "the back page."

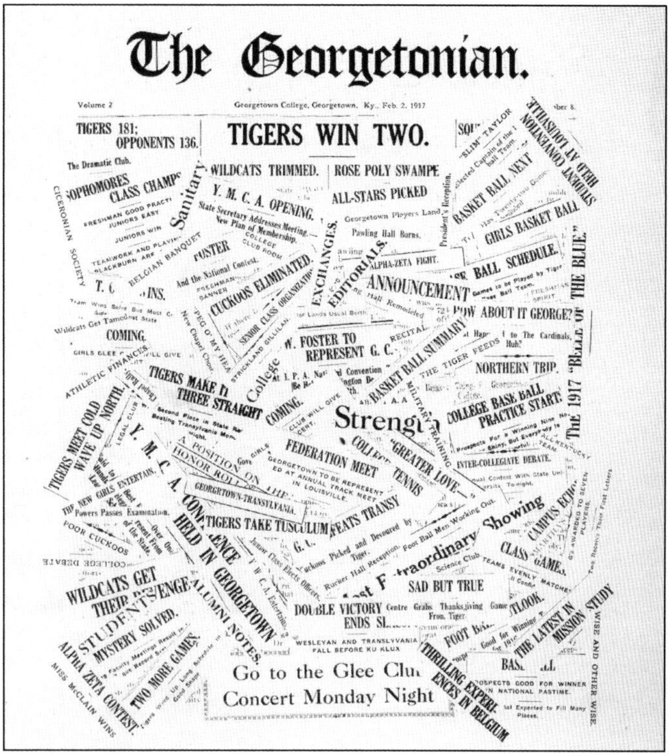

***GEORGETONIAN* TEXT.** The *Georgetonian* staff, larger in past years, worked long hours to print, layout, and deliver papers. Students in the 1940s remember printing by melting lead into molds and pressing them into the paper—if one malfunctioned, the printing staff would simply re-melt and begin the process again. To include a photograph in the paper, pictures were shipped to Cincinnati and molds sent back and then inserted into the already laid-out newspaper.

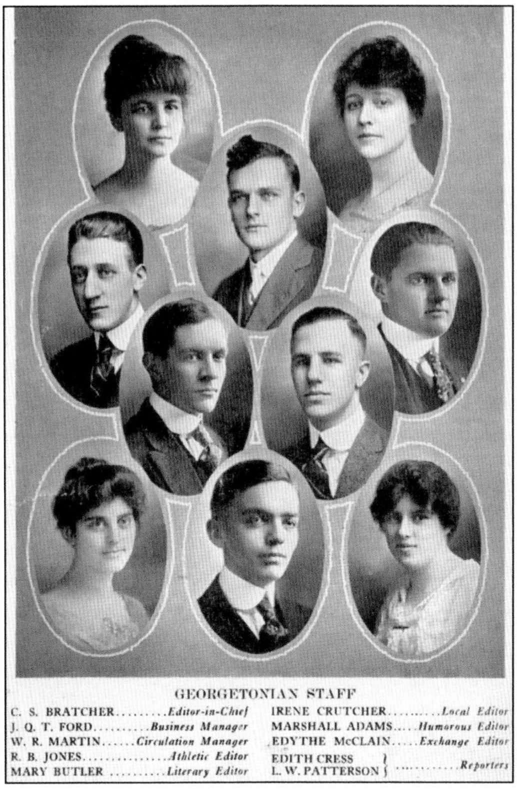

***GEORGETONIAN* STAFF.** The campus newspaper feeds students with the college news, gossip, and literary features. The 1917 *Georgetonian* staff pictured here includes C. S. Bratcher, J. Q. T. Ford, W. R. Martin, R. B. Jones, Mary Butler, Irene Crutcher, Marshall Adams, Edythe McClain, Edith Cress, and L. W. Patterson.

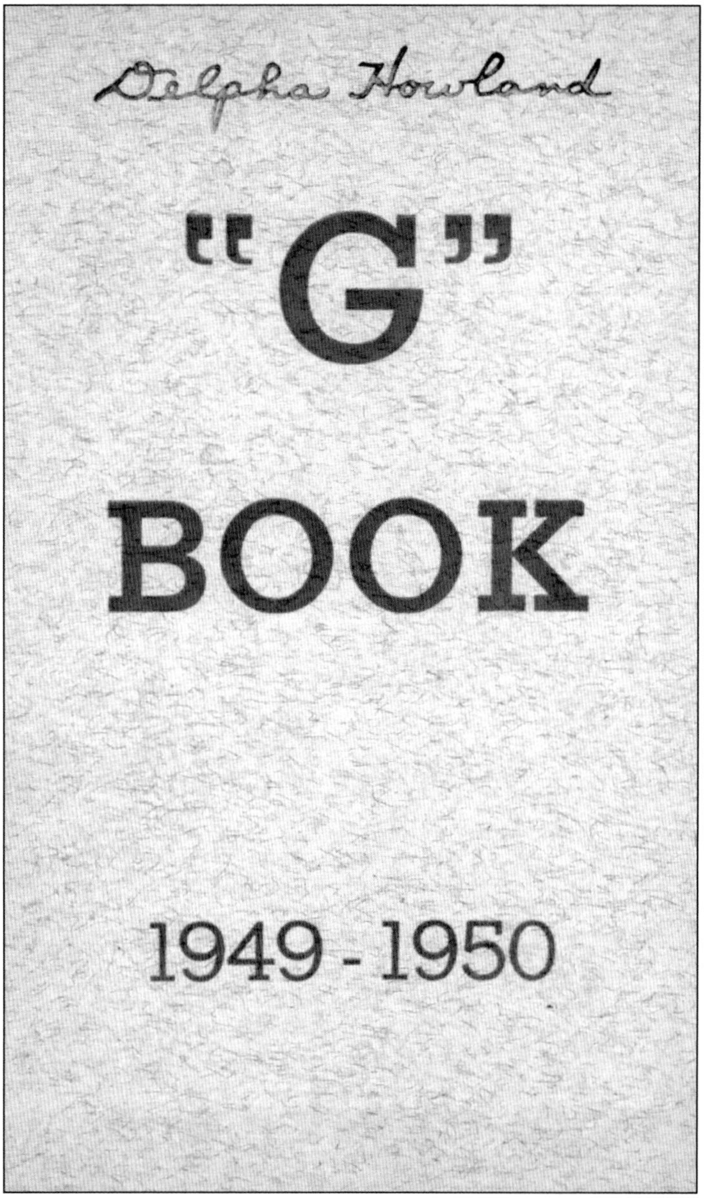

"G" Book. The tiny but compressed "G" book is much like today's agenda book at Georgetown, which provides information for students regarding the school calendar and school policy. This 1949–1950 book shows the much stricter and structured environment of Georgetown of the past. For example, male students were required to make arrangements with their housemother in order to invite a woman over any evening besides a Friday, Saturday, or Sunday. Groups were not permitted to leave campus for hikes, picnics, or parties without a chaperone. Women were not allowed to go to town at night alone and were also required to be in their own rooms after 10:30 with the lights out by 11. Alcohol, gambling, swearing, and dancing were completely banned, and smoking for women was prohibited. Also, women were allowed only a certain number of dates per month plus 12 "free" dates a year according to classification. This exemplifies the rigidity of students' social atmosphere in comparison to present rules.

Ten

THEN AND NOW

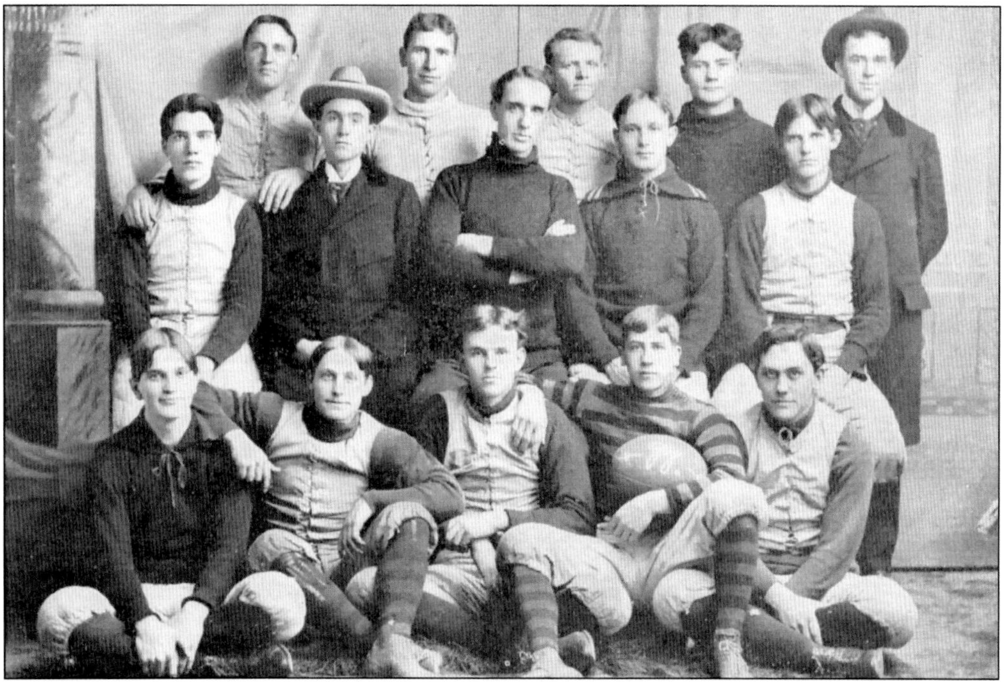

FOOTBALL TEAM. Though the group may look small and scraggly, the football team of 1897 to 1898 played a remarkable season, winning 7 out of 10 games with no coach. R. T. Hinton, who would later return to Georgetown and coach all sports teams, was elected captain and led the team to a successful season. Football was not as popular of a sport as it is today at Georgetown. It was discouraged by parents because its roughness, and there was low attendance at games. Pictured here from left to right are (first row) D. C. Hunter, S. M. Moorman, C. A. Beech, R. T. Hinton, and "Ward" McAllister; (second row) J. L. Hill, G. A. Williams (manager), J. A. Taylor, W. H. Vanlandingham, and C. T. Rule; (third row) H. Y. Harvin, George Green, I. N. Foreward, Robert Collins, and T. R. Snyder.

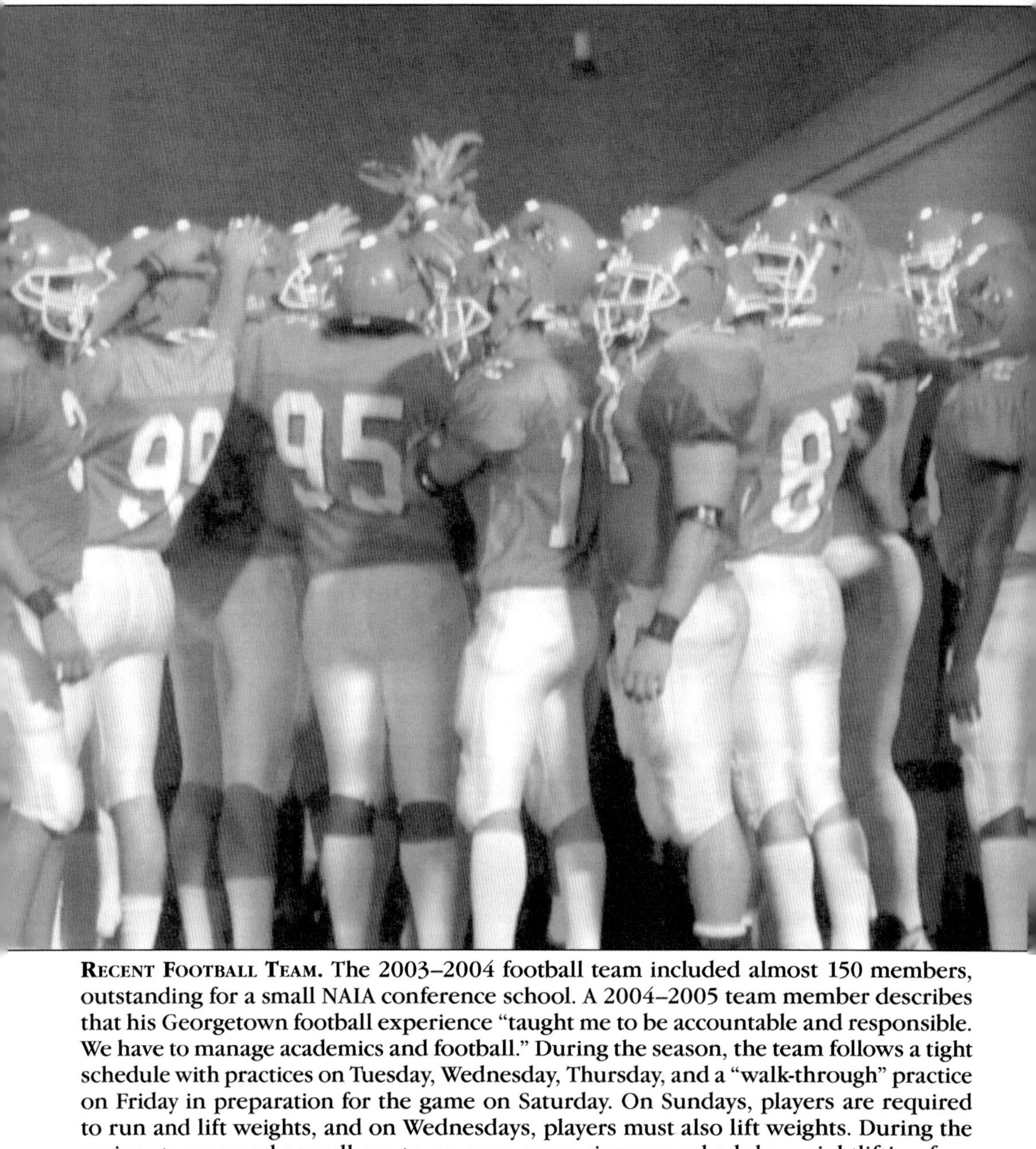

Recent Football Team. The 2003–2004 football team included almost 150 members, outstanding for a small NAIA conference school. A 2004–2005 team member describes that his Georgetown football experience "taught me to be accountable and responsible. We have to manage academics and football." During the season, the team follows a tight schedule with practices on Tuesday, Wednesday, Thursday, and a "walk-through" practice on Friday in preparation for the game on Saturday. On Sundays, players are required to run and lift weights, and on Wednesdays, players must also lift weights. During the spring, team members adhere to an even more rigorous schedule, weightlifting four times per week for one hour. The team practices on Tuesdays, Wednesdays, Thursdays, and Fridays, and a scrimmage is held on Saturdays.

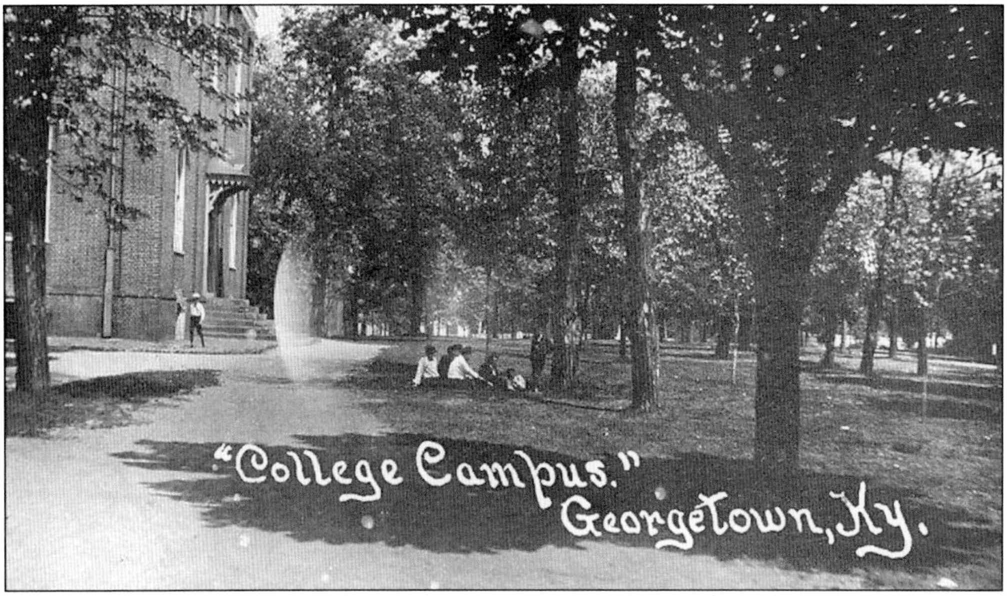

College Campus Postcard. Shaded by a host of trees, the lawn behind Giddings Hall was often frequented by students. Couples picnicked, students read, and many merely relaxed under the giant shade trees. Women carried a parasol of course, just in case the sun was to peep through. In the distance, one can notice the rear of Giddings Hall as well as a couple taking an afternoon stroll. (Postcard courtesy of Ron Morgan.)

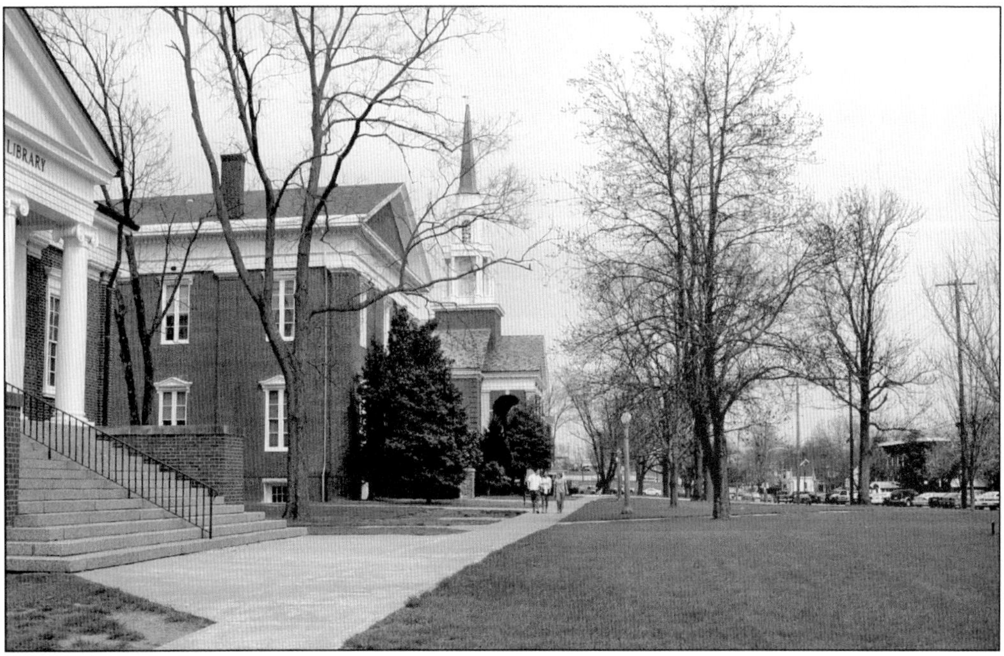

Recent College Campus. Today the campus layout is relatively the same, minus the wide clusters of trees that used to exist on campus. Now one finds cars throughout. Students often study outside their dorms rather than on this lawn in the photograph, while some play Frisbee golf and sand volleyball, two newer activities on campus. (Photograph courtesy of Jessica Ehleben.)

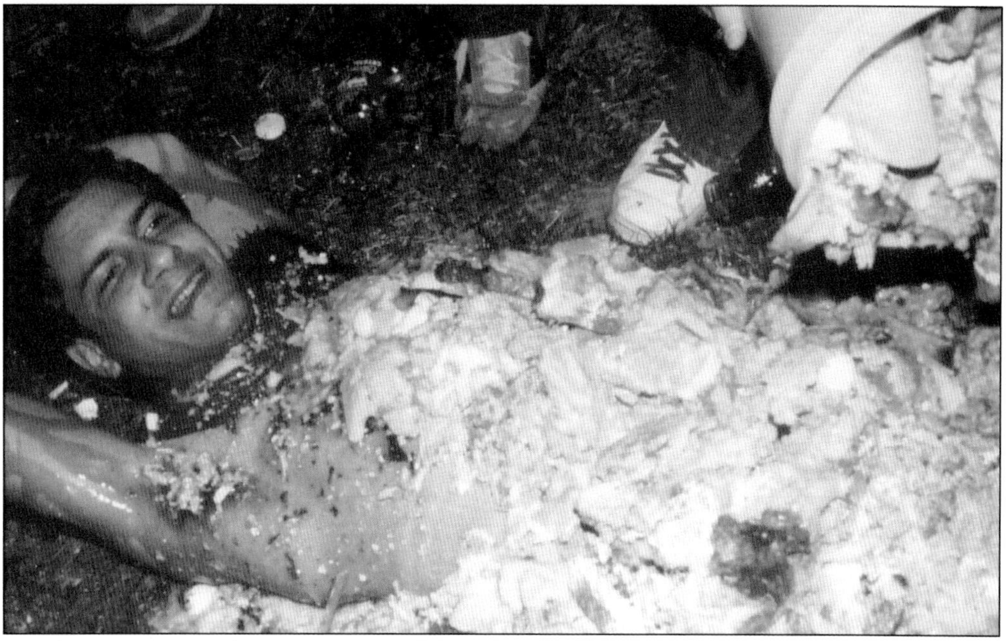

Phi Tau Stake Out. Phi Kappa Tau member Guthrie True, class of 1980, is playfully "staked-out" by his fraternity brothers as a "consequence" of becoming engaged to be married. The photograph, taken in 1981, depicts the array of substances poured on the victim.

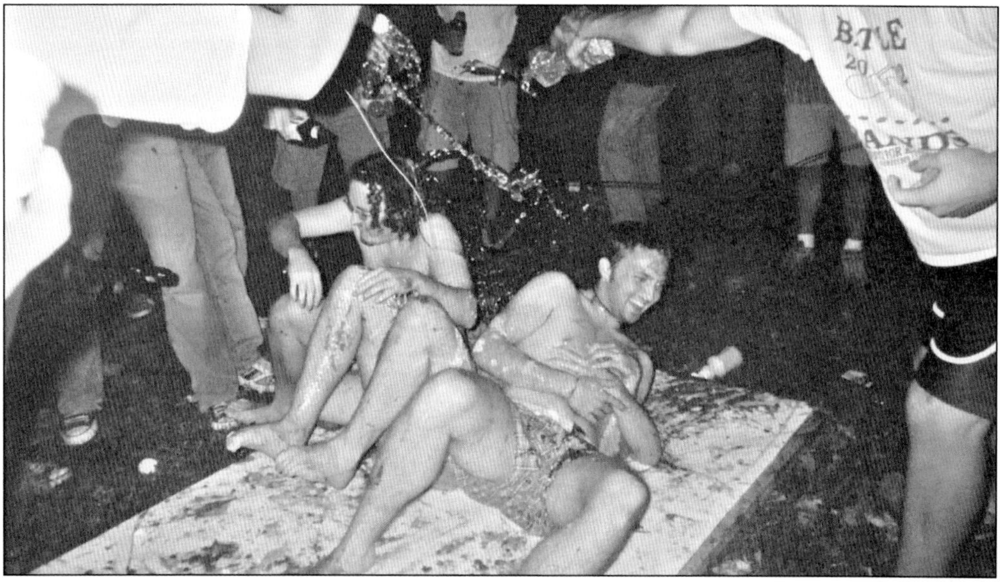

PHA Stake Out. Though not as frequent as in years past, engagements of a Georgetown fraternity boy were usually coupled with a "stake-out" in which every substance imaginable was poured on the poor man who had confessed his love. He was then left to hug his fiancée covered in the muck. Today fraternities observe a variety of "stake-out" procedures. This photograph gives a glimpse into the PHA "stake-out" of Roger Jasper, class of 2006. Roger (with only his legs showing) has "sacrificed" two of his fraternity brothers to endure the grotesque act, Justin Mulikin (seated left) and John Askew (seated right), both 2005 graduates of Georgetown. (Photograph courtesy of Roger Jasper.)

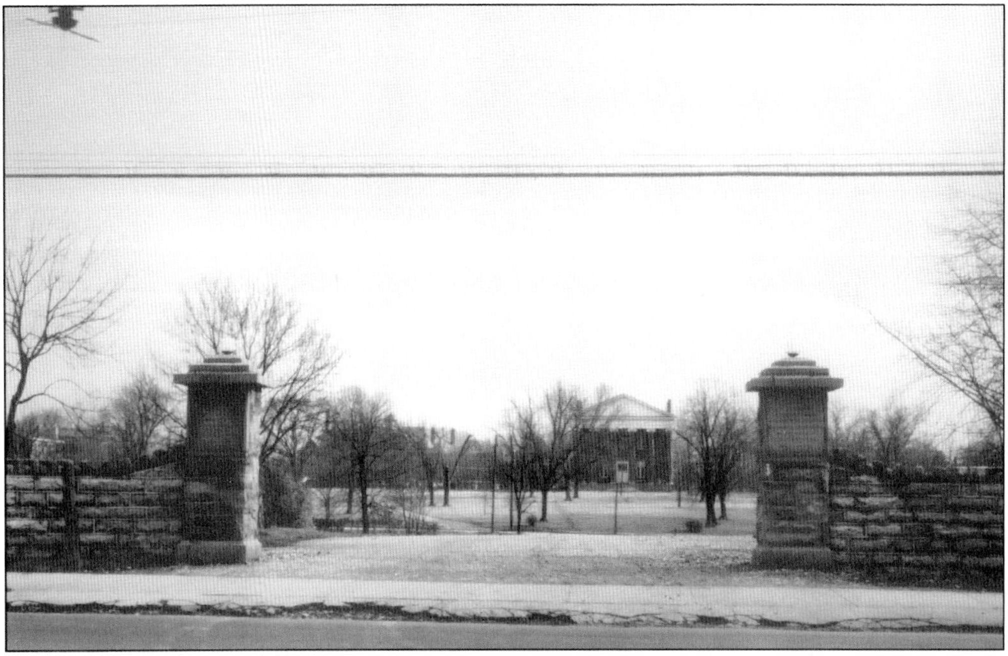

Entryway. The college entrance, lacking Giddings Circle, shows undeveloped green space. Today a larger and more visible sign sits at the front of Giddings Circle, welcoming all to the life and heart of Georgetown College.

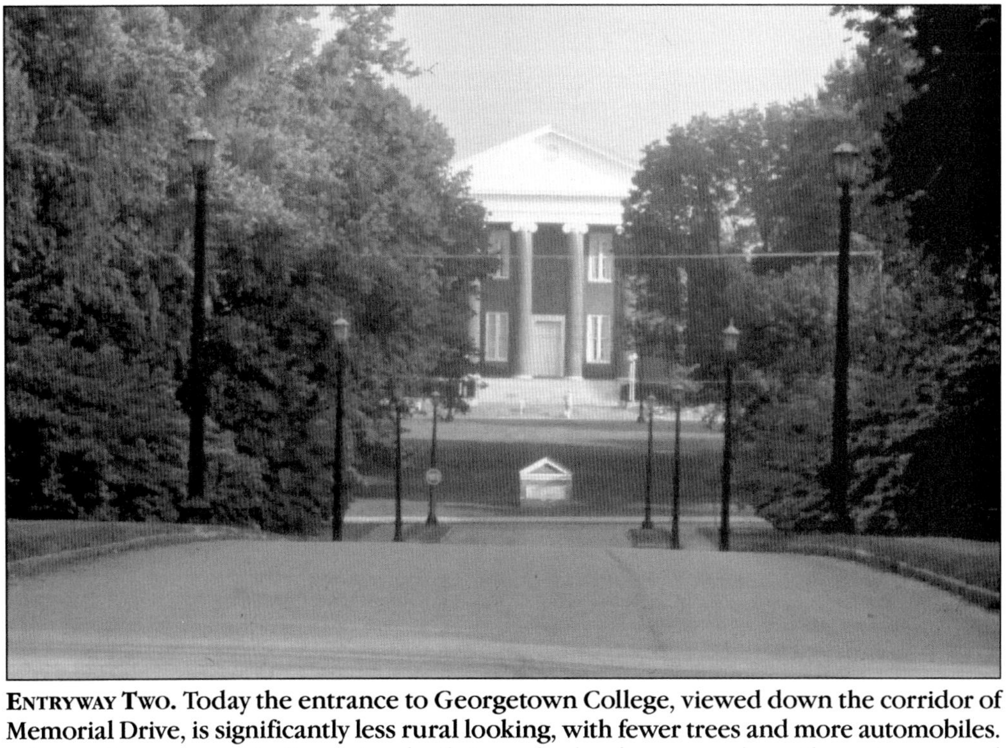

Entryway Two. Today the entrance to Georgetown College, viewed down the corridor of Memorial Drive, is significantly less rural looking, with fewer trees and more automobiles. A large Georgetown College sign built into the landscape anchors the entrance and draws attention to the stately Giddings Hall directly behind.

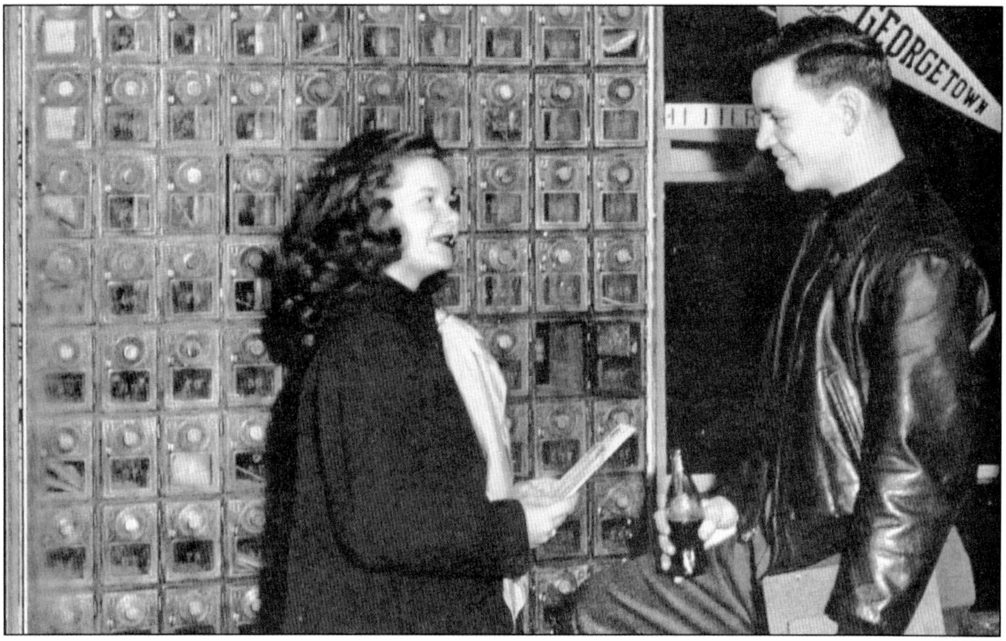

Mailroom. Much like today, the mailroom was as much a place for socializing as it was for receiving and delivering correspondence. In 1940, the mailroom was connected to the bookstore and a soda fountain. Today the mailroom is connected to the Grille, a popular student hangout, as well as the "C-store" and the college bookstore.

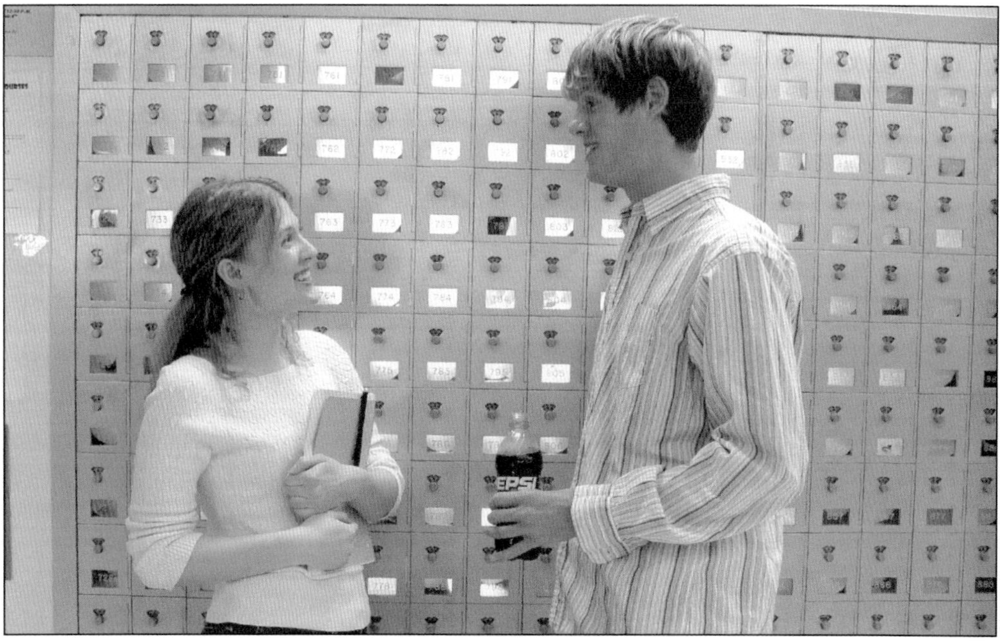

Recent Mailroom. Students Alex Smiley (left) and Darren Neel, both English majors while at Georgetown, converse in the mailroom after classes. Notice that Darren is holding a Pepsi in this photograph rather than a Coke because the college switched to Pepsi products in 2004. Also located behind the mailroom is a publishing and duplicating center. (Photograph courtesy of Jessica Ehleben.)

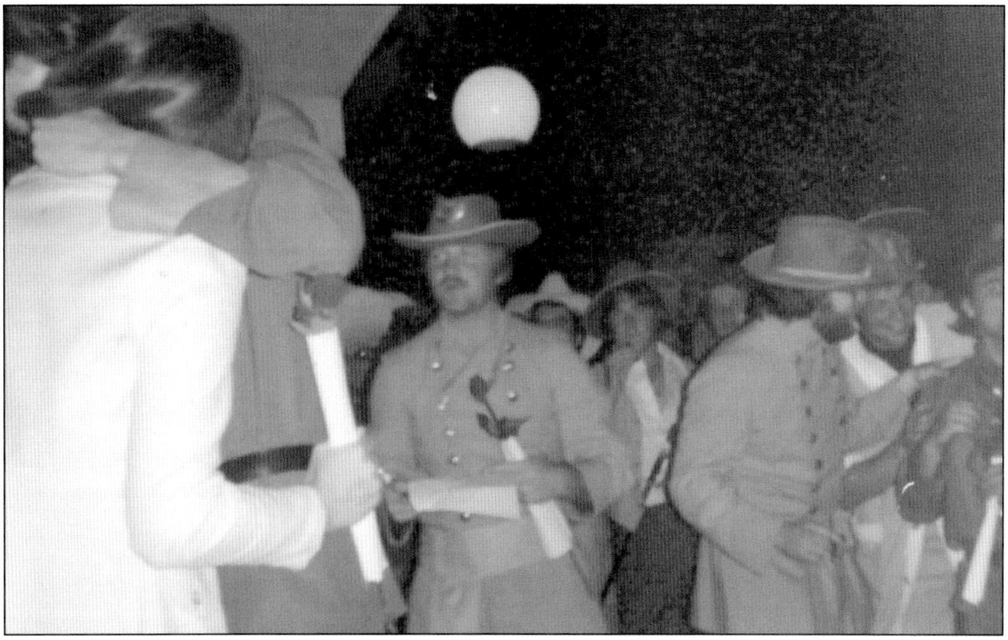

KA Rose Kiss, 1970s. Clifford Dale kisses Dana Snyder Dale as he asks her to accept the honor of the KA rose and of accompanying him to "Old South" weekend. The invitation to "Old South" remains a big excitement today at Georgetown. Girls adorned in hoop skirts and ruffles are serenaded by Confederate-dressed KAs. In the 1970s, during "Old South" week, the KAs wore their uniforms all week, neglected to shave, and serenaded the ladies' dorms at 7:00 in the morning.

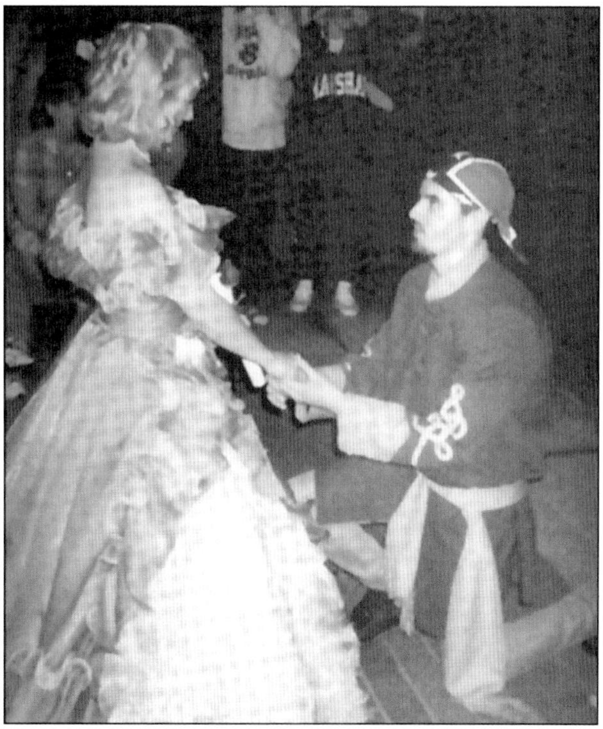

KA Rose Invite, 1998. Dressed in the traditional Confederate uniform, Kappa Alpha member Brad Mills asks Phi Mu Stephanie Borders to "accept this rose" and to accompany him to "Old South" weekend in Gatlinburg, Tennessee. Though recently the KAs have not made a showing of a horse-and-buggy procession or a memorial service, they still travel around campus with a symbolic cannon to request their dates' attendance to "Old South."

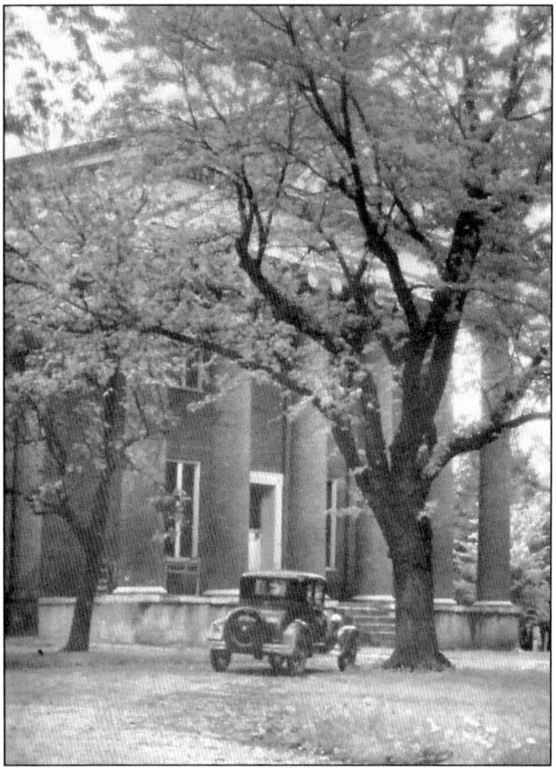

Giddings Hall With Car. Dr. Rockwood Giddings, who graduated from Waterville College and became a physician, rescued Georgetown College during his short term as president for only one year, from 1838 to 1839. A very busy man at the young age of 26, he pastored at Shelbyville Baptist Church. While president at Georgetown he managed to raise a large endowment. Giddings enlisted two more faculty members, Jonathan E. Farnham and Danford Thomas, to join the two existing faculty members at Georgetown. He also laid the plans to build an impressive Greek Revival structure, pictured here on the newly purchased tracts of land east of the old Rittenhouse property. However, the ill-fated death of Giddings on October 29, 1839, while preaching in the pulpit, prevented the young leader from seeing the building that now bears his name.

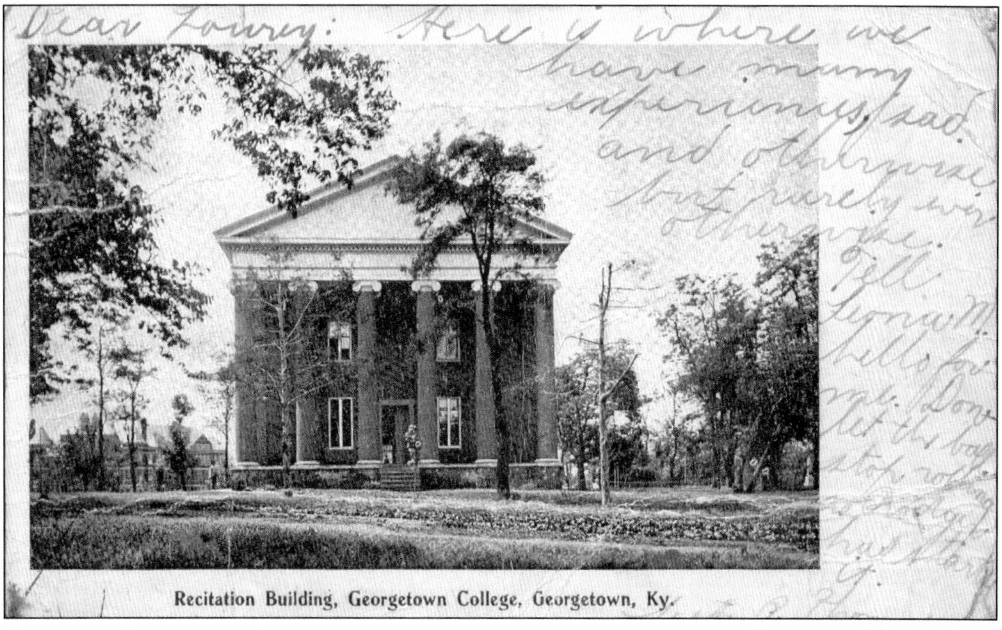

Giddings Postcard. Now an icon representing Georgetown College, Giddings Hall, constructed in 1841, captures the eye of observers as they enter the college on Memorial Drive. In this postcard, the hall's prominent columns lend an air of nobility and dignity. Formerly known as Recitation Hall, the old edifice was later named for its "father," Rockwood Giddings, who drafted plans for the structure in 1838.

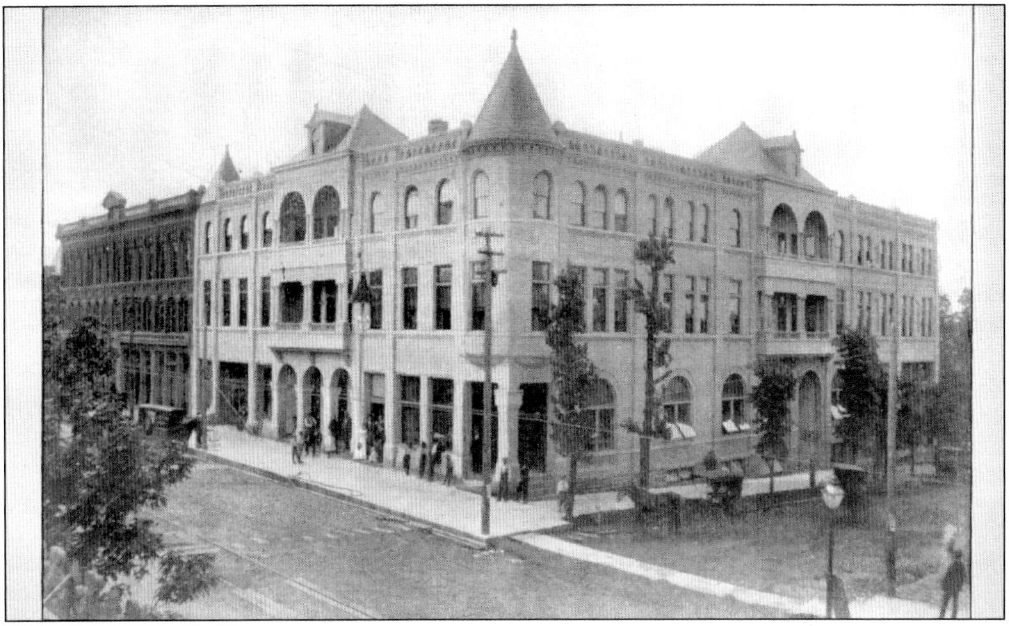

The Wellington. Downtown Georgetown was frequented by students in the 19th and 20th centuries more often than it is today. In the late 1860s, the downtown flourished and buildings sprouted at a high rate, making Scott County the 10th wealthiest county in Kentucky by 1882. This corner in downtown Georgetown, known as Wellington Block, has housed Farmers Bank since 1895. Prior to the bank, an apartment and hotel complex occupied all the floors of Wellington Block.

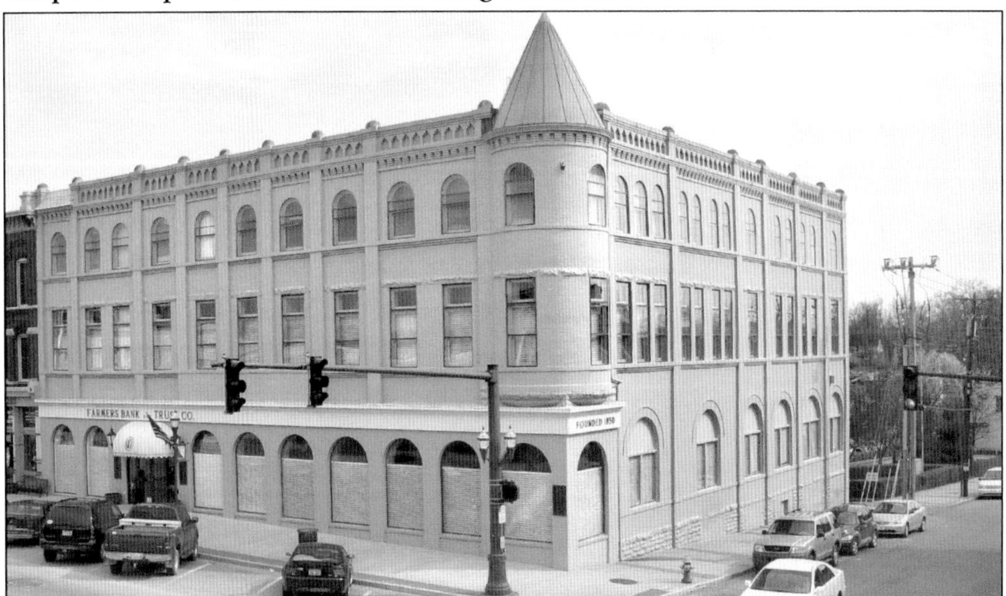

Farmers Bank. Today the Wellington Apartments have been fully converted into an expanded Farmers Bank, though its façade has experienced minimal changes. Across the street is an old bank, which closed in the heat of the early Depression. Today it functions as a coffee shop called Lock and Key.

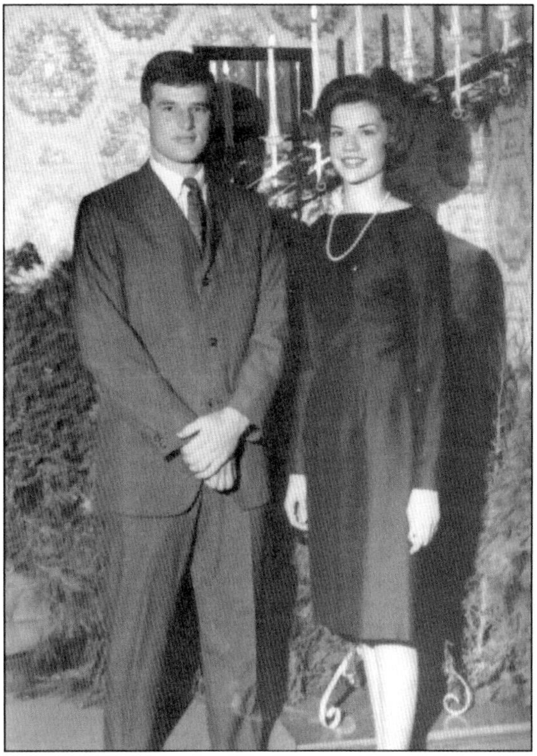

Anne and David Lee. Anne Barnett and David Lee both were extremely involved in student life while at Georgetown. Anne served as the Kappa Delta president and was also named Pi Kappa Alpha "Dreamgirl," and David, a member of Pi Kappa Alpha fraternity, played basketball for the Tigers as an All American in the 1960s. This photograph was taken of the couple at the 1965 Pi Kappa Alpha Christmas dinner. They married the following year. (Photograph courtesy of Anne Lee.)

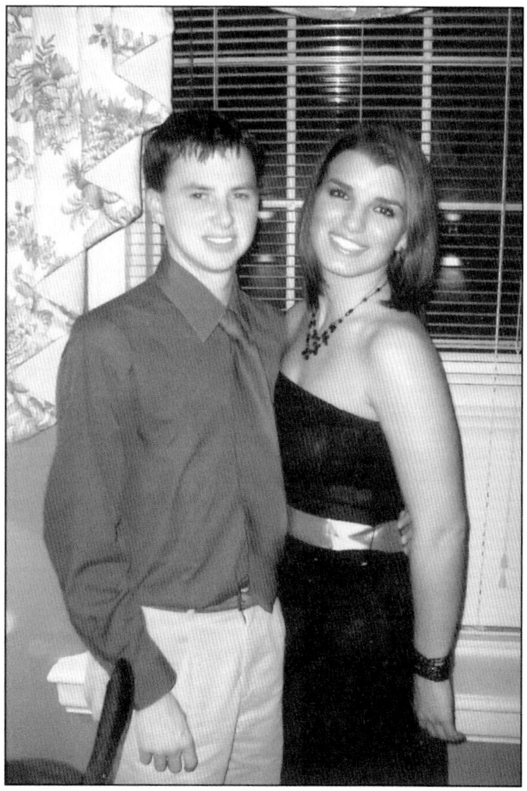

Recent PIKE Couple at a Dance. This photograph, featuring Travis Burton and Danielle Mann, was taken at a Pi Kappa Alpha dance in 2004. Danielle Mann, class of 2005, is a PIKE "diamond" and Burton served as the 2004–2005 Association of Georgetown Students president.

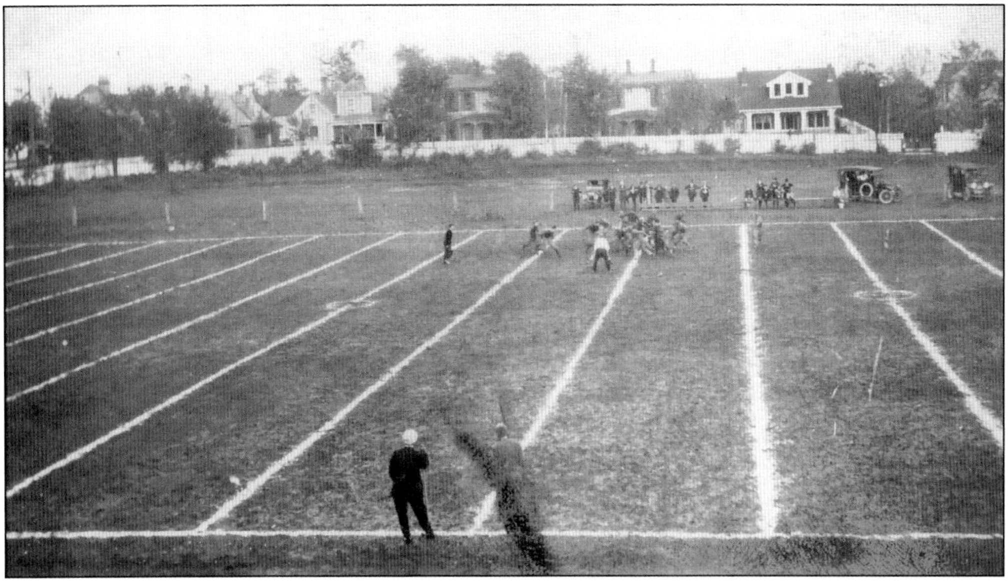

Old Football Field. Named for coach and athletic director Robert T. Hinton, who later became dean of students, Hinton Field was the center of excitement during football season. The field ran alongside Military Street, and in 1951, a bowling hall was added near the field. After World War II, under new athletic director Brad Jones, steel bleachers and lights were added to the field to seat fans and allow night games. The field originated out of students' need for outdoor exercise.

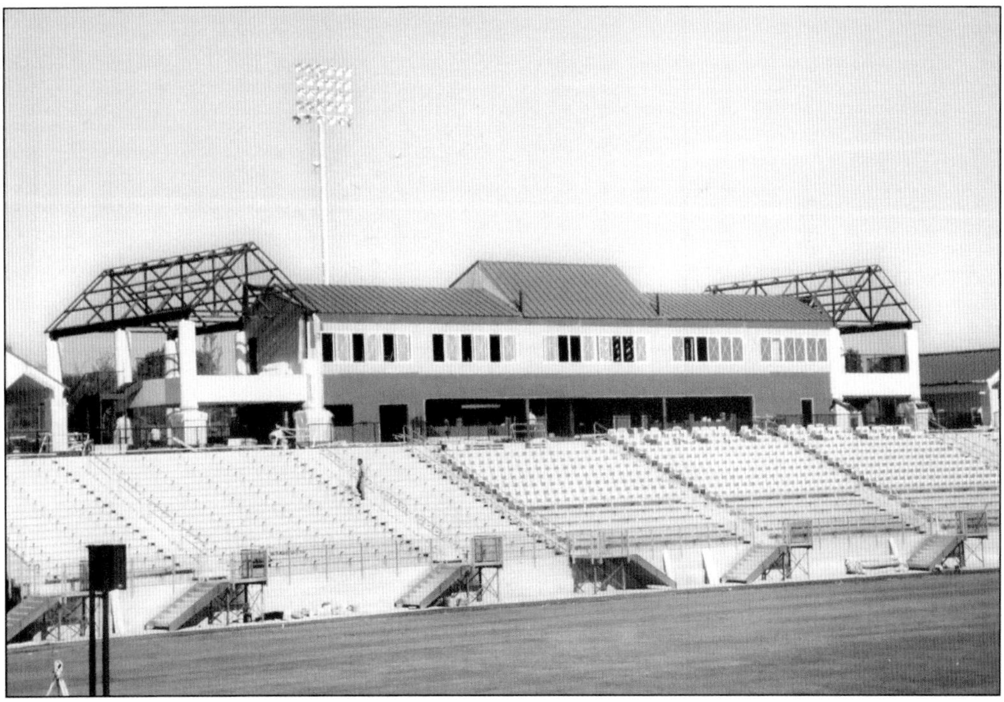

Rawlings Stadium. Today the football field, named Rawlings Stadium, functions also as a summer training center for the NFL's Cincinnati Bengals. The premium field is a stellar acquisition for Georgetown, considering the college's small size.

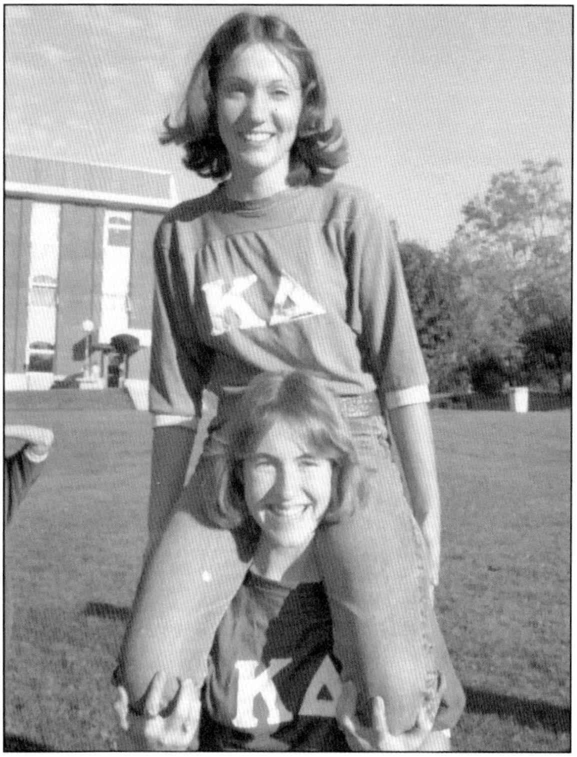

Fall Rush. Wendy Shelton (top) and Dana Snyder celebrate a successful 1977 fall recruitment for their sorority, Kappa Delta. During the fall semester, only upperclassmen women were allowed to "rush." During the previous spring semester, the women pictured were initiated into the sorority. Pledges were regularly called to perform "duties" for the actives, such as fluffing a pillow in the middle of the night.

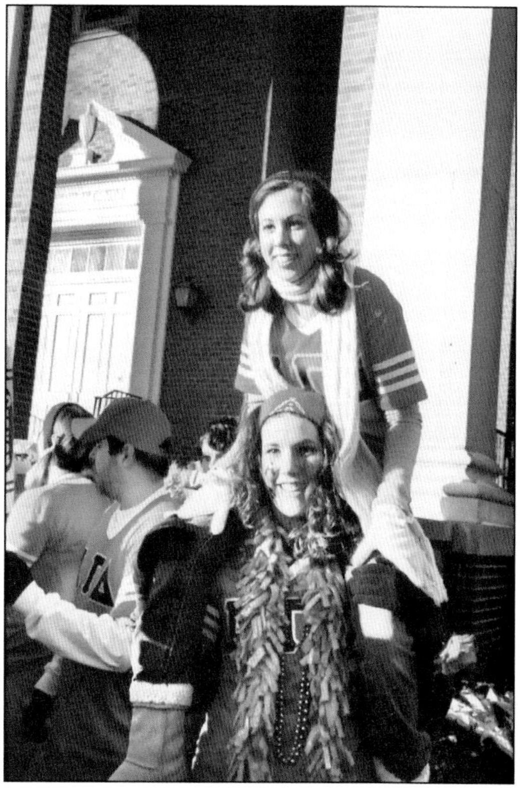

Spring Rush 2005. Spring rush 2005 proved exciting and successful for all four sororities on campus. At the end of recruitment week, clusters of women ran out of the chapel into their sisters' arms. The near week-long recruitment began with open house parties, continued with philanthropic and theme parties, and concluded with a preference night (when women choose their top two sororities to visit) and finally Chapel Day, at which the women reveal the sorority of their choice. Sororities spend hours in preparation decorating and rehearsing for the recruitment parties. Here two Alpha Gamma Deltas anxiously wait outside the chapel for the new "baby squirrels" to descend the chapel steps.

VIEW FROM GIDDINGS. The view from Giddings Hall prior to the construction of Memorial Drive was a scene of green pasture and sidewalks. Giddings Circle had not been paved either. Not until the science center and the Cralle Student Center were added did the buildings actually form a semi-circle. Dr. Robert Lee Mills renovated Giddings Hall in the 1970s. Lewis Auditorium, where the Maskrafters performed, was eliminated and was replaced by the Ruth Pierce Wilson Lab Theater. The space in Giddings Hall, previously occupied by the elegant auditorium, was converted to administrative offices.

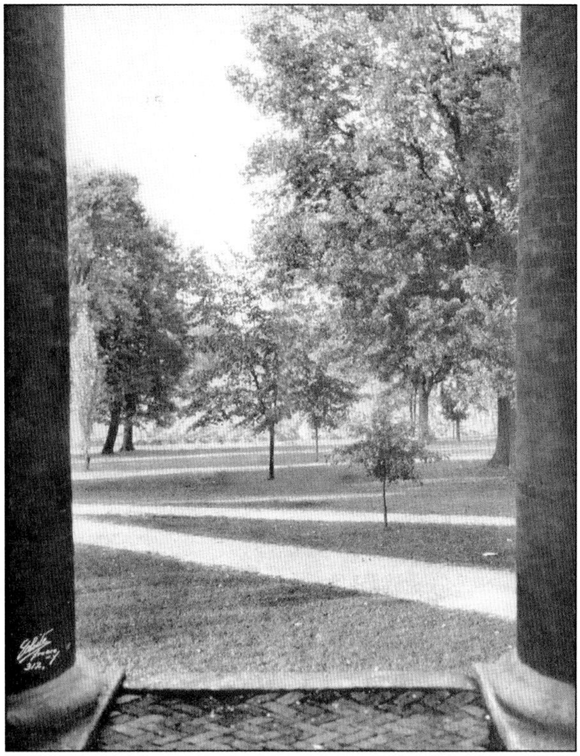

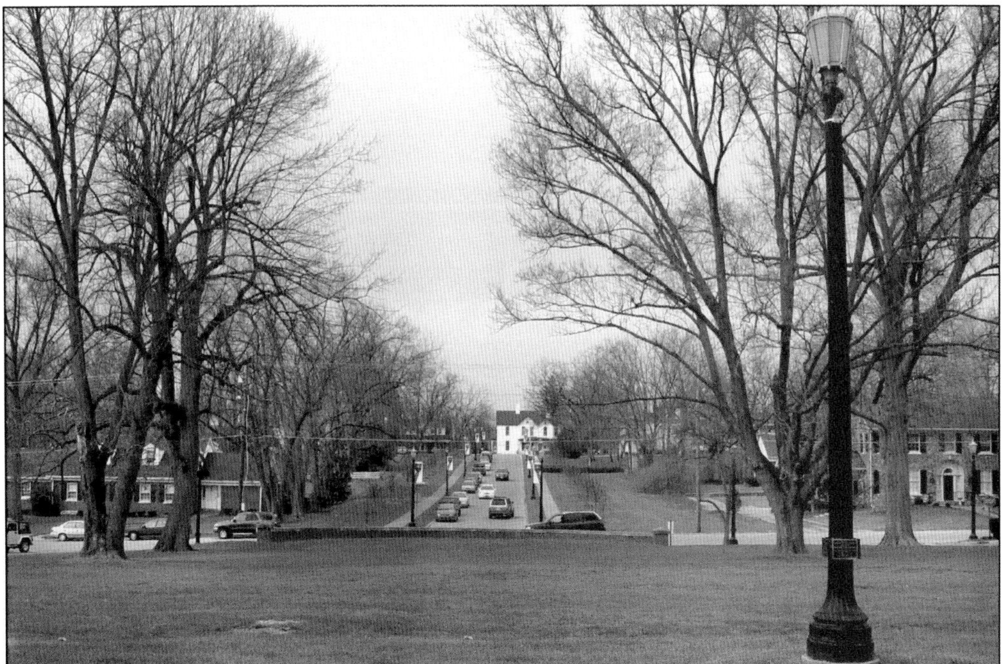

RECENT VIEW FROM GIDDINGS. The view from the steps of Giddings Hall conveys a much more metropolitan feeling than did the green fields of the 1930s and before. The streets are peppered with cars as more and more students bring their vehicles on campus.

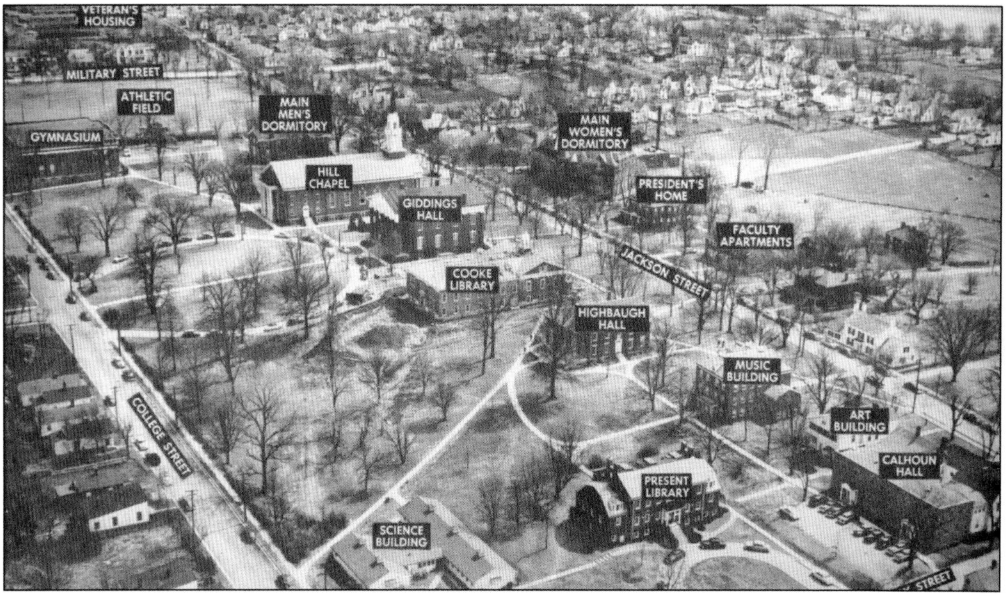

Aerial View of Old Campus. This view of campus from the late 1950s is more densely populated with trees than today. The view of Rucker Hall reveals the three separate wings of the dormitory as well as its massive size. Near the lower right of the view is Dudley Apartments, constructed in 1954 to provide faculty housing (labeled "Faculty Apartments" in the photo). The building was named in the honor of former President Dudley and was constructed on the former site of Dudley Cottage. Today Dudley Apartments serves as the Alpha Gamma Delta House.

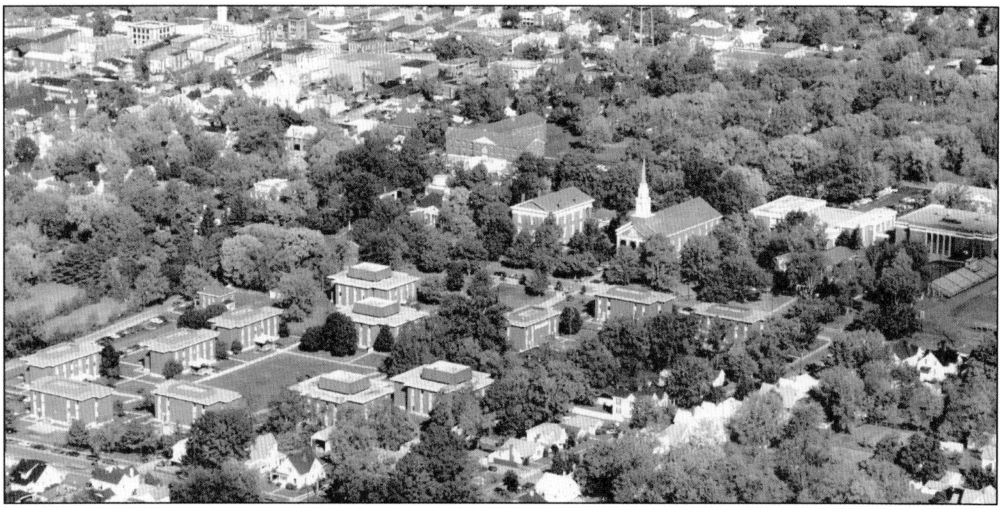

Recent Aerial View of Campus. In this more recent aerial view of campus, the new mini-dorms, constructed in the mid-1960s, are visible, and Rucker Hall no longer stands. Another property no longer existing at Georgetown is the old president's home, which stood in between Dudley Cottage/Apartments and Rucker Hall. These structures were demolished because of the need to build the mini-dorm complex and because of structural problems in the case of Rucker Hall. Other new additions to the campus since the mini-dorms are the science center, the Cralle Student Center, the fine arts building, the Ensor Learning Resource Center, and the Recreation Center (finished in 2001).